ColourSpectrums ™

Book 2: Stress Management and Conflict Resolution

Rob Chubb

Also in the ColourSpectrums series:

ColourSpectrums Personality Styles Book 1:
The Introduction

ColourSpectrums Personality Styles Book 3:
Brightening Pale Colours

◆ FriesenPress

Suite 300 - 990 Fort St
Victoria, BC, Canada, V8V 3K2
www.friesenpress.com

Copyright © 2016 by Rob Chubb
First Edition — 2016

All rights reserved.

No part of this publication may be reproduced in any form, or by any means, electronic or mechanical, including photocopying, recording, or any information browsing, storage, or retrieval system, without permission in writing from the publisher.

ISBN
978-1-4602-4986-4 (Hardcover)
978-1-4602-4987-1 (Softcover)
978-1-4602-5511-7 (eBook)

Distributed to the trade by The Ingram Book Company

To Mr. O and Mr. A

Contents

Acknowledgements . . . . *i*

How to Get the Most Out of This Book . . . . *iii*

Introduction to Book 2 . . . . *1*

Section 1: Stress Management — Look on the Bright Side *3*

It is not the destination. It is the journey within.

Stress is in the Eye of the Beholder 3
Writing a List of 10 Stressors 4
Bright Esteem Needs 6
Bright Stressors 13
Identifying Your Brightest Stressors 19
Identifying Your Other Bright Stressors 19
The Intensity Scale 21
Using Colours Assertively 23

Section 2: Bright Shadows — Understanding and Managing Them . . 25

> There are three things extremely hard:
> steel, a diamond, and to know one's self.
> — Benjamin Franklin

The Evolution of Stress: The Fight Response. 25
The Fight Response: For Better or Worse 28
Bright Shadow Characteristics. 28
Reviewing Your 10 Stressors For Fight Responses. 33
Recognizing Your Bright Shadow Characteristics. 33
Illuminating Bright Shadow Characteristics. 34
Understanding Principles of Perception 37
Bright Shadow Perceptions 39
Lighten-Up Phrases. 41
"Lighten-Up": A Paired Exercise 44
Dynamics of Palest to Brightest Colours 46
Being Assertive and Being Aggressive 46
Out-of-Esteem Bright Shadow Behaviour 48
Blue Emotions and Red Anger. 49
Bright Shadow Sticks and Stones. 53
Reframing Bright Shadow Sticks and Stones 54
Bright Shadow Self-Talk 59
Stress Management Cards: Look on the Bright Side 60

Section 3: Stress Management — Look on the Pale Side 63

> I am never in balance. I struggle to find
> a balance and the moment I find it I
> lose it again.

Pale Challenges 63
Pale Stressors. 68
Identifying Your Palest Stressors 72
Identifying Your Other Pale Stressors 73
Using Colours Passively. 93

Section 4: Pale Shadows — Understanding and Managing Them 95

Attempts to change others keep you from changing.

The Evolution of Stress: The Flight Response 95
The Flight Response: For Better or Worse 96
Pale Shadow Characteristics 96
Reviewing Your 10 Stressors for Flight Responses 102
Recognizing Your Pale Shadow Characteristics 102
Illuminating Pale Shadow Characteristics 103
Brighten-Up Phrases 104
"Brighten-Up": A Paired Exercise 107
Dynamics of Brightest to Palest Colours 109
Dynamics of Palest to Brightest Colours and Brightest to Palest Colours 110
Lighten-Up and Brighten-Up Combinations 113
Lighten-Up and Brighten-Up: A Paired Exercise 114
Lighten-Up and Brighten-Up Phrases: A Metaphor 117
A Matter of Perception 118
Being Passive and Being Passive Aggressive 118
Out-of-Esteem Pale Shadow Behaviour 120
Pale Shadow Sticks and Stones 121
Reframing Pale Shadow Sticks and Stones 121
Pale Shadow Self-Talk 126
Out-of-Esteem Bright and Pale Shadow Behaviours 127
Stress Management Cards: Look on the Pale Side 128

Section 5: Using ColourSpectrums to Improve Relationships 131

> Everything that irritates us about
> others can lead us to an understanding
> of ourselves.
>
> — Carl Jung

Perceptions and Perspectives 131
Stress Management Cards: Look on the Bright and Pale Sides 133
Finding a State of Balance 138

The Fight/Flight Shadow Connection 139
The Flight/Fight Shadow Connection 140
Illuminating Bright and Pale Shadows. 141
Chart of ColourSpectrums Continuums 141
Four Distinct and Separate Continuums 142

Section 6: Using ColourSpectrums to Improve Communication 149

You are a great communicator when you match colour and intensity. It is that simple. It is that challenging.

Great Communicators Match Colours. 149
300 Social Workers Can't Be Wrong 157
Great Communicators Match Colours and Intensities. 161
Effective People Match Intensities 164
Shifting to Match Intensity 166
Matching Colours 168
Paraphrasing and Active Listening. 169
Endings and Beginnings 170
ColourSpectrums Applications 170
Stress Management Card Set 177

Acknowledgements

I first started delivering ColourSpectrums workshops in 1990, first to my colleagues at what was then Grant MacEwan Community College. Over the years the approach changed somewhat, but the core idea of ColourSpectrums remained the same.

This series of books would not have been possible without all those people who have been part of ColourSpectrums along the way.

All my workshop participants — from the early MacEwan days and beyond — have made this book better by sharing their enthusiasm and feedback. Some of these people have shared their experiences, which are included in the book and make it more meaningful and relevant. My workshop facilitators have helped me deliver ColourSpectrums to more and more people, and their insights have improved my delivery materials.

My wife of 34 years, Laurie, has been unfailingly supportive as this venture took up more and more of my time and even as ColourSpectrums changed from a diversion to a career. Thank you, Laurie, for the colour you bring to my life and for our five wonderful children.

And speaking of those wonderful children — since I started working on these books, they've grown and the family has expanded to include grandchildren. Yes, it's taken longer than I would have expected to turn my notes into a bound book. Without the gentle nudging of my editor I might still be making "just one more change ... ." Thank you, Shelagh, for your direction, commitment and undying faith in this project.

Rob Chubb

How to Get the Most Out of This Book

Card Sets

In this book, I refer to the cards participants use in my workshops. A set of four two-sided stress management cards is provided on the last eight pages of this book. For a more hands-on ColourSpectrums experience, purchase coloured card sets at www.colourspectrums.com

This symbol indicates a written exercise. Complete written exercises to maximize your understanding and integrate your skills.

This symbol indicates a solitary exercise. Complete solitary exercises to integrate information and personalize your learning.

This symbol indicates a paired exercise in which you talk or interact with a partner. I encourage you to complete these paired exercises with someone important to you — your spouse, your best friend, your child, your brother or sister, your mom or dad, or a colleague. Sharing these experiences with someone will maximize your learning while enhancing your personal/professional relationship. For exercises that require a worksheet from the book, make a copy so you each have one.

Introduction to Book 2

The first book in the ColourSpectrums trilogy introduced the history and the background of ColourSpectrums and allowed you to assess and determine your own colour spectrum.

No doubt you, like so many other people introduced to ColourSpectrums, enjoyed the opportunity to learn something about yourself. One of the key insights is that we are all alike in being unique — and sometimes it is very easy to understand people like us and be very confused by those who are different.

In *ColourSpectrums Personality Styles Book 1: The Introduction*, you learned to recognize your different colours and rely on them at appropriate times, so that you are more effective.

Now, with *ColourSpectrums Personality Styles Book 2: Stress Management and Conflict Resolution*, you can gain more insight into yourself and others. You can learn how to identify your stress triggers so you can manage your stress. As well, you will learn how to improve your relationships and your communication skills to avoid conflict.

You can improve your life by understanding yourself and others and how you respond to certain situations. Let ColourSpectrums be your guide.

Section 1: Stress Management — Look on the Bright Side

Stress is in the Eye of the Beholder

ColourSpectrums can help you improve your life. Understanding your unique ColourSpectrums personality will help you identify and meet your needs and minimize your stress. Understanding other people's ColourSpectrums will help you appreciate their needs and minimize their stress. Mutual stress reduction enhances relationships and productivity.

Let me begin with the definition of a stressor. A stressor is any event that threatens or is perceived to threaten one's sense of balance and causes a person to respond in an effort to maintain or regain equilibrium. For example, if someone physically pushes you, you momentarily lose your balance and try to regain it. The event of being pushed is a stressor because it causes a stress response, the physical effort required to regain your balance. This is an example of bright red physical stress. The greater the physical effort required to regain your balance, the greater the physical stress you experience. A slight push causes a little stress. A violent push causes a great deal of stress, a great deal of physical effort required to return to a state of balance.

Your blue, green and yellow experience stress in much the same way. Your blue experiences blue emotional stress, your green experiences cognitive stress and your yellow experiences organizational stress.

It is evident by looking at the original ColourSpectrums attribute cards, included in the first book, that an event that is esteeming for one person may not be esteeming for another. In fact, an event that is highly esteeming for one person may be highly stressful for another person. It is not the situation that is inherently esteeming or stressful; rather, it is the experience of the situation that is esteeming or stressful. Esteeming experiences and stressful experiences are internal responses to external events.

Rob Chubb

Imagine two people discussing a problem in their relationship.

> "The problem with our relationship is... we spend too much time apart!"
>
> "The problem with our relationship is... we spend too much time together!"

These two people are in the same relationship and experiencing the same situation from two very different internal perspectives. We will come back and visit these two people later.

Writing a List of 10 Stressors

The following exercise will help you identify your sources of stress and potential solutions.

Complete this written exercise before reading further. You will be referring back to this stress check to complete the different parts of it after reading further explanations. For now, simply write 10 stressful situations in the centre column.

If you are working with a partner, you should each complete this written exercise separately.

Section 1: Stress Management — Look on the Bright Side

ColourSpectrums™   StressCheck

☞ In the centre column, write a list of 10 stressful situations.
Include a variety of environments: at home, at work, at school and in the community.
Include a variety of times: last week, last month, last year, in the past or in the future.
Consider a variety of events: the more diverse the better.

☞ There is one ground rule. You cannot blame another "colour" for your stress. Guard against this by describing the situations not the people.

10 Stressful Situations

Total Brightest Stressors

Total Personal Stressors

Total Palest Stressors

Bright Esteem Needs

We all have esteem needs. Esteem needs are not goals you can reach or outcomes that you can attain; rather, each colour is an esteeming state that needs to be experienced. It is not the experience of being loved that is empowering, it is the experience of loving. It is not the experience of receiving that is esteeming, it is the experience of giving; thus it is better to give than to receive. It is not the fish, but the fishing. It is not the destination out there, it is indeed the journey within.

> It is not the destination.
> It is the journey within.

Each colour is a source of esteem, and each colour provides a particular kind of esteem. When we use a colour, we experience the unique self-esteem and sense of empowerment that only that colour can provide. Your blue self can experience blue emotional and spiritual esteem. Your green self can experience green cognitive self-esteem. Your red self can experience red physical self-esteem and your yellow self can experience the pride of self-control and organizational self-esteem. So you can experience blue esteem, green esteem, red esteem and yellow esteem. You must use a colour in order to experience the associated state of self-esteem, self-fulfillment and satisfaction. In order to experience all four kinds of self-esteem and empowerment, you must use all four colours. The more colours you use, the more esteemed and empowered you will be.

Blue Esteem

The only way to experience blue esteem is to use your blue. The blue part of you needs to be experienced and esteemed to some extent. The brighter your blue is, the more it needs to be esteemed and the more you naturally seek opportunities to use and experience the esteeming state of blue. For example, you must use your blue to experience love, affection, intimacy, spirituality and tender loving care. The brighter your blue is, the greater your capacity to experience these esteeming events. Your blue can take a liking to, or have warm feelings towards, someone. Your blue can believe in love. Your bright blue can believe in love at first sight. In mutually bright blue relationships you can experience close friends, best friends, confidants, soul mates and intimacy. Your green, red and yellow do not have any capacity to experience these esteeming states, to experience love, affection, intimacy or spirituality.

Green Esteem

The only way to experience green esteem is to use your green. Your green needs to be experienced and esteemed. The brighter your green is, the more you seek opportunities to use and experience it. It is the experience of contemplating and analyzing an idea that is esteeming, not simply the experience of having an idea or being given an idea. As with the space shuttles, it is the voyage of discovery and the journey of the mind,

> " Think left and think right and think low and think high. Oh, the thinks you can think up if only you try! "
> — Dr. Seuss

not the destination of the planets or stars. Your green mind is more energized by the opportunity to explain an idea than to have an idea explained. The lecturer is more energized than the lectured. The explainer experiences more green esteem than the person who is listening to the explanation. Your green is interested in connecting the dots. If your green is bright, you are interested in connecting the dots differently each time.

People with bright green can make a long story short or a short story long. In either case they are energized by thinking, rethinking, inventing and reinventing. They are inclined to reinvent the wheel. You must use your green to experience mental competence, intellectual insight and cognitive understanding. The brighter your green is, the greater your capacity to experience these esteeming events. Your blue, red and yellow do not have the capacity to experience any mental competence, intellectual insight or cognitive understanding.

Red Esteem

The only way to experience red esteem is to use your red. The red part of you needs to be esteemed and empowered. The brighter your red is, the more it needs to be esteemed and the more you seek opportunities to use and experience the esteeming state of red. Your red is energized by being physically active. For example, you must put on your red game face to experience the adrenaline rush of physical competition, the hilarity of pulling off a practical joke, the gratification of being mechanically inclined or the simple pleasure of going for a walk. The brighter your red is, the greater your capacity to experience these esteeming events. The more you exert your muscles, the more your muscles grow and the more physically fit you become. The more you exercise your red physical coordination, the more coordinated you become.

Your blue, green and yellow do not have any capacity to perform physical activities, experience the adrenaline rush of physical competition, the hilarity of pulling off a practical joke, the gratification of being mechanically inclined or the physical pleasure of going for a walk.

Yellow Esteem

The only way to experience yellow esteem is to use your yellow. Your yellow needs to be esteemed and empowered. The brighter your yellow is, the more it needs to be esteemed and the more you naturally seek opportunities to experience the esteeming state of yellow. For example, it is the activity of organizing that esteems and energizes your yellow. You do not experience yellow esteem when someone does the organizing for you. Organizing is only esteeming for the person who does it. You must use your yellow to experience the pride of organizing, the integrity of completing a task on time and the prestige of being in charge or the self-satisfaction that comes with being responsible.

Your blue, green and red do not have any capacity to experience the pride of organizing, the integrity of completing a task on time or the satisfaction of being responsible and in charge.

Four Psychological Energies

Historically, in psychological literature, each colour is referred to as a primary psychological energy. Jung stated that "We cannot see psychic energies but we can see colours." We may not be able to see these psychic energies but we can certainly experience them. Your blue is the internal self, the entity, identity, inner spirit or inner energy that responds when your name is called. Your inner you is your blue.

You experience an increase in blue emotional energy when you become emotionally aroused, more emotive, more personal, more spiritual, or spiritually uplifted. You experience an increase in green intellectual energy when you become mentally aroused, when you become fascinated, when your interest is piqued, when you become curious and when you become intrigued by interesting ideas and unexplained mysteries. You experience an increase in red physical energy when you become physically aroused, when you become physically excited, when you react physically and when you are motivated to act. You experienced an increase in yellow energy when your organizational controls are aroused, when you experience an increased sense of responsibility, become more serious, become more focused on tasks and begin arranging, organizing and controlling.

> Your inner you is your blue.

You have esteem needs in all four dimensions so you need to use and experience all four colours, all four energies. Brighter colour needs are more important, more numerous and more self-fulfilling when satisfied. Paler colour esteem needs are less important to you, less numerous and less self-fulfilling when satisfied. You are self-fulfilled when you experience all your colours and satisfy all your needs in the right proportions.

Bright Blue Esteem Needs

Your blue esteem needs are met as you experience your blue. For example, the blue need "to be authentic" is being satisfied while you are being authentic. Being authentic is in and of itself, esteeming for your blue. Being authentic is a blue experience that arouses, energizes and empowers your blue. When your blue emotional and spiritual needs are met, your blue self is fulfilled.

Refer to the blue stress management card.

The following bright blue esteem needs are listed on the bright side of the blue stress management card.

BRIGHT BLUE ESTEEM NEEDS

To be authentic	To be personally valued
To be compassionate	To be spiritual
To be creative	To develop personally
To be empathic	To express emotions
To be friendly	To express the self
To be kind	To humanize events
To be loving	To relate personally

More Bright Blue Esteem Needs

To be accepted as a person
To be affectionate
To be appreciated
To be charitable
To be comfortable
To be genuine
To be human
To be included
To be intimate
To be liked
To be nurturing
To be peaceful
To be personally validated
To be self-aware
To establish rapport
To express affection
To give personal attention
To have a positive self-image
To have a positive sense of self
To have a sense of peace
To have faith
To have friends
To have genuine relationships
To have group cohesion
To have harmonious relationships
To have hope
To have personal contact
To have positive self-esteem
To have positive self-regard
To have time for self-reflection
To keep people first
To nurture self-esteem
To receive personal attention
To share feelings
To share personal experiences
To validate emotions

Bright Green Esteem Needs

Your green esteem needs are met as you experience your green. For example, the green need "to be innovative" is being satisfied while you have the esteeming experience of being innovative. Being innovative is in and of itself, esteeming. Being innovative is a green experience that arouses, energizes and empowers your green. When your green cognitive needs are met, your green self is fulfilled.

Refer to the green stress management card.

The following bright green esteem needs are listed on the bright side of the green stress management card.

BRIGHT GREEN ESTEEM NEEDS

To be innovative
To be intelligent
To be knowledgeable
To be logical
To be mentally active
To be sceptical
To challenge ideas
To conceptualize
To contemplate
To explain ideas
To ponder possibilities
To reason how
To think independently
To wonder why

More Bright Green Esteem Needs

To appreciate complexities
To ask questions
To ask why
To be autonomous
To be cognizant
To be impartial
To be independent
To be objective
To be precise
To be rationale
To be reasonable
To be unbiased
To challenge assumptions
To clarify meanings
To consider alternative ideas
To consider possibilities
To debate
To explain how
To explain thoughts
To explain why
To explore ideas
To explore possibilities
To explore thoughts
To figure things out
To have time to consider
To have time to think
To improve ideas
To investigate
To know why
To make sense
To research
To solve problems
To study information
To think about solutions
To think of implications
To think of strategies

Bright Red Esteem Needs

Your red esteem needs are met as you experience your red. For example, the red need "to act immediately" is being satisfied while you have the esteeming experience of acting immediately. Acting immediately is, in and of itself, esteeming. Acting immediately arouses, energizes and empowers your red. When your red physical needs are met, your red self is fulfilled.

Refer to the red stress management card.

The following bright red esteem needs are listed on the bright side of the red stress management card.

BRIGHT RED ESTEEM NEEDS

To act immediately
To be active
To be adventurous
To be enthusiastic
To be physical
To be playful
To be skillful
To be spontaneous
To be tactile
To have fun
To have impact
To live in the moment
To perform
To take risks

More Bright Red Esteem Needs

To act quickly	To have changes
To be competitive	To have new experiences
To be flexible	To have open spaces
To be free to move	To have room to move
To be hands-on	To keep busy
To be impulsive	To live here and now
To be in the action	To live it up
To be on stage	To live on the edge
To be on the go	To make it up
To be physically active	To move
To be quick	To push the limit/the envelope/one's luck
To do it	To react
To entertain	To respond immediately
To experience it	To respond quickly
To experience variety	To take chances
To give it a go	To test the waters
To give it a whirl	To touch it
To go for it	To try it

Bright Yellow Esteem Needs

Your yellow esteem needs are met as you experience your yellow. For example, the yellow need "to be a member" is being satisfied as you have the esteeming experience of being a member of an organization. Being a member in good standing is in and of itself esteeming. Being a member arouses, energizes and empowers your yellow. When your yellow organizational needs are met, your yellow self is fulfilled.

Refer to the yellow stress management card.

The following bright yellow esteem needs are listed on the bright side of the yellow stress management card.

BRIGHT YELLOW ESTEEM NEEDS

To be a member	To establish roles
To be loyal	To follow rules
To be neat	To follow traditions
To be on time	To maintain routines
To be responsible	To organize
To be safe	To plan
To complete tasks	To respect authority

More Bright Yellow Esteem Needs

- To arrange
- To attend to details
- To be accountable
- To be cautious
- To be dependable
- To be in control
- To be of service
- To be orderly
- To be organized
- To be predictable
- To be sequential
- To be serious
- To conform
- To define boundaries
- To follow correct procedures
- To follow directions
- To follow plans
- To follow protocols
- To follow rules
- To follow traditions
- To honour traditions
- To maintain standards
- To obey
- To have a clean environment
- To have detailed instructions
- To have predictable environments
- To have responsibilities
- To have stability
- To keep commitments
- To keep order
- To know who is responsible
- To maintain routines
- To make commitments
- To respect policies
- To stay on schedule
- To stay on task

Empowering Others to Meet Their Needs

Bright Esteem Needs

It is critical that you satisfy your esteem needs in proportions that are esteeming and empowering for you. When we are in situations or with people with whom we can experience our preferred intensities, we experience high self-esteem. This occurs most naturally when people use colours with the same intensities as we do. It also occurs when people accept, value and support us for using our colours with our preferred intensities. Workshop participants experience these high levels of self-esteem during brightest colour presentations in ColourSpectrums workshops when the audience values their presentation.

There are many roles and situations in which it is important for us to empower others to experience <u>their</u> colours and satisfy <u>their</u> esteem needs in proportions that are esteeming and empowering for them.

As Partners

In relationships, partners can create esteeming experiences for each other. If your partner's blue is energized by talking about your personal relationship, then listen, encourage and facilitate that blue experience so they can get in touch with their feelings. A true blue partner is a kindred spirit. If your partner's green is energized by explaining technical or clinical details, then express interest in your partner's explanations so they can experience their green energy, especially when his or her need to explain exceeds your need to have it explained. If your partner is energized by being physically active, quickly use your red and join right in. When your partner wants to plan and organize an event, support their behaviour so they can have that esteeming organizational experience.

Consider the big picture and encourage your partner to pursue career and life-long ambitions that are esteeming for them so they can experience life to the fullest. When you and your partner mutually support esteeming experiences for each other, you will both experience your colours with increasingly esteeming, empowering and satisfying intensities. Your relationship will grow.

As Parents

Parents have a unique opportunity to profoundly influence their children's lives. Parents can create enriched opportunities for their children to experience their colour spectrums in esteeming proportions. Parents can challenge and encourage children to develop their pale colours while supporting their natural skills and talents so they can grow up in a family environment that provides empowering experiences that will last a lifetime.

As Employers

Leaders, managers, supervisors and employers can provide staff members with opportunities to use their natural talents, to experience their natural sources of self-esteem and to feel highly regarded. When employees experience their natural sources of esteem they are empowered, energized, naturally motivated, engaged and highly committed. Staff morale is enhanced and productivity soars. Employers and supervisors can also recognize and effectively support the professional development of employees' paler colours.

Educators

Educators have a responsibility to maximize educational learning opportunities for students that will pique their intrinsic interests, maximize their potential and launch highly successful careers. Educators can use ColourSpectrums to help students recognize the challenges of using their pale colours and teach them how to use them more effectively.

It is in our best interests to create opportunities for ourselves and others, to experience colours in esteeming ways so everyone is empowered and productive. These opportunities present themselves in diverse roles. We can create esteeming experiences for our partners and children at home, our colleagues and employees at work, our students in schools, colleges and universities and our friends in the community.

Bright Stressors

A bright stressor is any situation that interferes with your bright esteem needs being met. A bright stressor puts your esteem needs at risk. More accurately, a bright stressor is a situation that keeps you from experiencing a colour as intensely as you prefer. The impact on you is bright stress. Bright colour needs are more important and more numerous than paler colour needs, so bright stressors cause greater stress. Pale colour esteem needs are less important and less numerous, so those unmet needs cause less bright stress.

Bright Blue Stressors

Bright blue stressors are situations that place blue esteem needs at risk. They interfere with people experiencing their blue as intensely as they prefer. Think of these bright stressors as situations in which blue esteem needs are not being met. For example, "arguments" are stressful because the esteem need "to be empathic" is not being met. It is not the external situation, or the "argument" that is inherently stressful. In fact I would argue that some people experience an argument as esteeming because it meets their needs to experience green mental stimulation as they rigorously debate ideas. An argument for one's blue, on the other hand, can be a bright blue stressor because it interferes with the internal blue need to experience harmony. Our green debates. Our blue has conversations.

A person with blue as a paler colour will experience an "argument" as less stressful because his or her need "to be empathic" is less. In addition, a person with blue as a bright colour, who has already satisfied many of his or her blue esteem needs, will already be in a state of high esteem. This person will experience these stressors as less threatening because they have blue esteem resources in reserve. A person who has not satisfied their blue esteem needs is already in a state of low esteem and will experience these blue stressors as more threatening because diminished blue resources are at a higher risk of being completely depleted. A person running on empty is running on emptiness.

The following bright blue stressors are listed on the bright side of the blue stress management card.

BRIGHT BLUE STRESSORS

Arguments	Lack of empathy
Disregard for people	Lack of genuineness
Human conflict	Loss of relationship
Impersonal interactions	Not being loved
Interpersonal conflicts	Not feeling unique
Lack of affection	Personal rejection
Lack of compassion	Unkindness

More Bright Blue Stressors

Being unloved	Impersonal communication
Betrayal	Impersonal service
Cruelty	Infidelity
Disagreements	Insensitivity
Disharmony	Lack of emotional stimulation
Disputes	Lack of friends
Disregard for feelings	Lack of group cohesion
Emotions not being validated	Lack of harmony
Group conflict	Lack of intimacy
Hostility	Lack of personal appreciation

Section 1: Stress Management — Look on the Bright Side

Lack of personal attention
Lack of personal contact
Lack of social interaction
No time for self-reflection
Not being liked
Not feeling understood
Personal confrontations
Personal criticism
Personal insults
Relationship conflicts
Relationship uncertainty
Restricted self-expression
Uncaring attitudes
Unfaithfulness
Unfriendliness
Unsympathetic attitudes

Bright Green Stressors

Bright green stressors are situations that are stressful because they place green esteem needs at risk. They interfere with people experiencing their green as intensely as they prefer. For example, "lack of debate" is stressful because the esteem need "to challenge ideas" is not being met. It is not the external situation, or the "lack of debate" that is inherently stressful. For some people, lack of debate is preferable so they can get on with the task at hand. It is the internal experience of not having the green esteem needs met that is stressful, of not being able to experience green with the preferred intensity.

A person with green as a paler colour will not experience a "lack of debate" as stressful because his or her need "to challenge ideas" is less. A person with green as a brighter colour, who already has many green esteem needs satisfied, will be in a state of high green esteem. This person will experience these stressors as less threatening because they have green esteem resources in reserve. A person who has not satisfied green esteem needs is already in a state of low green esteem and will experience these bright green stressors as more threatening because green resources are at higher risk of being depleted.

The following bright green stressors are listed on the bright side of the green stress management card.

BRIGHT GREEN STRESSORS

Having ideas ignored
Illogical thinking
Inability to explain
Inability to question
Inability to think
Inaccurate information
Lack of autonomy
Lack of debate
Lack of foresight
Lack of mental activity
Lack of objectivity
Lack of solitude
Not knowing why
Not understanding

More Bright Green Stressors

Ambiguous meanings
Appearing foolish
Appearing stupid
Confused thoughts
Explaining the obvious
Faulty reasoning
Guesswork
Having ideas misunderstood
Illogical reasoning
Illogical thought
Inadequate problem solving
Inadequate research
Irrational conclusions
Irrational thinking
Lack of independence
Lack of information
Lack of mental stimulation
Lack of quiet time
Lack of vision
Losing train of thought
Loss of concentration
Not being able to analyze
Not being able to concentrate
Not being able to contemplate
Not having time to think
Off topic
Quick decisions
Redundant ideas
Redundant ideas
Scattered thoughts
Unclear meanings
Unclear questions
Unethical behaviour
Unprincipled behaviour
Unreasonable behaviour
Vague ideas

Bright Red Stressors

Any situation that interferes with bright red needs being met is a bright red stressor. People with bright red need a free hand to act so any situation that ties their hands is a bright red stressor. People with bright red can't wait to act. They experience a loss of energy when they have to wait. Time flies when they have a good time. They actually get bored of waiting, get tired when they are not doing anything. When they don't have room to move, they are cooped up, get cabin fever and climb the walls.

Situations that are stressful because red esteem needs are not being met include "lack of enthusiasm," stressful because the esteem need "to be enthusiastic" is not being met. It is not the external situation, or the "lack of enthusiasm" that is inherently stressful. For some people, lack of enthusiasm is appealing because it gives them more time to think things over. It is the internal experience of not having the red esteem needs met that is stressful.

A person with red as a paler colour will experience a "lack of enthusiasm" as less stressful because his or her need "to be enthusiastic" is less. A person with red as a brighter colour, who has already satisfied many red esteem needs will be in a state of high red esteem. This person will experience these stressors as less threatening because they have red esteem resources in reserve. A person who has not satisfied red esteem needs is already in a state of low red esteem and will experience these bright red stressors as more threatening because resources are at risk of being depleted.

The following bright red stressors are listed on the bright side of the red stress management card.

Section 1: Stress Management — Look on the Bright Side

> **BRIGHT RED STRESSORS**
>
> | | |
> |---|---|
> | Inactivity | Lack of spontaneity |
> | Lack of adventure | Lack of variety |
> | Lack of competition | Moving too slowly |
> | Lack of energy | Negative attitudes |
> | Lack of enthusiasm | Physical confinement |
> | Lack of fun | Restricted activity |
> | Lack of humour | Waiting |

More Bright Red Stressors

Being confined	Limited opportunities to perform
Being fenced in	Low energy
Being held back	Not being able to act
Being inactive	Not enough activity
Delayed action	Not enough challenges
Delayed gratification	Not enough changes
Delayed reactions	Not enough play
Delays	Not enough risk
Going slow	Not having enough to do
Immobility	Physical confinement
Inability to bargain	Physical disabilities
Inaction	Physical limitations
Inflexible activities	Physical restrictions
Lack of freedom to move	Quiet/silence
Lack of momentum	Repetitive activities
Lack of new challenges	Restraint
Lack of physical activity	Restricted physical movement
Lack of physical stimulation	Stopping

Bright Yellow Stressors

Bright yellow stressors are situations that place yellow esteem needs at risk. Think of these bright stressors as situations in which yellow esteem needs are not being met. For example, "being off task" is stressful because the esteem need "to be on task" or "to complete tasks" is not being met. It is not the external situation of "being off task" that is inherently stressful. Some people experience being off task as a welcome break from tedious tasks. It is the internal experience of not having yellow esteem needs met that is stressful.

A person with yellow as a paler colour will experience "being off task" as less stressful because his or her need "to complete tasks" is less. A person with yellow as a brighter colour, who has already satisfied many yellow esteem needs will be in a state of high yellow esteem. This person will experience these stressors as less threatening as well because they have yellow esteem in reserve. A person who has not satisfied yellow esteem needs is already in a state of low yellow esteem and will experience these bright yellow stressors as more threatening because resources are at a greater risk of being depleted.

The following bright yellow stressors are listed on the bright side of the yellow stress management card.

BRIGHT YELLOW STRESSORS

Being late	Irresponsible behaviour
Being off task	Lack of control
Disrespect for authority	Lack of discipline
Inability to organize	Lack of order
Inability to plan	Lack of routine
Inattention to details	Undefined roles
Incomplete tasks	Unpredictability

More Bright Yellow Stressors

Being off schedule	Lack of follow up
Broken rules	Lack of standards
Change of plans	Lack of structure
Cheating	Not being prepared
Clutter	Not enough rules
Directions not being followed	Not knowing who is in charge
Disarray	Policies not being adhered to
Discontinuity	Poor planning
Disloyalty	Procedures not being followed
Disorder	Things out of place
Disorganization	Unclear boundaries
Disrupted routines	Unclear responsibilities
Frequent changes	Undefined roles
Instability	Unfinished business
Intrusions	Unpredictable environments
Lack of closure	Unprofessional behaviour
Lack of commitment	Unsafe conditions
Lack of direction	Wasted resources

Section 1: Stress Management — Look on the Bright Side

Identifying Your Brightest Stressors

1) Refer to the ColourSpectrums StressCheck on page 5 that you completed earlier. Write the name of your brightest colour in the box at the top of the left-hand column.

2) Review the list of 10 stressful situations you wrote in the centre column and place check marks in boxes in the left-hand column to indicate situations that are stressful as a result of your brightest colour esteem needs not being met. (Refer to your brightest colour's list of bright esteem needs and list of bright stressors to help you identify these situations.)

   For example:

   If blue is your brightest colour, then you would check off a situation such as "arguments" as a bright blue stressor because your blue esteem need "to be friendly" is at risk.

   If green is your brightest colour, then you would check off a situation such as "having ideas ignored" as a bright green stressor because your green need "to explain ideas" is at risk.

   If red is your brightest colour, then you would check off a situation such as "being inactive" as a bright red stressor because your red need "to be active" is at risk.

   If yellow is your brightest colour, then you would check off a situation such as "being late" as a bright yellow stressor because your yellow need "to be on time" is at risk.

3) When you have checked off your brightest stressors in the left-hand column, add up the check marks and write the total number of bright stressors at the bottom of the left-hand column.

Identifying Your Other Bright Stressors

In the previous exercise you identified situations that are stressful because your brightest colour needs are not being met. You did not identify situations that are stressful because your other colours' needs are not being met.

You need to experience your other colours' needs too. Your second colour's needs, although less intense and less frequent, must still be met. When those needs are not met, your second colour also experiences bright stress. When your third colour's needs are not met, it experiences bright stress as well. And yes, even your palest colour must be experienced to some extent, so on those rarer occasions when your palest colour's needs are not met, your palest colour will experience bright stress.

You can review your list of 10 stressors on page 5 again and follow the same procedure to identify other colours' unmet needs and bright stressors.

We tend to blame external influences, such as other people and unfortunate circumstances, as the cause of our esteem needs not being met. Consider, however, that each of your colours has an internal relationship with each of your other colours.

It is important to acknowledge these power differentials. There is a tendency for your brighter colours to outshine and overshadow your paler colours, meeting their own needs at the expense of your paler colours' needs. Just as significantly, however, your paler colours are quick to submit and surrender their needs in the overwhelming presence of your brighter colours. When you focus your energies on meeting your brighter colours' needs, you may be unknowingly doing so at the expense of your paler colours' needs. Because your brighter colours are naturally stronger and more influential, they can easily dominate the paler colours within you. In a real sense your bright colours can dominate, intimidate and even bully your pale colours into submission. Your own bright colour behaviours can cause your paler colours to experience the bright stress of unmet needs. In these cases the mere presence of your bright colours can be bright stressors for your own paler colours.

Because each of your colours' needs are met only by experiencing the colour, you can quickly determine if you are experiencing bright stress in any situation by asking yourself four basic questions:

1) "Am I experiencing too little blue?"
   If yes, then you are experiencing bright blue stress.
2) "Am I experiencing too little green?"
   If yes, then you are experiencing bright green stress.
3) "Am I experiencing too little red?"
   If yes, then you are experiencing bright red stress.
4) "Am I experiencing too little yellow?"
   If yes, then you are experiencing bright yellow stress.

The answers to these four basic questions will identify which needs are not being met. With this awareness you have choices. You can choose a specific course of action to meet your specific needs. The strategy for meeting green needs is distinctly different than the strategy for meeting red needs and so on.

You may also need to recognize that your needs may not be met in a specific situation or relationship. In this case you might consider meeting your needs in other situations or in other relationships. It is important to have a variety of experiences and diverse relationships because not all of your needs can be met in one situation or in one relationship. One of the keys to wellness and balance is to engage in blue, green, red and yellow experiences so all of your colours are stimulated and all of your colours' needs are met.

Simply identifying your unmet needs without taking further action can alleviate some stress. Making sense of stressful experiences naturally alleviates the anxiety and tension associated with confusion. It is important to note that not all stress is the result of bright colour needs not being met. Other significant sources of stress will be identified later.

Section 1: Stress Management — Look on the Bright Side

Multiple bright stressors

You can experience multiple bright stressors at the same time.

For example, if you have green and yellow as bright colours, you could experience back-to-back business meetings, classes or appointments as multiple bright stressors. In this situation you could experience the "inability to organize" as a bright yellow stressor because your bright yellow need "to organize" is not being met as you rush from one commitment to another. Simultaneously you could experience "not having time to think" as a bright green stressor because your bright green need "to contemplate" is not being met as you hurry from one appointment to the next, making split second decisions with no time to think.

If you have blue and red as bright colours, you could experience a disagreement as a multiple bright stressor. An "argument" can be a bright blue stressor because your bright blue need "to be friendly" is at risk. Simultaneously the "lack of fun" can be a bright red stressor because your bright red needs "to have fun."

A review of your 10 stressful situations may reveal some situations that are especially stressful due to two or more colours' esteem needs not being met at the same time.

The Intensity Scale

Colours move up and down and vary in brightness depending on how intensely they are being used. Refer to the illustration of the intensity scale that follows.

When a colour is used more intensely, it moves up and becomes brighter. These brightened intensities can be experienced as pleasant or unpleasant. An increase in blue emotional energy can be "uplifting" or "upsetting." An increase in green cognitive energy is experienced when you "make up your mind," give it a "heads up" or are "quick on the uptake." Intense green thoughts can also be pleasant or unpleasant: "I think this makes sense," "This is really confusing and it doesn't make any sense whatsoever." An increase in red physical energy is experienced when you get "warmed up," "worked up" or "fired up," are "up and about," "up for it," "upbeat" or "up in arms." Again, an increase in red energy can be experienced as pleasant and empowering or unpleasant and disempowering. An increase in yellow organizational energy is experienced when you are "up to the task," "up for a promotion" or "uptight." Intense yellow can be experienced as empowering and disempowering.

When a colour is used less intensely, it moves down and becomes paler. A decrease in blue emotional energy is experienced when emotions "subside" or "calm down." A decrease in green cognitive energy can be experienced as "mental down time." A decrease in red physical energy can be "slowing down" or "lying down." A decrease in yellow organizational energy can be "down time."

Different situations require different colours and different intensities. When colours are used appropriately with effective intensities they are functional and considered to be "in the light." Colours used within this illuminated range are positive and productive human attributes. The original four ColourSpectrums attribute cards describe the positive qualities of each colour when they are used effectively, "in the light."

The intensity scale ranges from "0" to "10."

```
                    Intensity Scale

        Assertive      10        ○    ↑
                                 ○
        Mid-range       5
                                 ○
        Passive         0        ○    ↓
```

Passive Intensity of "0"

When you use a colour with minimal energy, you use it with an intensity of "0." The colour at the lower end of this intensity scale is being used passively. There are times when it is appropriate and effective to use colours passively. When you are not being personal, emotional or empathic, when you are not feeling too much one way or the other, you are using your blue passively. When you are not analyzing or simply not thinking too much about anything, you are using your green passively. When you are not being active, not taking action, not doing much, not doing anything or just sleeping, you are using red passively. When you are not organizing, not arranging or not controlling the order of things, you are using your yellow passively. You use your paler colours more passively more often than your brighter colours.

Mid-range Intensity of "4, 5, or 6"

When you use or experience a colour with medium intensity, you use it in the mid-range intensity of 4, 5 or 6 — being somewhat emotional, thinking about some things, being somewhat active and being sort of prepared. Colours can be used effectively in this mid-range. You often use your middle colours with these intensities.

Assertive Intensity

When you use a colour with high energy, you use it with an intensity of "10." The colour at the upper end of the intensity scale is being used assertively. Using colours assertively can be effective. When you are empathic, emotional or spiritual, you are using your blue assertively. When you are reasoning, rationalizing and analyzing, you are using your green assertively. When you are being physically active, vigorous and enthusiastic, you are using your red assertively and when you are organizing, arranging, and following through on deadlines and commitments, you are using your yellow assertively. You use your brighter colours more assertively more often than your paler colours.

Using Colours Assertively

There are good reasons to use colours assertively.

When you can use your colours assertively, you can be effective in diverse situations. You can be effective when you are able to use your bright blue assertively to provide genuine compassion and emotional support when it is needed. You can be effective when you use your bright green assertively to think about implications and problem solve strategies for the future. You can be effective when you use your bright red to quickly call for help in an emergency or actually pick up the phone and make the phone call you have been avoiding. You can be highly effective when you are able to use your bright yellow to assertively take charge, organize your day and put your house in order.

You will be more effective when you use a colour assertively to match and communicate with a person who is using it intensely. If you use a colour passively with someone who is using it assertively, you will not be able to communicate effectively. I will say more about the key to great communication later.

Using colours assertively can meet your needs. When the needs of one of your colours are not being met, brightening that colour and using it assertively can be an appropriate response and an effective way to meet that colour's esteem needs. Being assertive is clearly communicating your needs in a firm and persistent manner. It is not the same as being aggressive and hostile and it is not the same as being demanding or overbearing and getting your needs met at someone else's expense.

Section 2: Bright Shadows — Understanding and Managing Them

The Evolution of Stress: The Fight Response

What happens when your assertive efforts to cope with a situation just aren't enough? What happens when your best efforts to satisfy your esteem needs fall short and you continue to experience the bright colour stress of unmet needs?

To understand our response to stress today we need to understand the evolution of stress. The physiologist Walter Cannon coined the phrase "fight or flight" to describe the nervous system's autonomic response to external stimuli as a physiological phenomenon that mobilizes energy to either defeat the stressor or to get away from it. Any perceived threat to your needs can trigger this response. It is a normal, adaptive response to environmental stimuli.

Imagine you are a cave dweller gathering cool, juicy tropical fruit in the hot and humid prehistoric jungle. Your mouth drools with delicious anticipation. Suddenly you find yourself face-to-face with a saber-toothed tiger! As bad luck would have it, while you were gathering, the tiger was hunting. You face imminent physical danger!

Thanks to millions of years of evolution, you have a secret biological weapon that has prepared you for this very moment. You have a highly developed fight/flight response system that you inherited from your ancestors (ancestors with poorly developed fight/flight response systems didn't live long enough to bear children.)

The fight/flight response occurs in two distinct stages:

1) The physiological response stage
2) The behavioural response stage.

1) The physiological response stage

Your biological fight/flight response immediately triggers a rapid sequence of physiological responses throughout your entire body:

- **You are frozen with fear.** You shiver with chills running up and down your spine as your brain fires a series of rapid electrical discharges that pulse through your spinal cord to alert the nervous system. Your nervous system paralyzes your body so you can't move and so the tiger that was stalking your every move can hardly see you. Being immobilized keeps you from getting yourself into even more trouble than you already are.
- **Your hair stands on end.** A chill ripples through your skin. The resulting goose bumps stand your hair on end, making you appear bigger and more intimidating. Lucky for you, if the tiger sees you he will get the full visual effect because you are totally naked. Unlucky for you the tiger gets goose bumps too and having more hair creates a higher intimidation factor... a hair-raising experience for both of you!
- **Your eyes bulge out of your head.** Your eyes open wide to expand your peripheral vision. Your pupils dilate to let in more light. Your hearing and sense of smell become supersensitive... you can hear the tiger breathing and you can smell the tiger's breath and it smells like trouble.
- **You turn white as a ghost.** Blood vessels under your skin constrict, forcing blood away from the surface of your skin to large muscle groups deeper below. This will keep you from bleeding to death if you are inflicted with a serious flesh wound. Your muscles are engorged with blood and fueled for action.
- **You feel numb with fear.** Pain receptors turn off to reduce sensations of pain.
- **You break into a cold sweat.** Sweat makes you slippery and hard to get a hold of.
- **Your heart races.** Your racing heart increases blood flow and quickly distributes oxygen-enriched blood and nutrient-rich fat cells to essential muscles and organs.
- **Your knees shake.** Your muscles tighten and you start to shake and feel edgy as your muscles become spring-loaded and quiver under the tension... ready to spring into action.
- **Your fingers are clenched.** Clenched fingers squeeze blood from your hands so more blood is diverted to major muscle groups. With less blood your hands are harder for hitting and will bleed less when cut. The clench reflex forms fists, which are stronger for hitting than open hands.
- **You feel a sudden surge of energy.** Blood sugars rise rapidly to provide energy to major muscle groups.
- **You gasp!** The deep inhalation reflex primes your lungs with fresh oxygen and you breath rapidly.
- **You get butterflies in your stomach.** Your digestive system shuts down and abdominal muscles tighten to protect internal organs from a frontal assault.
- **You are ready to fight or flee.** The blood supply to the frontal parts of your brain that are responsible for higher levels of reasoning is reduced, inhibiting green logical functioning. The blood supply to the more primitive parts of the brain at the brainstem is increased, stimulating automatic and instinctive behaviour. Isn't this just great! Now you can't even think straight. Your brightened red takes you out of your head so you can react without thinking.

In this high state of tension you cannot physically do nothing. You are not only ready to fight or flee; you <u>must</u> fight or flee. The physiological arousal stage of the fight/flight response is complete. This physiological response stage has prepared your body for physical action. This is your red physical functioning at its best. Fighting and fleeing both require this same biological readiness. Whether you fight or flee is not the point. Your supercharged body is highly charged and must expend the energy quickly by taking either course of vigorous action.

2) The behavioural response stage

The saber-toothed tiger salivates and licks its lips. Terrified by its two long protruding teeth, you are suddenly inspired to grasp one in each hand and twist both with all of your might. Caught off guard and off balance by the element of surprise, the tiger loses its balance as you flip it onto its back. Dazed and confused, the tiger struggles to its feet and takes flight into the safety of the jungle. This scenario illustrates the cave dweller's <u>fight</u> response. This scenario also illustrates the tiger's <u>flight</u> response.

The red physical fight or flight response prepares us for physical action to protect the physical body. We have evolved and come a long way socially and technologically since the prehistoric days of gathering fruit in the jungle and escaping the teeth of saber-toothed tigers. As we have evolved, however, the fight or flight response mechanism that helped us survive the physical threats of the prehistoric jungle has remained relatively unchanged for millions of years and it is still biologically wired in us today.

Emotional and Psychological Stressors

It is rare nowadays for us to be actually faced with physical threats or life and death situations. Take a look at the 10 stressors you wrote on your StressCheck. Is there anything on your list of 10 stressors that is life threatening? Probably not. Is there anything on your list of 10 stressors that is even remotely physically threatening? Probably not.

The stressful situations you have listed are emotional stressors, mental stressors, physical stressors and organizational stressors. These are the saber-toothed tigers in <u>your</u> life. Although your 10 stressful situations are not physically threatening, they do trigger the same physiological arousal stage of the fight or flight response mechanism, the same response as if physically threatened. The natural resolution of this physical state of tension would be a physical course of action — a physical fight or a physical flight. Physical responses are not usually suitable options...even though you may have imagined them. So here you are with a list of 10 stressors...all stressed up and no place to go. Now what?

The Fight Response: For Better or Worse

When you use a colour more assertively in an effort to satisfy that colour's needs, that colour becomes brighter within you. The fight response can bring out the best in us and motivate us to be appropriately assertive and highly effective. If bright stressors continue to threaten your bright esteem needs, your unconscious fight response continues to brighten that colour in a desperate last-ditch effort to meet your needs. The greater the threat is perceived to be, the greater the stress and more intense the physiological arousal stage becomes.

While the fight response can bring out the best in us, it can also bring out the worst in us. What happens when we continue to brighten a colour? As a colour becomes increasingly intense it moves upward, away from the light, and into the bright shadow. Welcome to the dark side!

Bright Shadow Characteristics

Carl Jung used the term "shadow side" to describe the hidden dark side of human awareness. He believed that the negative personal qualities that we are not consciously aware of are veiled in the shadows. This dark side of human nature has been described in a number of ways in the past. Freud used the term alter ego. Others have referred to this phenomenon as the lower self, the id and the repressed self.

Bright shadow characteristics appear when a colour is used, or is perceived as being used, too intensely. The more intense the colour, the larger and darker the shadow.

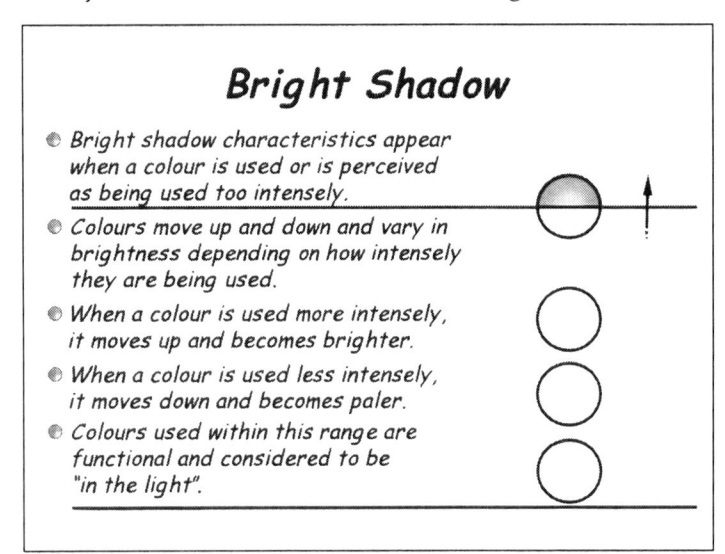

Bright Shadow

- Bright shadow characteristics appear when a colour is used or is perceived as being used too intensely.
- Colours move up and down and vary in brightness depending on how intensely they are being used.
- When a colour is used more intensely, it moves up and becomes brighter.
- When a colour is used less intensely, it moves down and becomes paler.
- Colours used within this range are functional and considered to be "in the light".

When any of your colours' esteem needs are threatened by bright stressors, your fight response can be triggered. An assessment of the threat, your available resources and the odds of prevailing determine your course of action.

Section 2: Bright Shadows — Understanding and Managing Them

There are two reasons your brighter colours are more likely to respond with a fight response than your paler colours. First, your brighter colour needs are more important to you. Your bright colour needs are worth fighting for so when those needs are threatened you are highly motivated and more likely to rise to the challenge. Second, your brighter colours are your greatest strengths and your odds of prevailing seem better. You are more capable of using them intensely and effectively in a fight response.

When your blue needs are threatened, the fight response brightens your blue emotional behaviour. When your green esteem needs are threatened, the fight response triggers increasingly brighter green cognitive behaviour. When your red needs are threatened, the fight response brightens your red physical behaviour, and when your yellow needs are threatened, your yellow fight response is triggered and your organizational behaviour becomes more intense.

> You fight with bright.

Generally speaking a stressor is any event that causes a stress response. More specifically a bright stressor is any event that triggers a fight response and causes a colour to become brighter. This reaction causes a person to display bright shadow characteristics.

Bright Blue Shadow Characteristics

Consider what happens when you use, or are perceived as using, your blue too intensely. A bright blue shadow appears and you will be perceived as having bright blue shadow characteristics. People using blue with less intensity will perceive your bright blue shadow before you do. The greater the difference in intensity is perceived to be, the larger your bright blue shadow will appear to be. In the light, blue is a good thing. But, too much of a good thing... is not a good thing.

The following bright blue shadow characteristics are listed on the bright side of the blue stress management card.

BRIGHT BLUE SHADOW CHARACTERISTICS

Ashamed	Moody
Codependent	Over accommodating
Defensive	Overly emotional
Depressed	Overly sensitive
Emotionally conflicted	Self-conscious
Emotionally fragile	Self-doubting
Excessively helpful	Victimized

More Bright Blue Shadow Characteristics

Being a pushover
Dwelling on feelings
Easily offended
Emotional outbursts
Emotionally distraught
Emotionally distressed
Emotionally needy
Emotionally reactive
Emotionally unstable
Feeling defensive
Feeling downhearted
Feeling guilty
Feeling hopeless
Feeling hurt
Feeling sorry for self
Feeling unloved
Helpless
Meek
Narcissistic
Over-personalizing
Overly friendly
Overly helpful
Placating
Pleasing everyone
Sad
Self absorbed
Self pity
Self sacrificing
Socializing too much
Submissive
Temperamental
Too agreeable
Too passive
Too personally involved
Too sensitive
Too trusting

Bright Green Shadow Characteristics

When you use, or are perceived as using, green too intensely, a bright green shadow appears. You will be perceived as having bright green shadow characteristics. People using green with less intensity will perceive your bright green shadow before you do. The greater the difference in intensity is perceived to be, the larger your bright green shadow will appear to be.

The following bright green shadow characteristics are listed on the bright side of the green stress management card.

BRIGHT GREEN SHADOW CHARACTERISTICS

Argumentative
Arrogant
Condescending
Controversial
Cynical
Eccentric
Manipulative
Opinionated
Overly analytical
Overly sceptical
Pessimistic
Too abstract
Too technical
Too theoretical

Section 2: Bright Shadows — Understanding and Managing Them

More Bright Green Shadow Characteristics

Calculating	Mentally abusive
Close minded	Obstinate
Complicating the simple	Over-explaining
Conniving	Over rationalizing
Conspiring	Patronizing
Contentious	Plotting
Cunning	Quibbling over semantics
Devil's advocate	Sarcastic
Devious	Scheming
Diabolical	Shrewd
Double talk/speak	Sinister
Facetious	Sly
Fault finding	Smug
Hard headed	Thinking too much
Indignant	Tough-minded
Intellectualizing	Verbose
Long-winded	Wily
Lost in thought	Wordy

Bright Red Shadow Characteristics

When you use, or are perceived as using, red too intensely, a bright red shadow appears. You will be perceived as having bright red shadow characteristics. People using red with less intensity will perceive your bright red shadow before you do. The greater the difference in intensity is perceived to be, the larger your bright red shadow will appear to be.

The following bright red shadow characteristics are listed on the bright side of the red stress management card.

BRIGHT RED SHADOW CHARACTERISTICS

Angry	Reckless
Chaotic	Restless
Disruptive	Shocking
Distracted	Showy
Erratic	Too competitive
Hyperactive	Too fast
Impatient	Too impulsive

More Bright Red Shadow Characteristics

Abrupt	Inattentive
Agitated	Interrupting
Clowning around	Intrusive
Cocky	Loudmouth
Distracting	Manic
Exhibitionist	Overzealous
Extremist	Pleasure seeking
Fidgety	Provocative
Flippant	Pushy
Fly-by-night	Rambunctious
Foolhardy	Rebellious
Frantic	Rowdy
Frenetic	Sporadic
Frivolous	Too hasty
Goofing off	Too loud
High risk	Too outrageous
Hostile	Violent
In your face	Wild

Bright Yellow Shadow Characteristics

When you use, or are perceived as using, yellow too intensely, a bright yellow shadow appears. You will be perceived as having bright yellow shadow characteristics. People using yellow with less intensity will perceive your bright yellow shadow before you do. The greater the difference in intensity is perceived to be, the larger your bright yellow shadow will appear to be.

The following bright yellow shadow characteristics are listed on the bright side of the yellow stress management card.

BRIGHT YELLOW SHADOW CHARACTERISTICS

Authoritarian	Possessive
Bureaucratic	Punitive
Controlling	Regimented
Judgmental	Rigid
Materialistic	Rule bound
Overly responsible	Stingy
Overly strict	Uptight

Section 2: Bright Shadows — Understanding and Managing Them

More Bright Yellow Shadow Characteristics

Admonishing others	Nitpicky
Autocratic	Obsessive
Blind allegiance	Old fashioned
Blind obedience	Over planning
Bossy	Over preparing
Cheap	Overly cautious
Compulsive	Overly compliant
Constrained	Overly obedient
Dictatorial	Petty
Disciplining	Rigid adherence to timelines
Dogmatic	Rigid enforcement of rules
Domineering	Stern
Excessive conformity	Stuck in a rut
Guarded	Subservient
Hoarding	System bound
Inflexible	Taskmaster
Ironhanded	Territorial
Miserly	Too serious

Reviewing Your 10 Stressors For Fight Responses

Refer to the ColourSpectrums StressCheck on page 5 that you completed earlier and take note of the stressful situations you checked off in the left-hand column. You will recall that those situations are stressful because your brightest colour needs are not being met. These are also the situations that are most likely to trigger your fight response causing you to display bright shadow characteristics.

Review your brightest colour's list of bright shadow characteristics to identify the bright shadow characteristics that you display in response to the bright stressors you have checked off.

Recognizing Your Bright Shadow Characteristics

As you brighten your colours and use them more intensely in a genuine effort to meet your needs or in an effort to be more effective, it will seem to you as if your increased intensity is appropriate for the situation. For example, as your blue becomes more emotive because you need to express your blue emotions, as your green opinions become opinionated because your green needs to state opinions, as your red becomes more competitive and feisty because it likes to win to earn hard-fought bragging rights, and as your yellow becomes more authoritarian because your yellow needs to experience more order... your needs are increasingly satisfied. Because your needs are being satisfied your behaviour is rewarded and you will have the perception that you are doing the right thing. As far as you are concerned — that is, from your perspective — using that colour with increasing intensity is an appropriate response to the situation.

While you perceive yourself being in the light, others may perceive you as being in the bright shadow. Your blue has a need to accommodate others. When you brighten your blue and perceive yourself as being more accommodating, a person using less blue may perceive you as being a pushover. While you perceive you are being kind, a person with less blue may perceive you as kind to a fault. While you feel welcoming by putting out the welcome mat, someone using less blue may perceive you as being walked on and being a doormat.

While you think you are analyzing, someone using less green may think you are "anal-yzing."

While you experience your red as a carefree troubleshooter, someone using less red sees you as a careless, overly impulsive, cavalier trouble maker. While you perceive yourself as an avid sports fan, someone with paler red perceives you as a sports fanatic.

While you take pride in being traditional, a person using less yellow may judge you as old-fashioned or old school. While you perceive you have an established routine, a person with less yellow may judge you as stuck in a rut or entrenched. There is a fine line between a groove and a rut. While you take pride in your established regimes, someone with less yellow might perceive you as set in your ways and regimented. When you perceive yourself sticking to the plan, someone using paler yellow may perceive you as stuck to the plan. While you perceive yourself attending to details with a fine-toothed comb, someone else perceives you as an overbearing, finicky stickler for details. You might perceive yourself as being neat while someone with paler yellow perceives you as being a neat freak. When you go over the rules or make a ruling, a person with paler yellow may perceive themselves as being overruled or ruled over. And when you simply mean business, you may come across as simply mean.

So, how can you know if you are using, or are perceived as using, a colour too intensely? How can you possibly recognize your own bright shadow characteristics when the experience is highly esteeming for you and satisfies your needs? The more intensely you experience your bright colours and the more esteeming and self-satisfying the experience is, the less objective you are.

As it turns out, your own perspective is only half of the story. While you perceive yourself as using a colour assertively, people using that same colour less intensely may perceive you as using it aggressively...and that is the other half of the story.

Illuminating Bright Shadow Characteristics

When you are in the bright shadow, you are in the dark. Behaviours and characteristics that are hidden in the shadows are out of conscious awareness, so we cannot make conscious choices about them. Jung believed that everything in our conscious awareness is "in the light." Raising awareness of bright shadow characteristics from an unconscious level to a conscious level brings them to light and illuminates them. When you acknowledge your bright shadow, you shed light on these shady behaviours. This does not eliminate bright shadows, but it does illuminate them.

> Not being known doesn't stop the truth from being true.
>
> — Richard Bach

Section 2: Bright Shadows — Understanding and Managing Them

> "Don't fear the darkness if you carry the light within."
> — Siyanda

When you are enlightened, you are empowered to make conscious and informed choices. When it dawns on you, you can see the light. You can choose to continue and strengthen behaviours that are effective, and you can choose to diminish or stop behaviours that are ineffective. Either way, with increased awareness, you have increased choices.

Forming Good Habits

Many of our behaviours are habits. We use them routinely and are so familiar with them that we don't notice how frequently and intensely we actually use them. It is this lack of awareness that gives habits their power. We cannot change what we do not acknowledge. We can only break old habits or make new habits by raising our awareness of them from an unconscious level to a conscious level.

We are least aware of what we do most often.

What behaviours are you unconsciously aware of at this very moment? This question is difficult to answer because the moment you become conscious of an unconscious behaviour, it is no longer an unconscious behaviour. Simply put, you cannot be consciously aware of your own bright shadow behaviour because, by definition, those behaviours are in the shadow of unconscious awareness. The moment you become aware of your shadow behaviours, they are illuminated and no longer in the shadow.

An Exercise in Awareness

You have probably not been aware of your breathing for the last few minutes. Stop reading for a moment and simply notice your breathing for 10 seconds. Go ahead! Notice your breathing for 10 seconds before reading further.

What happened to your breathing when you consciously attended to it? Did you notice that your breathing changed? Perhaps your breathing rate increased or perhaps it decreased. Maybe your breathing became deeper... or shallower. The point is, when we become consciously aware of unconscious behaviour, it is natural for us to change that behaviour.

When you raise awareness of your other behaviours from an unconscious to a conscious level, you will notice you have a natural tendency to change those behaviours too. Not convinced? Try the next exercise.

You have not been consciously aware of the position of your left foot until I brought it to your attention just now.

Stop reading and notice the position of your left foot for 10 seconds.

Did you change the position of your left foot simply because you attended to it? Chances are you did. Consciously attending to your left foot gives it conscious energy. Of course as you brought your left foot into conscious awareness, you may also have become consciously aware of your right foot. Shedding light on one unconscious behaviour has the positive effect of illuminating related shadow behaviours that are in close proximity, bringing them into the light of conscious awareness as well.

35

Consider how this phenomenon of conscious awareness can benefit your behaviours. When you become consciously aware of your bright shadow behaviours, you will be inclined to change them. You will tend to change your behaviours for the better because it is difficult to continue behaving ineffectively when you become consciously aware of ineffective behaviour and perceive more effective options. Increased levels of conscious awareness consistently lead to positive changes in behaviours. It is my experience and belief that people are naturally inclined to change their behaviour so it is more positive and productive. When people have more options, they make <u>better</u> choices. As human beings we are naturally drawn toward the light. You can minimize your bright shadow characteristics and maximize effective behaviours by attending to them and being more consciously aware.

Brightest Colours: Our Greatest Strengths and Greatest Weaknesses

Our brightest colours can be our greatest strengths and our greatest weaknesses. They can be our greatest strengths when we use them with the balancing influences of our paler colours. All four of our colours interact and influence each other in a dynamic dance of balances and counterbalances. We are all familiar with these internal tensions and conflicts — "Should I spend more time with my friends or more time working?" "Should I act more quickly or think it over more thoroughly?" These modifying influences help us stay in balance and safeguard us from bright shadow characteristics.

Our paler colours modify our bright colours so they are less intense, reducing our risks of becoming too emotional, too logical, too physical or too rigid. When we use our brighter colours without the balancing effects of our paler colours, we are at risk of moving toward the bright shadow.

Using colours too intensely over prolonged periods can cause psychological problems and make you sick. When you are in the bright blue shadow for prolonged periods, you may experience emotional exhaustion, depression and intense mood swings. Prolonged green shadow behaviour exerts a toll and can lead to mental exhaustion, headaches, altered or distorted perceptions, disillusionment and memory loss. Prolonged red shadow behaviours can lead to hyperactivity, physical exhaustion, anger and physical aggression. Prolonged exertion of bright yellow behaviours can lead to organizational fatigue, obsessiveness, compulsiveness, increased insecurities, hypertension and high blood pressure.

Being in any bright shadow for extended periods can lead to generalized symptoms including insomnia, negative attitudes, stomach disturbances, uncharacteristic or extreme behaviours and a marked decrease in individual capability and effectiveness. The overuse of any colour can lead to burnout. When colours become exhausted we can experience emotional collapse (burnout has been described as "the collapse of the human spirit"), mental collapse, physical collapse or organizational collapse. Using a balance of colours, on the other hand, helps reduce emotional, mental, physical and organizational stress and potential burnout, increasing health, wellness and effectiveness.

Section 2: Bright Shadows — Understanding and Managing Them

> Life is a classroom. You just don't know what the next lesson is going to be.
>
> If you don't learn the lesson you will repeat the class again and again and again and ...

When you use your brightest colour you are esteemed and empowered. Your brightest colour is a remarkable resource and you have used it with great success. Remember, however, that your brightest colour can only perform those colour functions. It cannot do everything. Far from it. If you cannot accomplish something, it might not be because you are not using a colour intensely enough. It might be because you are using the wrong colour.

A Definition of Insanity

Albert Einstein defined insanity as "doing the same thing over and over again and expecting different results."

The next time things are not going well ... acknowledge your bright shadow:

1) Notice what colour you are using.
2) Notice it isn't working.
3) Use another colour.

You are the expert on using your brightest colour too intensely. Although it is possible to use any colour too intensely, it is likely that you use your brightest colour too intensely more often. When you perceive that you are in the bright shadow, you can move toward the light simply by giving it a rest and doing less of what you have been doing. Doing less or doing nothing at all is sometimes a better option.

Understanding Principles of Perception

In Book One I described how our five senses function — simultaneously but separately with no duplication of services — as a way of understanding how our four colours function. Now consider how our five senses actually perceive events, because that is also how our four colours perceive events.

The following paired exercise will demonstrate what I mean.

Choose one person to be the instructor for the following exercise. Only the instructor should read the directions.

Instructor: You are going to give your partner two different instructions simultaneously. You will give your partner the verbal instruction "Put a finger on your chin." You will also give your partner the visual instruction to put a finger on his or her cheek by demonstrating (by putting one of your fingers on your cheek).

Rehearse giving these two instructions in private first.

When you are ready, sit and face your partner and give both instructions at the same time. (As you give the verbal instruction "put a finger on your chin," demonstrate the visual instruction by putting one of your fingers on your cheek).

Debrief the exercise.

What just happened? The instructor gave two messages. The other person heard the auditory message "put a finger on your chin." That message goes in the ears and is processed in a region of the brain called the primary auditory cortex. The person saw the visual message to put a finger on the cheek. That message goes in the eyes and is processed in the visual cortex of the brain. The message that gets processed first actually blocks the other message from being processed, at least for a while until the other message works its way through the brain and then...wait a minute...you told me to do one thing while showing me something different. We perceive a conflict and because we don't like internal conflict, we settle on one message and ignore the other. So if visual processing is faster, the person placed a finger on his or her cheek just as he or she was shown. If the person's auditory processing is faster, the person placed a finger on his or her chin just as he or she was told.

Our four colours perceive and process information in much the same way. People give you four colour messages all the time. Your bright colours are highly perceptive so you perceive and respond quickly to those messages. Your pale colours are not as perceptive so you do not perceive, process or respond to those messages as quickly. Your bright colours' efficient processing blocks your paler colours from perceiving and processing paler colour messages.

Consider the previous exercise. Rather than responding to only one message or the other, how could you respond to both messages at the same time? How could you put a finger on your chin as you are told and put a finger on your cheek as you are shown? If you can't put your finger on the solution...put your fingers on the solutions.

Of course! You can use your ears to perceive and respond to the auditory message by putting one finger on your chin _and_ you can use your eyes to perceive and respond to the visual message by putting another finger on your cheek. The solution is to respond to _both_ messages rather than limiting your response to only one at the expense of the other. The messages themselves don't conflict; they are simply different messages. We only interpret the messages as conflicting when we misinterpret the difference between our sense of sight and sense of hearing as conflict. The conflict we perceive in the messages is simply a reflection of our own inner conflict. That inner conflict forces us to respond to one _or_ the other. When we accurately interpret the messages as simply different, then we can perceive and respond to one _and_ the other.

This is the key to using your colours effectively to communicate. Instead of responding to blue, green, red _or_ yellow messages, you can be highly effective by perceiving and responding to blue, green, red _and_ yellow messages. You will be more perceptive and experience less internal conflict when you appreciate that different colour messages are not conflicting messages...they are different messages

Consider again how your five senses perform separate and simultaneous functions to perceive the world around you. Your eyes see, your ears hear, your skin touches, your nose smells and your tongue tastes. Although we experience all five senses simultaneously, we can easily distinguish between what our eyes are seeing, our ears are hearing, our skin is touching, our

> We only perceive and are only perceived colour to colour. The implications are profound.

Section 2: Bright Shadows — Understanding and Managing Them

tongue is tasting and our nose is smelling because each of our five senses is physically located in different parts of the body. We don't get confused. We know we don't see sounds and we know we do not hear colours and so on. This sensory knowledge is so deeply integrated into our human functioning that we intuitively use the right sensory function for the right task. So if you want to see something better, you naturally use your eyes to look more closely. If you want to hear better you lend an ear. If you want to feel something you simply reach out and touch it with your hand. If you want to smell something you hold it up to your nose and if you want to taste something you use your tongue.

This is the solution for using your four colours effectively. Use your colours in the same manner and you will be a highly perceptive communicator. Use your blue to perceive and respond to blue messages, your green to perceive and respond to green messages, your red to perceive and interact with people's red and of course use your yellow to perceive and respond to yellow messages.

It sounds pretty straightforward, but unlike our five senses that are easily differentiated (because they are located in different parts of the body), our blue emotions, green cognition, red physical actions and yellow organizational functions are not as easily differentiated. Until now. Now you know the language of ColourSpectrums. ColourSpectrums enhances your perceptual powers by enabling you to clearly distinguish between each colour's function so you can use the right colour for the right job. Empowered with this perceptual clarity, you will be a highly perceptive and effective communicator.

Bright Shadow Perceptions

Each of your colours perceives the corresponding colour in others. Your colours are also sensitive to differences in intensities. Your blue intuitively senses when someone is using blue more intensely than you are. Your green understands when someone is using green more intensely. Your red notices when someone is using red more intensely than you are and your yellow takes note when someone is using yellow more intensely.

When one of your colours perceives someone using that colour with a great deal more intensity, your colour will often have the impression the other person is using that colour <u>too</u> intensely and will perceive that colour's bright shadow.

Because your perceptions are based on perceived differences in intensities, your paler colours perceive corresponding bright shadows in others more often than your brighter colours do.

> **For example:**
>> The paler your blue is, the more often you perceive bright blue shadow characteristics in others. The paler your green is, the more often you perceive bright green shadow characteristics in others. The paler your red is, the more often you perceive bright red shadow characteristics in others and the paler your yellow is, the more often you perceive bright yellow shadow characteristics in others.

The greater the difference in intensity is perceived to be, the larger the bright shadow appears to be. When you perceive a small difference in intensity, you perceive a small bright shadow in the other person. When you perceive a large difference in intensity, you perceive a large bright shadow.

Bright Shadow Perceptions: A Case in Point

The phenomenon of bright shadow perceptions is evident in ColourSpectrums workshops. You will recall that participants work in brightest colour groups and make group presentations to the audience on the priorities, delights and talents of using their brightest colours. When a brightest colour group makes their presentation, everyone in the audience has that colour as a paler colour, as their second, third or even palest colour. Regardless of the colour that is being presented, audience members perceive the presenting group's brightest colour as more intense than their own. This perceived difference in intensity can cause audience members to perceive bright shadow characteristics in the presenting group.

The perception of these bright shadows becomes evident during the question period following each presentation. After each presentation the presenting group remains at the front of the room so audience members can ask them questions. At this point in the workshop, audience members are wearing nametags with four colour dots in vertical order that represent their colour spectrums. When audience members ask questions it is easy to determine whether the bright colour that has been presented is the audience member's second, third or palest colour. The paler that colour is for the audience member, the more likely he or she will perceive bright shadow characteristics in the presenters.

Audience members' perceptions are revealed by the way they ask questions. Audience members who have blue as a second colour are able to use their blue to closely identify with the bright blue presentation on the priorities, delights and talent of using blue. Audience members who have blue as a third colour identify less closely with the bright blue presentation and audience members who have blue as their palest colour can find it challenging to understand the bright blue presenters' priorities, delight and talents. They ask the presenting group questions such as, "Don't you feel you are too emotional?" and "Why do you take things so personally?" The tone of these questions strongly suggests that the audience members asking these questions perceive the presenters as using blue too intensely. These audience members perceive the presenters as displaying bright blue shadow characteristics.

During the bright green presentation audience members who have green as a second colour are able to understand the priorities, delights and talents of using green because it is fairly bright for them too. Audience members who have green as a third colour identify less closely with the green presentation. Audience members who have green as their palest colour can find it challenging to identify with the bright green presentation. While presenters with bright green have a way with words, audience members with pale green do away with

> People who think they know everything are a great annoyance to those of us who do.
>
> — Isaac Asimov

words. These audience members are often puzzled by the bright green explanatory, and seemingly wordy, presentation and ask such questions as, "Don't you get tired of thinking so much?" and "Why do you need to explain everything?" Again the tone of these questions suggests these audience members perceive these presenters as using too much green, as displaying bright green shadow characteristics.

When participants with bright red make their presentation, audience members who have red as a second colour resonate and identify with the presentation. Audience members who have red as a third colour identify less closely. Those who have red as a palest colour can be overwhelmed by the high physical energy and loud volume of the red presentation. They ask, "Don't you ever get tired of being so enthusiastic and physically active?" "Why do you take so many risks?" The tone of the questions suggests these audience members perceive the presenters as displaying bright red shadow characteristics.

Audience members who have yellow as a second colour also value the organized bright yellow presentation on the priorities, delights and talents of using bright yellow. Audience members who have yellow as a third colour identify less closely with this presentation. Audience members who have yellow as their palest colour can find it challenging to identify with the priorities, delights and talent of using yellow so intensely. These audience members ask the group presenting bright yellow, "Don't you think you take life too seriously?" and "Why do you have to be so organized?" These questions indicate audience members perceive these presenters as displaying bright yellow shadow characteristics.

Lighten-Up Phrases

When we perceive someone using a colour more intensely than we do, we may not appreciate and value that intensity for what it is. Instead, we tend to focus on the difference in intensity, the difference between our intensity and the other person's. We are inclined to be more subjective than objective. We are also inclined to perceive the difference as a negative rather than a positive. Because we prefer to perceive ourselves as being in the light ... we are forced to perceive the other person as being in the bright shadow. We would rather perceive the other person as using the colour too intensely than perceive ourselves as not using that colour intensely enough.

When we perceive someone's bright shadow, we often react by trying to close the gap. When we perceive the other person as responsible for the difference, we pressure the person to use that colour with less intensity rather than pressuring ourselves to use that colour more intensely — expecting less of others, rather than expecting more of ourselves. There are many common phrases we use in everyday language to convey these messages, to coax and persuade others to use colours less intensely and come back into the light where we are. These are "lighten-up phrases."

When our paler blue attempts to persuade someone's brighter blue to be less intense, we use blue lighten-up phrases. These messages emanate from our paler blue, not from our paler green, red or yellow.

The following blue lighten-up phrases are listed on the bright side of the blue stress management card.

> **BLUE LIGHTEN-UP PHRASES**
>
> *"Don't feel bad."*
> *"Don't be so sad."*
> *"Don't be so sensitive."*
> *"Don't be so emotional."*
> *"Don't feel so defensive."*
> *"Don't take it personally."*
> *"Don't be so self-conscious."*

When our paler green pressures someone's brighter green to be less intense, we use green lighten-up phrases. These messages originate from our paler green, not from our paler blue, red or yellow. The following green lighten-up phrases are listed on the bright side of the green stress management card.

> **GREEN LIGHTEN-UP PHRASES**
>
> *"Don't think so much."*
> *"Don't be so sceptical."*
> *"Stop intellectualizing."*
> *"Don't be so technical."*
> *"Don't be so theoretical."*
> *"Stop analyzing everything."*
> *"Don't ask so many questions."*

When our paler red attempts to persuade someone's brighter red to be less intense, we use red lighten-up phrases. These messages come from our paler red, not from our paler blue, green or yellow. The following red lighten-up phrases are listed on the bright side of the red stress management card.

> **RED LIGHTEN-UP PHRASES**
>
> *"Not so fast."*
> *"Slow down."*
> *"Take it easy."*
> *"Wait a minute."*
> *"Don't be so impulsive."*
> *"Don't be so competitive."*
> *"Don't be in such a hurry."*

When our paler yellow pressures someone's brighter yellow to be less intense, we use yellow lighten-up phrases. These messages come from our paler yellow, not from our paler blue, green or red. The following yellow lighten-up phrases are listed on the bright side of the yellow stress management card.

> **"YELLOW LIGHTEN-UP PHRASES**
> *"Don't be so rigid."*
> *"Don't be so strict."*
> *"Don't be so uptight."*
> *"Don't be so controlling."*
> *"Don't be so judgmental."*
> *"Don't be so materialistic."*
> *"Stop being so responsible."*

Note: These lighten-up phrases are listed here as examples so you will recognize them and their variations when you hear them or say them in everyday language. They are **not** recommended things to say. In fact, as you will see, these are phrases that ought to be avoided because they can trigger the fight response.

We pressure people to use colours with less intensity so their intensity matches ours.

We pressure people to use bright colours less so we don't have to use them more.

Lighten-up phrases are stated with a level of insistence that is directly proportional to the perceived difference in intensity. When we perceive someone using a colour with somewhat more intensity, we use lighten-up phrases with some insistence. When we perceive someone using a colour with a great deal more intensity, we use lighten-up phrases with a great deal more insistence.

What Lighten-up Phrases Do You Use?

What colour of lighten-up phrases do you use the most often to persuade your partner or other people to lighten up? The lighten-up phrases that <u>you</u> use the most often reveal <u>your</u> paler colours.

What colour of lighten-up phrases does your partner use or other people use the most often to persuade you to lighten up? The lighten-up phrases that <u>other</u> people say to you reveal <u>your</u> brighter colours.

The Intent of Lighten-up Phrases

It seems that our paler colours are on a mission to influence other people to use those colours with less intensity, just as we do. It appears, on the surface, that these lighten-up phrases are attempts to get people to change. But consider this... How often do people use a colour with less intensity just because you **tell** them to? Probably not very often. And how often do <u>you</u> use a colour with less intensity just because someone tells you to? Again, probably not very often.

If you were consoling someone who seemed overly emotional, wouldn't you be surprised if they became less emotional simply because you said "Don't feel bad"? If you thought someone was being overly analytical, would you really expect him or her to stop analyzing just because you said, "Don't think so much"? If you noticed someone being reckless, would you really expect him or her to slow down just because you said "Hold your horses! Not so fast!" And wouldn't you be taken aback if a person became less rigid because you said "Don't be so rigid"?

So if other people don't use colours with less intensity because you tell them to lighten up, and if you don't use your colours with less intensity just because someone tells you to lighten up... why do you suppose we continue pressuring each other in these ways? Why do we use these lighten-up phrases so often? What is going on? There must be another reason we keep up the pressure; there must be something about these interactions that reinforces this common everyday language and behaviour. The following exercise sheds light on this dynamic.

"Lighten-Up": A Paired Exercise

Complete the following exercise with a partner before reading further. You will need to refer to the lighten-up phrases that are listed on the stress management cards.

1) Stand with your partner and face each other.
2) Hold the palm of your left hand up against your partner's right palm so your hands are pressing gently against each other.
3) Take note of your partner's brightest colour and read that colour's first lighten-up phrase aloud to your partner as if persuading him or her to use that colour less intensely. As you read the phrase, push against your partner's right palm to physically emphasize the lighten-up phrase.
4) Read the second lighten-up phrase with increased insistence and push against your partner's right palm with increased physical pressure.
5) Continue reading the lighten-up phrases in order with increasing insistence and continue pushing your partner's right palm with increasing forcefulness each time.
6) Reverse roles and repeat the exercise.

Before reading further, apologize to each other, tell each other you didn't mean it and that you will never pressure each other again.

Newton's third law of motion states, "For every action, there is an equal (in energy) and opposite (in direction) reaction." This principle holds true in human dynamics. In physics and in relationships forces always come in pairs - equal and opposite action-reaction force pairs. So when you pressure a person to use a colour less intensely you provoke an equal and opposite reaction. It is important to note that the equal (in energy) means not only equal in intensity but equal in colour; it means equal in colour because blue, green, red and yellow energies are different energies and because interactions are always colour to colour. A blue lighten-up phrase provokes a bright blue reaction, a green lighten-up phrase provokes a bright green response, a red lighten-up phrase provokes a bright red reaction and a yellow lighten-up phrase provokes a bright yellow reaction.

Section 2: Bright Shadows — Understanding and Managing Them

How did your partner respond in this exercise? With each increasingly insistent lighten-up phrase and increasingly vigorous push, your partner probably responded with an equal (in colour) and opposite (in direction) reaction. (In this exercise your red physical push provoked a red physical push back.) This is your partner's fight response. A partner who is passive at first will eventually resist and react if pushed long enough and hard enough; even a pushover will push back!

Pushing the palm of your partner's hand is like pushing someone's buttons: blue, green, red and yellow buttons. A person who is antagonized may become defensive and perceive the best defense as a good offense...and become offensive. Pushing a person too far provokes a backlash. The fight response kicks in and the person reacts. Let's face it! No one likes to be pushed around.

When you trigger a person's fight response, the colour that you perceived as too bright becomes even brighter. The bright shadow characteristics you perceived as too intense become more intense. When you provoke a person's fight response, you get back even more of what you say you do not want. The question then still remains: Why do we pressure people to use colours less intensely if all we get in response is more of what we say we do not want? What is going on?

In this exercise, you stated the lighten-up phrases with increasing insistence and your partner reacted by asserting their position with equal and opposite intensity. You also asserted your own position with increasing intensity. The standoff is the payoff! As each of you takes a stand by defending and fortifying your preferred positions, you both experience your preferred esteeming intensities with increasingly satisfying intensities.

As it turns out, lighten-up phrases are not attempts to change the other person. They are attempts to esteem yourself and guard against change in the face of a perceived external threat. When you try to change other people, you actually entrench your own esteeming position. Attempts to change others demonstrate your refusal to be changed.

Before reading further, make sure you and your partner have reversed roles in the previous exercise. It is important that both of you experience both perspectives — the experience of pressuring your partner to change and the experience of being pressured to change.

Dynamics of Palest to Brightest Colours

Think of yourself as the "self" on the left side of this illustration. Imagine using your palest colour to interact with someone who has it as a brightest colour. What are the potential irritants? What are the potential delights?

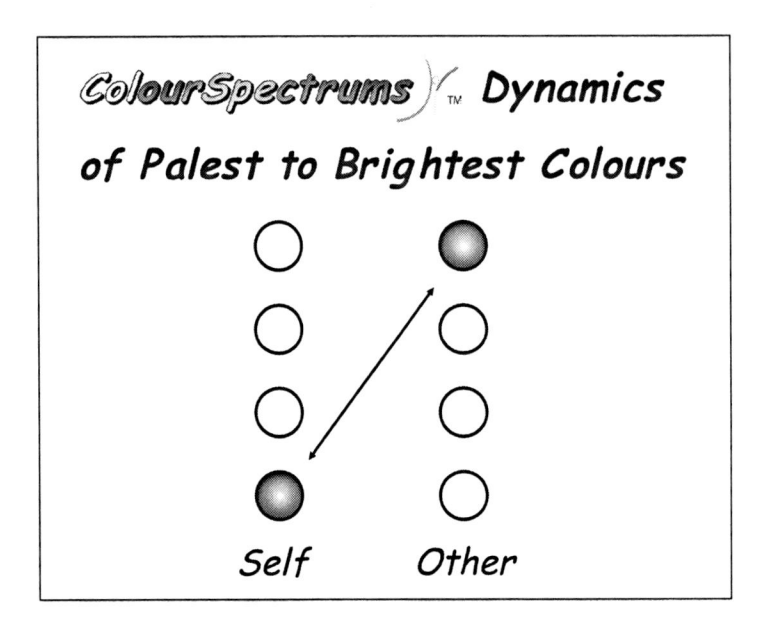

ColourSpectrums™ Dynamics of Palest to Brightest Colours

Self   Other

Visualize interacting with this person as you pressure him or her to use his or her brightest colour with less intensity. Remember that perception and communication only occur colour to colour. When you use pale blue, you may be easily frustrated by people who use bright blue because their priorities, delights and talents are different. When you use pale green, you may be easily frustrated by people who are using bright green because their priorities, delights and talents are different. When you use pale red, you may be frustrated by people who use bright red, and when you use pale yellow you may be easily frustrated by people who use bright yellow.

Being Assertive and Being Aggressive

When we use colours with minimal intensity we use them passively. When we use colours with somewhat greater intensity we use them in the mid-range of the intensity scale. Colours that are used with even greater intensity are used assertively. Assertive behaviours can be highly effective and are considered to be "in the light." When our fight response is triggered and we brighten our colours even more, we become aggressive. Our colours go over the top and off the scale as represented by the brightest colour in the following illustration. Rather than asserting our will in interactions, we impose our will against <u>their</u> will. Just as being assertive can bring out the best in us, being aggressive can bring out the worst in us.

Section 2: Bright Shadows — Understanding and Managing Them

Intensity Scale

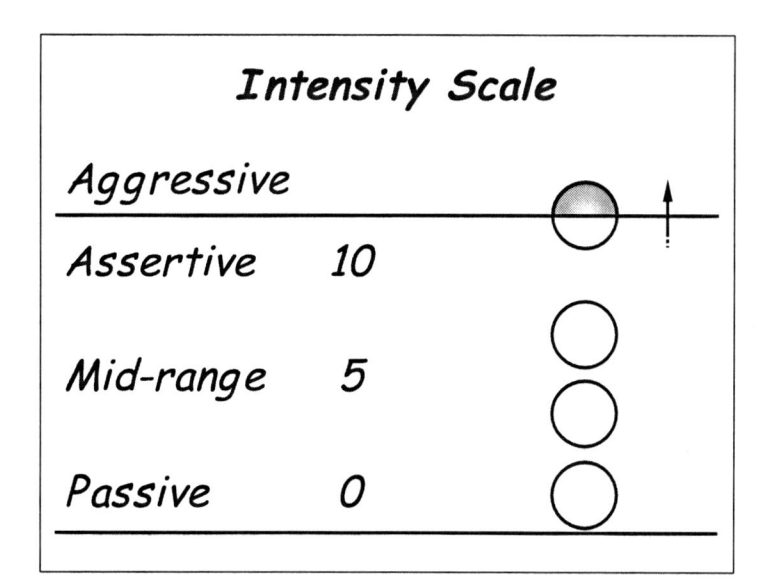

Aggressive		○ ↑
Assertive	10	○
Mid-range	5	○
Passive	0	○

For example:

As assertive behaviours become more intense, they move up into the bright shadow and become aggressive behaviours.

	Assertive Behaviours	Aggressive Behaviours
Blue	Cooperative behaviours Self-awareness Empathic responses	become overly accommodating becomes self-consciousness become overly sympathetic, feeling pity or feeling sorry for someone
Green	Analyzing Reasoning Scepticism	becomes overly analytical becomes too theoretical becomes pessimism
Red	Physical activity Risk taking Spontaneity	becomes hyperactivity becomes reckless becomes too impulsive
Yellow	Organizing Collecting Routines	becomes controlling becomes hoarding become regimented

In the light our blue influences how people feel. In the bright blue shadow our blue attempts to control how people feel. In the light our green influences what and how people think. In the bright green shadow our green attempts to manipulate what and how people think by pulling the wool over people's eyes. In the extreme this is mental manipulation. In the light our red influences people's actions. In the bright red shadow our red attempts to physically overpower people's physical actions. In the light our yellow influences the order of things and how people are organized. In the bright yellow shadow our yellow controls the order of things by controlling people and ordering them around by giving orders.

Jung says that the acts of a person's shadow should not be taken as acts by the person. He suggests that shadow behaviours are best understood as unconscious, rather than conscious, acts of aggression. When you have the perception a person is acting aggressively or displaying bright shadow characteristics, it can be enlightening to realize the other person perceives he or she is only acting assertively. Also consider that a person displaying bright shadow behaviours is likely experiencing bright stress.

Out-of-Esteem Bright Shadow Behaviour

Self-esteem is only experienced in the light. It is not experienced in the shadow. Bright blue, green, red and yellow shadow behaviours are out-of-esteem behaviours. The greater the bright shadow becomes, the less self-esteem is experienced.

In the following illustration the circle at the top represents a colour that is increasing in intensity and moving up into the bright shadow. The top half of the circle that extends up into the bright shadow represents desperate aggressive "out-of-esteem" bright shadow behaviours. The lower half of the circle that is still in the light represents the colour's assertive "in esteem" behaviours.

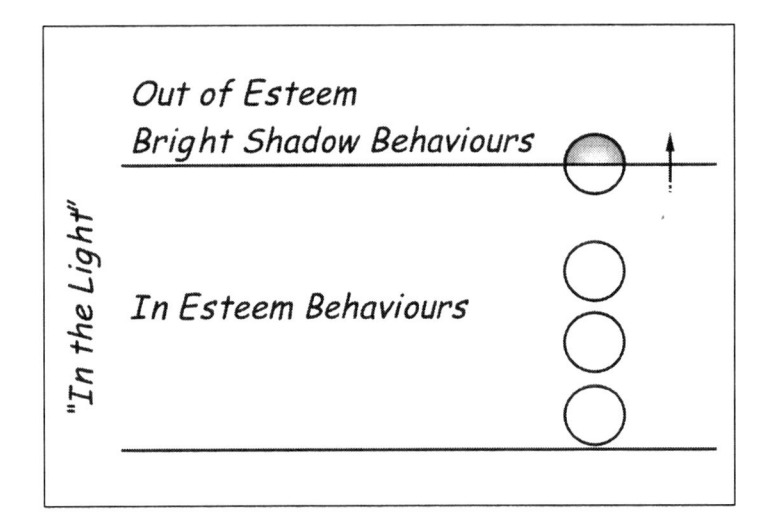

Blue Emotions and Red Anger

Emotions play a unique and vital role in our human experience and they warrant additional consideration in this discussion. We often think of emotions as positive or negative, but we can gain more insight by considering another perspective.

Think of your emotions as empowering or disempowering. Empowering blue emotions include love, affection, fondness, kindness, compassion, intimacy, joy and so on. Disempowering emotions include hurt, embarrassment, humiliation, disappointment, shame, grief, sorrow and yes... feeling blue and singing the blues. In short, empowering emotions feel good and disempowering emotions feel bad.

When your blue is a bright colour, you experience a roller coaster of emotions. Our spectrum of emotions only occurs along the blue continuum, not along the green, red or yellow continuum. Intense empowering and disempowering emotions are experienced at the bright end of the blue continuum, while less intense empowering and disempowering emotions are experienced at the pale end of the blue spectrum. Bright blue emotions are intense and high energy while pale blue emotions are less intense and low energy.

As emotions become more intense, they accumulate and saturate the bright end of the blue spectrum. When the bright end of the blue spectrum becomes saturated with positive, empowering emotions, the red spectrum becomes stimulated and the person is motivated to perform random acts of kindness. The person acts on their emotions and displays spontaneous physical expressions of love, compassion, and affection — spontaneous warm embraces and hugs, for example. A hug is a red physical expression of blue emotional affection. Hugging with open arms physically opens our heart to the other person's heart and wrapping our arms around the other person surrounds and encircles the person's heart with blue energy. When we hug, our hearts are as physically close as they can possibly be. The person is literally near and dear to our heart.

We strive to maintain an overall sense of empowerment. When the bright end of the blue spectrum becomes emotionally charged with overwhelming unpleasant disempowering emotions, our fight response attempts to compensate by empowering our red fight responses. The physical red spectrum becomes agitated. Your red cannot, however, perceive an emotional threat. It can only perceive a physical threat so when it becomes agitated it senses the presence of a physical threat where there is none but it acts as if there is.

> " We all boil at different temperatures. "
> — Ralph Waldo Emerson

Anger, rage and outrage are out-of-esteem... "out of steam" behaviours. Rage is red, and anger is only one letter short of danger. You experience your bright red shadow when you "see red," when something "burns you up," when you get "fired up," when you "flare up," when you get "hot under the collar," have a "hot temper," have a "temper tantrum," are "embroiled" in a heated argument, when your "blood boils" or when you hit the red panic button.

When you act angry, your red physical fight response triggers the other person's red physical fight response of anger and rage. Anger and rage are not emotions and are not experienced along the blue spectrum; rather, they are red physical fight responses that occur at the bright end of the red spectrum. When emotions run high, intense blue emotions can trigger red fight responses.

Just as no one can think clearly when his fists are clenched, no one can feel clearly, act clearly, or plan clearly when his or her fists are clenched. When any colour is used in the bright shadow, it has the potential to incapacitate paler colours.

> "No man thinks clearly when his fists are clenched."
>
> — George Nathan

Anger can manifest as displays of physical intimidation, physical posturing, belligerence and bravado that attempt to compensate for emotional, mental, physical and organizational vulnerability. It is when anger becomes hostile that it becomes volatile and detrimental. Anger can also empower us to take appropriate positive action when it is tempered with a balance of other colours. Anger mobilizes us to act. We can act assertively. We can act aggressively. Anger can literally motivate us to take a stand and stand up for ourselves. Anger can give us the courage to take effective action to advocate or be an activist for a worthwhile cause. Without the mobilizing effects of red anger, we can become immobilized by disempowering emotions, disempowering thoughts and disempowering yellow organizational controls.

When we say we "feel angry," we are misperceiving our internal experience. We are actually experiencing disempowering emotions such as hurt and disappointment while experiencing the empowering physical reactions of anger and rage. The fact is we feel hurt and act angry. When disempowering emotions move up into the bright shadow, we become unaware of them. While physical red anger is expressed, we become less aware of feeling hurt or ashamed and more aware of acting angry. We misinterpret the experience because our intense disempowering emotions are experienced at the same time as intense empowering and overpowering physical reactions of anger. When we experience disempowering blue emotions and empowering physical red, visceral gut reactions simultaneously, we cannot distinguish between them even though they are experienced along distinct and separate continuums. The pale blue shadow of an emotionally abusive backhanded comment occurs along the blue continuum while the bright red shadow of a physically abusive backhand occurs along the red continuum. One is emotional abuse, the other is physical abuse; both can occur simultaneously.

It is important to differentiate between what your blue emotions are feeling and what your red physical body is doing. Distinguishing between blue emotions and red anger brings clarity to the human experience and provides choices in human behaviour.

Section 2: Bright Shadows — Understanding and Managing Them

For example:

Blue Emotions in the Light	Red Anger in the Bright Shadow
When we feel disappointed	we may also act angry
When we feel embarrassed	we may also act angry
When we feel humiliated	we may also act angry
When we feel hurt	we may also act angry
When we feel insulted	we may also act angry
When we feel personally offended	we may also act angry
When we feel sad	we may also act angry
When we feel self-conscious	we may also act angry

When your blue experiences intense disempowering emotions and you brighten your red to compensate by raising your voice in anger or becoming physically agitated, your red becomes empowered but your blue remains disempowered. Anger and rage distort our internal experience, creating the self-deception and false impression to others that we are empowered when our blue is actually feeling disempowered. As you act infuriated, your red physical actions become more demonstrative; as you act out in a fury, your authentic, genuine blue emotions retreat into the bright shadow and are suppressed into unconscious awareness. Interestingly enough, however, because your red and blue function along two parallel but distinct and separate continuums, no amount of empowering red rage can express or empower your blue emotions.

While this discussion has centred on disempowered blue emotions triggering red anger, the same dynamics can be seen to a somewhat lesser degree to disempowered green thoughts, disempowered red behaviours and disempowered yellow organizational functions. People with bright green may act angry when their green is disempowered, when their ideas are ignored, when they are confused or when they perceive themselves as stupid. People with bright yellow may act angry when their yellow is disempowered, when they experience disorganization, lack of control or disrespect for their positions of authority. Of course, people with bright red may act angry when their red is disempowered, when they are physically challenged, threatened or intimidated directly without blue, green or red being disempowered first.

As long as you recognize and express genuine emotions, they remain in the light. When you do not recognize or express genuine emotions, they retreat into the bright shadows and out of conscious awareness. When a person is angry, there are often emotional undercurrents hidden in the bright blue shadow. Acknowledging and validating those underlying, unconscious hidden emotions brings them back into the light, empowers the blue spectrum, and dissipates the need for the charade of red physical anger. The solution for balance is to express your true blue emotions before your red acts out. Anger management is not just about managing anger...it is about "managing" (and I don't mean controlling) your blue emotions, brightening and nurturing your blue so you can acknowledge and genuinely express emotions in a clear, appropriate and assertive manner. The bright red shadow of anger dissipates in the presence of genuinely expressed emotions. As long as people are expressing disempowering blue emotions, expressing anger in appropriate ways to let off steam, expressing disempowering green thoughts or confusion and expressing disempowering yellow organizational needs or loss of control, they don't need to resort to physical intimidation or physical violence.

I use the word "emotions" rather than "feelings" to clearly differentiate blue emotions as a blue function and not a green, red or yellow function. Your green, red and yellow cannot "feel" anything emotional. Emotions are not what we think, not what we do and not what we organize. People often begin speaking as if they are going to express emotions by saying, "I feel..." but they end up explaining their green thoughts ("I feel...it is a good idea"), reporting red actions ("I feel...I have to get going"), or stating yellow plans ("I feel...we should do the right thing and complete the task"). Although these statements begin with the blue phrasing, "I feel..." none of these statements reports blue emotions.

It is one thing to realize that expressing emotions is important. It is another thing to do it. There is a short phrase that can go a long way in helping you accurately express genuine emotions. Whether you are acknowledging your own emotions or helping others express theirs, the following format will help.

Simply use the following template and fill in the blank with one word of emotion.

"I feel _____."

For example:
"I feel <u>happy</u>."
"I feel <u>sad</u>."
"I feel <u>proud</u>."

If you add more than one word, you will not be expressing an emotion. You will end up explaining what your green is thinking, describing what your red is doing or detailing what your yellow is organizing.

Empowering Emotions

The following is an alphabetical list of pleasant emotions, empowering emotions that people experience when their blue needs are being met. These emotions can be experienced less intensely at the pale end of the blue spectrum and with stronger intensity at the bright end of the blue spectrum. Use these when you feel good. To express a blue emotion, simply insert the appropriate emotion to complete the statement:

"I feel _____."

affectionate	elated	joyful	sentimental
affirmed	encouraged	loving	serene
appreciated	friendly	mellow	spiritual
blessed	fulfilled	open-hearted	tender
blissful	glad	optimistic	touched
cheerful	good	passionate	tranquil
comfortable	gracious	peaceful	unique
compassionate	grateful	pleased	warm
confident	happy	proud	wonderful
delighted	hopeful	reassured	yearning

Section 2: Bright Shadows — Understanding and Managing Them

Disempowering Emotions

The following is an alphabetical list of disempowering emotions that people experience when their blue needs are <u>not</u> being met. These emotions can be experienced less intensely at the pale end of the blue spectrum and with stronger intensity at the bright end of the blue spectrum. Use these when you feel bad. Simply insert the appropriate emotion to complete the statement:

"**I feel _____.**"

abandoned	despair	forlorn	jealous
agony	detached	fragile	lonely
alienated	devastated	gloomy	phony
anguished	disappointed	grief	remorseful
ashamed	discouraged	guilty	sad
bereaved	disheartened	heartbroken	self conscious
bitter	distraught	heartsick	sorrowful
defensive	embarrassed	helpless	uncomfortable
dejected	envious	hopeless	unhappy
depressed	foreboding	hurt	worthless

When the above disempowering emotions are experienced intensely and not acknowledged or expressed, the bright red shadow of anger can emerge.

Bright Shadow Sticks and Stones

When an object obstructs light, it casts a shadow. When our personal perspective obstructs our perception, we also cast a shadow. We cast a shadow on others when we insist on standing in the light. When we perceive ourselves as being in the light we cast a shadow and project bright shadow characteristics onto others. The bright shadows you perceive in others are not a true reflection of the person; rather, they are a projection of the shadows you fail to perceive in yourself.

> Easily seen are others' faults,
> hard indeed to see are one's own.
>
> — Buddha

When we judge and criticize a person's bright shadow behaviour, we often judge and criticize the person as well. One of the ways we devalue and malign a person's character is by making disparaging remarks and applying degrading labels. These negatively charged labels are the sticks and stones we throw to devalue and offend others for using colours too intensely. In short ... name-calling.

Rob Chubb

Reframing Bright Shadow Sticks and Stones

Bright Blue Sticks and Stones and Reframes

It is only your blue that perceives someone else's blue. Your blue, like the other colours, is sensitive to differences in intensities. When it perceives someone else's blue as too intense your blue can feel defensive and overwhelmed. If the best defense is a good offence, then your pale blue may go on the attack and become offensive. Bright blue sticks and stones are thrown by your pale blue to devalue someone's bright blue. These are also the sticks and stones thrown by someone else's pale blue to devalue your brighter blue.

In the left-hand column is an alphabetical listing of bright blue sticks and stones — negative labels that your pale blue might use to devalue, ridicule and offend a person's bright blue. On the right are positive reframes.

1) For each of the sticks and stones on the left, write a positive reframe in the centre column before checking the suggested reframe on the right.

2) Complete each reframe one at a time and practise as you go.

   If you are working on your own complete this exercise before reading further.

   If you are working with a partner complete this exercise together by discussing each reframe before reading further.

Bright Blue

Sticks and Stones	Your Positive Reframe	Suggested Positive Reframe
Bleeding heart		Tender heart
Cry baby		Emotionally responsive
Daydreamer		Imaginative
Do-gooder		Compassionate
Lovey dovey		Romantic
Melodramatic		Expressive
Mushy		Tender
Navel-gazer		Self-reflective
Peacenik		Peacemaker
People pleaser		People person
Pushover		Accommodator
Sap		Tender-hearted
Softy		Soft-hearted
Touchy feely		Affectionate
Tree hugger		Environmentalist
Whiner		Emotionally expressive
Wimp		Soft spoken
Wishy-washy		Diplomatic

Section 2: Bright Shadows – Understanding and Managing Them

The positive reframing exercise above brightened your blue because you had to use your blue more intensely to perceive each negative label in a more positive light. Your blue became brighter with each reframe so reframing became progressively easier with practice. Brightening your blue enhances your ability to perceive bright blue characteristics in positive ways and diminishes the appearance of negative bright blue shadow characteristics.

Bright Green Sticks and Stones and Reframes

When your green is confused, perplexed, puzzled and stymied in an interaction, it may interpret that the other person is using green too intensely.

In the left-hand column is an alphabetical listing of bright green sticks and stones — negative labels that your pale green might use to devalue people for using too much green. On the right are positive reframes.

1) For each of the sticks and stones on the left, write a positive reframe in the centre column before checking the suggested reframe on the right.
2) Complete each reframe one at a time and practise as you go.

   If you are working on your own complete this exercise before reading further.

   If you are working with a partner complete this exercise together by discussing each reframe before reading further.

Bright Green

Sticks and Stones	Your Positive Reframe	Suggested Positive Reframe
Big-headed	_____	Self-assured
Bookworm	_____	Well read
Brain	_____	Intelligent
Bullheaded	_____	Confident
Cynic	_____	Sceptical
Eccentric	_____	Interesting
Einstein	_____	Brilliant
Geek	_____	Whiz kid
Hard-headed	_____	Strong minded
Headstrong	_____	Determined
Know-it-all	_____	Knowledgeable
Nerd	_____	Technical
Pessimist	_____	Questioning
Sly fox	_____	Wise
Smart-aleck	_____	Witty
Smarty Pants	_____	Smart
Thick-headed	_____	Pensive
Tough-headed	_____	Well-reasoned

Rob Chubb

The positive reframing exercise above brightened your green because you had to use your green more intensely to perceive each negative label in a more positive light. Your green became brighter with each reframe. With this practice your green becomes brighter as you progress down the list and you are more able to perceive the positive benefits of bright green characteristics. Brightening your green also diminishes the appearance of negative bright green shadow characteristics in others.

Bright Red Sticks and Stones and Reframes

When your red becomes overly stimulated, agitated, rattled or shaken up in an interaction, it may spontaneously perceive the other person as using too much red.

In the left-hand column is an alphabetical listing of bright red sticks and stones — negative labels that your pale red might use to devalue people for using too much red. On the right are positive reframes.

1) For each of the sticks and stones on the left, write a positive reframe in the centre column before checking the suggested reframe on the right.

2) Complete each reframe one at a time and practise as you go.

   If you are working on your own complete this exercise before reading further.

   If you are working with a partner complete this exercise together by discussing each reframe before reading further.

Bright Red

Sticks and Stones	Your Positive Reframe	Suggested Positive Reframe
Bull in a china shop		Freewheeling
Childish		Childlike
Class clown		Comedian
Daredevil		Brave
Exhibitionist		Entertainer
Fanatic		Fan
Flighty		Free and easy
Goofball		Joker
Hyperactive		Mover and shaker
Juvenile		Youthful
Kamikaze		Go-getter
Loose cannon		Troubleshooter
Maniac		Enthusiast
Menace		Risk taker
Rowdy		Energizer
Showboat		Performer
Show-off		Show-man
Wing nut		Free spirit

Section 2: Bright Shadows — Understanding and Managing Them

The positive reframing exercise above brightened your red. With practice your red became brighter and brighter so that reframing becomes easier as you go. Brightening your red enhances your ability to perceive bright red characteristics in positive ways and diminishes the appearance of negative bright red shadow characteristics.

Bright Yellow Sticks and Stones and Reframes

When your yellow perceives it is being overwhelmed, controlled and judged your paler yellow may react defensively and ironically judge the person as being too judgmental and controlling. Even when your yellow is pale it still has the capacity to be judgmental.

In the left-hand column is an alphabetical listing of bright yellow sticks and stones — negative labels that your pale yellow might use to devalue people for using too much yellow. On the right are positive reframes.

1) For each of the sticks and stones on the left, write a positive reframe in the centre column before checking the suggested reframe on the right.

2) Complete each reframe one at a time and practise as you go.

If you are working on your own complete this exercise before reading further.

If you are working with a partner complete this exercise together by discussing each reframe before reading further.

Bright Yellow

Sticks and Stones	Your Positive Reframe	Suggested Positive Reframe
Anal retentive		Detailed
Bureaucrat		Manager
Cheapskate		Frugal
Control freak		Take charge
Iron fisted		Steadfast
Miser		Frugal
Money-grubber		Budget conscious
Nit-picker		Meticulous
Pencil pusher		Administrator
Penny-pincher		Penny-wise
Scrooge		Economical
Skinflint		Thrifty
Square		Conservative
Stick-in-the-mud		Steady
Stingy		Prudent
Stuffed shirt		Professional
Taskmaster		Task oriented
Workaholic		Strong work ethic

The positive reframing exercise above brightened your yellow. Just as your other colours brightened with use, your yellow becomes brighter with practice so each subsequent reframe becomes easier. Brightening your yellow enhances your ability to perceive bright yellow characteristics in a more positive light, diminishing the appearance of negative bright yellow shadow characteristics.

I mentioned earlier that the reframing exercise above would brighten each of your colours. What does that mean and how does that work? Consider something that we all have an opinion on... money. If you perceive "saving money" from a pale yellow perspective, you will characterize it in a "negative light" and perceive it as "stingy." When you brighten your yellow you are able to reframe "saving money" as a positive behaviour, as "thrifty." The actual behaviour of "saving money" remains the same but your perception changes. When you change your perception, other people appear to change.

We characterize other people's behaviours as positive or negative depending on how bright or pale their colours are compared to ours. In the previous reframing exercises the sticks and stones that are the easiest to reframe are those of your brighter colours because your priorities, delights and talents are already closely aligned with them. You perceive those positive reframes easily and naturally. The sticks and stones that are the most difficult to reframe in a positive ways are those of your paler colours because the bright priorities, delights and talents of those bright colours are not closely aligned with your pale perspective.

Think about how you have devalued others by using these bright sticks and stones, these negative labels. You may have devalued others by saying these words out loud. More often, however, you may have devalued others by consciously thinking them in silence, or you may have devalued others unconsciously.

> "Appreciation is a wonderful thing: it makes what is excellent in others belong to us as well."
> — Voltaire

When your self-esteem is based on comparisons with others, then devaluing others may seem gratifying because it enhances your comparative value. Devaluing others, of course, does nothing to enhance your value. The self-deception can be temporarily gratifying nonetheless. But truth be known, putting someone down does not lift you up.

Devaluing others has deeper implications for you. When you reframed the negative labels in positive ways, you brightened that colour within you. So it's true: when you value others, you value yourself. The implication is that when you devalue someone else's bright colour, you devalue that colour in yourself as well. Negative talk about others is actually negative <u>self</u>-talk. In spite of the illusion that devaluing others enhances your own value, the truth is that devaluing others devalues you.

The bright colours you are quick to devalue in others are already your paler colours. Devaluing others for using those colours too intensely requires you to diminish those colours within you even further. They are already your paler colours and at risk of not being used intensely enough. You are the one who can least afford to diminish them.

> When you belittle others you must be little yourself.

Section 2: Bright Shadows — Understanding and Managing Them

Bright Shadow Self-Talk

We are engaged in an ongoing internal dialogue of "self-talk." There are four "conversations" occurring simultaneously and they involve much more than just green words. Blue self-talk includes impressions, emotions, moods, and personal reflections. Green self-talk includes fleeting and fragmented thoughts as well as lucid and coherent streams of intellectual consciousness and trains of thought. Red self-talk is true body language consisting of physical urges, reflexes and impulses. Yellow self-talk is your guiding inner voice that tells you what is right and what is wrong — your conscience, if you will. It follows the "shoulds," shouldn'ts," "supposed tos" and "have tos" and other organizational controls that maintain self-discipline and order. It is as if our four colours are having a conversation. Sometimes they talk all at once and sometimes they take turns. Your brighter colours can dominate the discussion. This continuous spontaneous conversation takes place just below our conscious level of awareness. This "self-talk" comes into the light of conscious awareness from time to time and then retreats to the shadow of unconscious awareness.

> "When the mind is thinking it is talking to itself."
> — Plato

Self-talk in the Moment

You can illuminate your unconscious self-talk and bring this rich resource into conscious awareness simply by attending to it. Just as other people recognize your bright shadows before you are consciously aware of them, your subconscious also recognizes your bright shadows before you are consciously aware of them. Listen to these inner voices. By tapping into this unconscious stream of awareness, you can heighten awareness of your bright shadow characteristics and minimize the negative impact of those behaviours.

Listen to these inner voices. They alert you to the presence of your bright shadows in the moment. You have four colours of unconscious bright shadow awareness available: bright blue shadow awareness, bright red shadow awareness, bright green shadow awareness and bright yellow shadow awareness. Each one communicates different experiences in different ways.

For example:

When your blue feels "overly emotional," it may be in the bright blue shadow. When your green thinks, "I am over analyzing" it may be in the bright green shadow. When your red suddenly catches itself and senses it is "going too fast!" it may be in the bright red shadow. When your yellow admonishes itself and judges, "I shouldn't be so rigid," it may be in the bright yellow shadow. Consciously noticing these diverse internal messages is like having a smoke detector that alerts you to possible hot spots, intense bright shadow behaviours.

Self-talk After the Fact

Have you ever reacted in a way that you thought was appropriate at the time, only to realize later that you overreacted? Of course! We all have.

In the heat of the moment, when you are in the bright shadow, you are unaware of your extreme behaviours. Only afterwards, when you come to your senses (blue emotional senses, green cognitive senses, red physical senses and yellow organizational senses) do you say to yourself, "that wasn't like me," "I can't believe I did that!" "I overreacted." That is your bright shadow speaking.

When your blue feels it has been in the bright blue shadow, it might say, "I took that comment too personally." When your green thinks it has been in the bright green shadow you might find yourself thinking, "I really was analyzing too much." When it suddenly hits your red that it has been in the bright red shadow it might strike you, "I was too impulsive!" When your yellow judges it has been too intense your yellow self-talk might be heard to say, "I was being too strict."

> When it is dark enough, you can see the stars.
>
> — Ralph Waldo Emerson

It is only after our intense energy has calmed down, when the colour comes back into the light, that we "realize" we have used a colour too intensely and displayed bright shadow characteristics. This process of self-reflection in which we acknowledge our ineffective behaviours is the process of enlightenment, the process of bringing unconscious bright shadow behaviours into the light where we can see them more clearly. It is in the "realizing" that we "illuminate" bright shadows. Without awareness you cannot initiate change. Illuminating bright shadow behaviours creates opportunities for change.

Stress Management Cards: Look on the Bright Side

An Exercise in Using the Bright Sides of the Stress Management Cards

Turn the four stress management cards over so the heading "Bright Esteem Needs" is at the top of each card. Then position the four cards in their respective quadrants as indicated below.

Section 2: Bright Shadows — Understanding and Managing Them

Four Stress Management Cards — Look On the Bright Side

BLUE	GREEN
BRIGHT ESTEEM NEEDS **BRIGHT STRESSORS** **BRIGHT SHADOW CHARACTERISTICS** **LIGHTEN-UP PHRASES**	**BRIGHT ESTEEM NEEDS** **BRIGHT STRESSORS** **BRIGHT SHADOW CHARACTERISTICS** **LIGHTEN-UP PHRASES**
BRIGHT ESTEEM NEEDS **BRIGHT STRESSORS** **BRIGHT SHADOW CHARACTERISTICS** **LIGHTEN-UP PHRASES**	**BRIGHT ESTEEM NEEDS** **BRIGHT STRESSORS** **BRIGHT SHADOW CHARACTERISTICS** **LIGHTEN-UP PHRASES**
RED	YELLOW

You can use these cards to manage bright colour stressors, yours and others. Simply start at any point on the bright side of these stress management cards and refer to the related elements.

For example:

If you are having trouble coping with a situation because there are "interpersonal conflicts," locate that bright blue stressor under "Bright Stressors" on the blue stress management card and review that side of the card to identify the related "Bright Esteem Needs," "Bright Shadow Characteristics" and "Lighten-Up Phrases."

For example:

When a person appears "overly analytical," locate that bright green shadow characteristic under "Bright Shadow Characteristics" on the green stress management card and review the related "Bright Esteem Needs," "Bright Stressors" and "Lighten-Up Phrases."

You can use all of the stress management cards in a similar manner to quickly locate and identify each colour's bright esteem needs, bright stressors, bright shadow characteristics and lighten-up phrases at a glance.

Section 3: Stress Management — Look on the Pale Side

Before reading further, ensure you have completed the StressCheck on page 5 by writing a list of 10 stressful situations. You will refer to this written list later.

Pale Challenges

Your brighter colours seem the most natural. They are well developed and easy to use. Your paler colours seem less natural. They are less developed and more challenging to use. Pale colours are the most difficult to use. Pale challenges are the difficulties we experience in using pale colours effectively. All colours experience challenges from time to time.

Pale Blue Challenges

Pale blue challenges are emotional and spiritual challenges. The following pale blue challenges are listed on the pale side of the blue stress management card. The paler your blue is, the greater and more frequent these challenges will be. If blue is your palest colour, these are your greatest challenges.

PALE BLUE CHALLENGES

Being artistic	Being spiritual
Being compassionate	Demonstrating empathy
Being friendly	Displaying affection
Being intimate	Expressing emotions
Being loving	Reading body language
Being personal	Relating personally
Being physically close	Validating emotions

More Pale Blue Challenges

Being accommodating
Being benevolent
Being caring
Being charitable
Being consoling
Being cozy
Being emotional
Being gentle
Being genuine
Being good natured
Being harmonious
Being intuitive
Being kind hearted
Being merciful
Being nurturing
Being passionate
Being reverent
Being romantic
Being self-disclosing
Being self-aware
Being self-expressive
Being self-reflective
Being sensitive
Being sentimental
Being social
Being sympathetic
Being tender
Believing
Establishing personal rapport
Expressing compassion
Expressing fondness
Expressing tenderness
Feeling attached
Having faith
Trusting feelings
Using people skills

Pale Green Challenges

Pale green challenges are cognitive and intellectual challenges. The following pale green challenges are listed on the pale side of the green stress management card. If green is your palest colour, these are your greatest challenges.

PALE GREEN CHALLENGES

Analyzing
Being abstract
Being hypothetical
Being intellectual
Being logical
Being philosophical
Being strategic
Being technical
Being theoretical
Conceptualizing
Contemplating
Explaining why
Researching
Scrutinizing

Section 3: Stress Management — Look on the Pale Side

More Pale Green Challenges

Articulating	Deliberating
Being cognizant	Deciphering data
Being factual	Explaining complexities
Being innovative	Explaining concepts
Being inventive	Exploring possibilities
Being knowledgeable	Formulating ideas
Being mentally active	Interpreting data
Being objective	Investigating clues
Being precise	Making meaning
Being rational	Making sense
Being sceptical	Reasoning
Being scientific	Seeing the big picture
Being strong minded	Speculating
Calculating	Thinking clearly
Clarifying ideas	Thinking critically
Comprehending	Thinking independently
Considering implications	Thinking outside the box
Contemplating possibilities	Understanding complexities

Pale Red Challenges

Pale red challenges are physical challenges. The following pale red challenges are listed on the pale side of the red stress management card. If red is your palest colour, these are your greatest challenges.

PALE RED CHALLENGES

Assembling things	Being physically active
Being competitive	Being spontaneous
Being energetic	Improvising
Being enthusiastic	Moving rapidly
Being hands-on	Multitasking
Being immediate	Responding quickly
Being impulsive	Taking risks

More Pale Red Challenges

Being active
Being adventurous
Being animated
Being boisterous
Being brave
Being courageous
Being daring
Being excited
Being full of life
Being in the moment
Being lively
Being loud
Being on the go
Being physical
Being playful
Being quick
Being resilient
Being upbeat

Being vigorous
Competing
Going with the flow
Handling tools
Having fun
Hurrying
Initiating action
Initiating activities
Living it up
Living on the edge
Operating equipment
Physical exertion
Physical labour
Playing it by ear
Reacting quickly
Responding immediately
Taking chances
Winging it

Pale Yellow Challenges

Pale yellow challenges are organizational challenges. The following pale yellow challenges are listed on the pale side of the yellow stress management card. If yellow is your palest colour, here are your greatest challenges... in alphabetical order (you're very welcome).

PALE YELLOW CHALLENGES

Adhering to timelines
Attending to details
Being accountable
Being responsible
Completing tasks
Committing to plans
Establishing boundaries

Following routines
Maintaining order
Obeying rules
Organizing
Planning
Setting limits
Staying on task

More Pale Yellow Challenges

Assigning tasks	Controlling
Arranging	Coordinating tasks
Being authoritative	Delegating responsibilities
Being consistent	Disciplining
Being dutiful	Enforcing rules
Being neat and tidy	Following almost anything
Being obedient	Following directions
Being on time	Following procedures
Being orderly	Following rules
Being prepared	Judging right from wrong
Being self-disciplined	Maintaining self-control
Being sequential	Maintaining standards
Bringing closure	Making commitments
Budgeting	Respecting authority
Completing paperwork	Saving
Complying with authority	Scheduling
Complying with regulations	Staying in line
Conforming to roles	Staying in role

Projecting Pale Challenges

If blue is one of your paler colours, you may find it challenging to carry on personal conversations for any length of time. As you interact personally, you begin to perceive the other person as "being too personal." But a closer look reveals something quite different. As you interact personally, your pale blue becomes saturated and challenged. It is your pale blue that experiences "being too personal" because you have exceeded your blue capacity for being personal. As you detach, disown and externalize this experience, you project it on to the other person and mistakenly perceive the <u>other</u> person as being "too personal." You would rather perceive the other person as "being too personal" than perceive yourself as not being personal enough.

When you have the perception that a person is being too technical, consider that you are experiencing the pale green challenge of being too technical...for you. When you have the perception a person is being too impulsive, consider that it may be your paler red that is being overly stimulated and exceeding your comfort level, exceeding your pale red capacity to respond effectively and being confronted with your own pale red challenge. When you judge that a person is being too rigid, consider that it may be your paler yellow that is being overly stimulated and that <u>you</u> are having the experience of being too rigid...for you, that <u>you</u> are experiencing your own pale yellow challenge. If you had a greater capacity to use yellow, you would not perceive the other person as being too rigid.

These perceptual experiences are classic examples of projection. Your inability to recognize your own pale challenges of not being able to use a colour intensely enough causes you to perceive the other person as using it too intensely. We hold the other person responsible for our experiences rather than taking ownership and being accountable. We prefer to perceive the other person as using a colour too intensely than to perceive ourselves as not using a colour intensely enough. As long as we hold others responsible for our experiences, we cannot be responsible for ourselves. This leaves others in charge of our experiences. "If everyone else changes...I will be fine." Ask yourself, "Do I need people to be different in order for me to be okay?" These projections are distortions that keep us from taking charge of our own behaviour, taking charge of our lives.

As much as we like to react and complain about people using our pale colours too intensely, their bright behaviours also liberate us from the challenge of having to use that colour more intensely ourselves. If they use it, we don't have to.

Summary of Pale Challenges

Your pale blue can be emotionally challenged.

Your pale green can be mentally challenged.

Your pale red can be physically challenged.

Your pale yellow can be organizationally challenged.

Pale Stressors

A pale stressor is any situation that calls on you to use your pale colour effectively. These situations cause you to experience your pale colour more intensely than you prefer as you rise to the occasion. Pale stressors rapidly exceed your pale colour's capacity to cope. The impact on you is pale stress. The greater the challenge and paler the colour, the higher the pale stress will be.

Your palest colour experiences pale stress the most often and most intensely. Your third colour experiences pale stress less frequently and less intensely. Your second colour can experience some pale stress and even your brightest colour can be challenged on occasion and experience some pale stress.

Pale Blue Stressors

The following situations require bright blue responses. The paler your blue is the more challenging these pale blue stressors will be and the greater your pale blue stress will be. The following pale blue stressors are listed on the pale side of the blue stress management card.

Section 3: Stress Management — Look on the Pale Side

PALE BLUE STRESSORS

Displays of emotion	Personal issues
Group dynamics	Personal relationships
Group interactions	Social gatherings
Holistic approaches	Spiritual environments
Interpersonal dynamics	Too much accommodating
Personal attention	Too much harmony
Personal interactions	Too much self-disclosure

More Pale Blue Stressors

Being cared for	Overfriendliness
Being embraced	Personal discussions
Being loved	Personal encounters
Being personally appreciated	Personal interactions
Being physically close	Personal rapport
Close physical proximity	Personal self-disclosure
Continuous interactions	Prolonged group interactions
Displays of affection	Receiving affection
Friendliness	Receiving personal feedback
Group work	Relationship dynamics
Interpersonal relationships	Romantic situations
Intimacy	Self disclosure
Intimate settings	Sentimentality
Intimate situations	Social chit chat
Kindliness	Social occasions
Lack of personal space	Tender moments
Lack of privacy	Too much group work
One-on-one situations	Too much personal information

Pale Green Stressors

The following situations require bright green responses. The paler your green is the more challenging these pale green stressors will be and the greater your pale green stress will be. These are situations in which you experience information overload, mind-boggling experiences that cause your eyes to glaze over. These are also listed on the pale side of the green stress management card.

PALE GREEN STRESSORS

Abstract concepts	Technology
Complex data	Too many facts
Conceptual models	Too many ideas
Intellectual discussions	Too much information
Philosophical debates	Too much logic
Politics	Too much theory
Technical explanations	Too much thinking

More Pale Green Stressors

Algebra	Hypothetical scenarios
Big words	In-depth analysis
Complex formulas	Lectures
Complex ideas	Mathematics
Complex information	Mind maps
Complex problems	Philosophical discussions
Complexities	Political debates
Complicated explanations	Research data
Complicated issues	Science
Conceptual models	Scientific research
Data	Statistics
Debates	Technical information
Detailed investigations	Technology
Emails	Theoretical concepts
Equations	Theories
Explanations	Too much exploration
Formulas	Too much independence
Hypothetical discussions	Too much time to think

Pale Red Stressors

The following situations require bright red responses. The paler your red is the more challenging these pale red stressors will be and the greater your pale red stress will be. These are also listed on the pale side of the red stress management card.

Section 3: Stress Management — Look on the Pale Side

PALE RED STRESSORS

Being rushed	High energy
Competition	Noisy environments
Constant change	Non-stop action
Crises	Physical activity
Dynamic environments	Rapid transitions
Frequent interruptions	Surprises
Hands-on activities	Urgencies

More Pale Red Stressors

Abrupt changes	Impromptu situations
Being bumped	Intense sensory stimulation
Being hurried	Large operating equipment
Being jostled	Living moment to moment
Being pushed	Loud machinery
Being shoved	Loud noises
Being startled	Mechanical devices
Commotion	Physical labour
Competitive atmosphere	Perpetual motion
Constant motion	Physical stimulation
Continuous activity	Playful situations
Emergencies	Racket
Fast-paced surroundings	Risks
Frequent changes	Sensory distractions
Frequent distractions	Sensory overload
Hustle and bustle	Spontaneity
Immediacies	Spur-of-the-moment events
Immediate demands	The unexpected

Pale Yellow Stressors

The following situations require bright yellow responses. The paler your yellow is the more challenging these pale yellow stressors will be and the greater your pale yellow stress will be. These are also listed on the pale side of the yellow stress management card.

PALE YELLOW STRESSORS

Administrative details	Restrictions
Budgeting	"Right" vs "wrong"
Bureaucracy	Routines
Formal procedures	Schedules
Limits	Too many rules
Paperwork	Too many plans
Policies	Too much organization

More Pale Yellow Stressors

Authority figures	Obligations
Boundaries	Official ceremonies
Commitments	Official procedures
Controls	Predictable environments
Detailed directions	Prohibitions
Detailed instructions	Red tape
Detailed plans	Regulations
Detailed tasks	Responsibilities
Duties	Sequential procedures
Establishment	Shoulds
Formal proceedings	Shouldn'ts
Formal situations	Strict rules
Formalities	Timelines
Highly organized settings	Too many details
Imperatives	Too many limits
Inflexible rules	Too much order
Institutional settings	Too much structure
Judgments	Traditions

Identifying Your Palest Stressors

There are many reasons we may have to use pale colours more intensely than we prefer. Simply put, you must be able to feel, think, act and organize effectively in order to respond successfully to diverse situations, at home, at work, at school and in the community.

1) Refer to the ColourSpectrums StressCheck on page 5 that you completed earlier.

   Write the name of your palest colour in the box at the top of the right-hand column.

2) Review the list of 10 stressful situations you wrote in the centre column and place check marks in the boxes in the right-hand column to indicate the situations

that are stressful as a result of your palest colour being challenged. (Refer to your palest colour's list of pale challenges and list of pale stressors to help you identify these situations).

For example:

If blue is your palest colour, then you would check off a stressful situation such as "social gatherings" as a pale blue stressor because "relating personally" is a pale blue challenge.

If green is your palest colour, then you would check off a stressful situation such as "too much technology" as a pale green stressor because "being technical" is a pale green challenge.

If red is your palest colour, then you would check off a stressful situation such as "non-stop action" as a pale red stressor because "being physically active" is a pale red challenge.

If yellow is your palest colour, then you would check off a stressful situation such as "too many plans" as a pale yellow stressor because "planning" is a pale yellow challenge.

A stressor that has already been checked off in the left-hand column (a bright colour stressor in which bright colour needs are not being met) may be checked off again at this time in the right-hand column if the situation is also a stressor because it challenges your palest colour.

For example:

A "change in job" may already be checked off in the left-hand column as a bright blue stressor because your bright blue need "to relate personally" is at risk; a change in job or a promotion can mean a loss of personal acquaintances, relationships or friends. When your blue is bright, personnel changes are personal changes.

A "change in job" may be checked off again at this time in the right hand column because it is challenging for your pale red to "take risks" or "be adventurous."

3) When you have checked off your palest stressors in the right hand column, add up the check marks and write the total number of pale stressors at the bottom of the right hand column.

Identifying Your Other Pale Stressors

The written exercise above only helps you identify situations that are stressful because your palest colour is being challenged. You can follow the same process to identify situations that are stressful because your other colours are being challenged. Your third colour can be a challenge to use so it can experience pale stressors and pale stress. Your second colour can also be challenged from time to time. Even your brightest colour can be challenged and experience pale stress on occasion.

Pale Colour Exhaustion

All situations require us to use the appropriate colour intensely enough to be effective. If you can rise to the challenge and brighten the appropriate pale colour for a brief period of time, you can be effective in the short term. Maintaining a pale colour with bright intensity over the long term is much more challenging, and before too long a pale colour becomes exhausted. If your blue is pale, you may welcome visitors for a short visit but when they stay too long they wear out their welcome as your blue welcoming capacity wears out. When exhaustion sets in, it becomes difficult to maintain sufficient intensity, and as the colour fades it becomes less effective. We can experience blue emotional exhaustion, green mental exhaustion, red physical exhaustion and yellow organizational exhaustion.

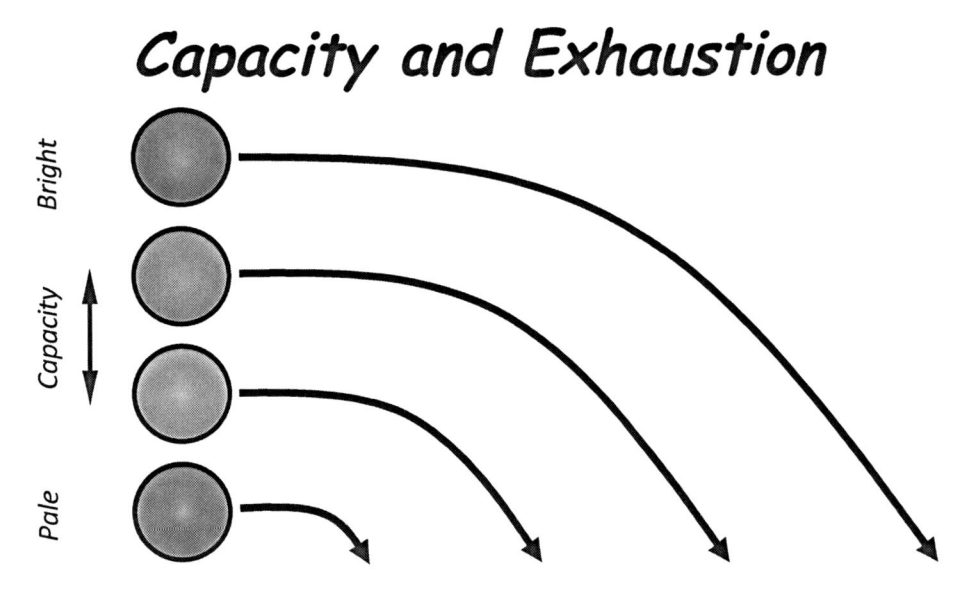

Capacity and Exhaustion

Brighter colours have greater capacity and endurance. Paler colours have less capacity and become exhausted sooner. We experience blue emotional, green mental, red physical and yellow organizational exhaustion at different rates.

Pale Challenges and Pale Stressors

Each colour's pale challenges and pale stressors are experienced along that colour's continuum. Pale blue challenges and pale blue stressors are only experienced along the continuum of the blue spectrum. Your green, red and yellow do not perform any blue functions so they do not experience pale blue challenges or pale blue stressors. This principle applies to the pale challenges and pale stressors of all the colours, each colour experiencing unique pale challenges and pale stressors.

Although you have the capacity to use your brightest colour with a great deal of intensity for long periods of time, it can also become exhausted. Think of an interaction you have had with someone who was using your brightest colour even more intensely than you. The challenge of trying to maintain the intensity of your brightest colour in order to keep up with that person would be a pale challenge. You would experience being with that person as a pale stressor because even your brightest colour can be overwhelmed when it pales in comparison. Your experience of trying to keep up with that person is useful information for you because that is how other people experience trying to keep up with you when your brightest colour is one of their paler colours. There are also many situations (not just people) that require you to use your brightest colour more intensely than you prefer. Situations that exceed your brightest colour's capacity to be effective are also experienced as pale challenges and pale stressors.

Just as you can identify bright stress by asking four basic questions, you can also identify pale stress by asking yourself four basic questions.

1) "Am I experiencing too much blue?"
   If yes, then you are experiencing pale blue stress.
2) "Am I experiencing too much green?"
   If yes, then you are experiencing pale green stress.
3) "Am I experiencing too much red?"
   If yes, then you are experiencing pale red stress.
4) "Am I experiencing too much yellow?"
   If yes, then you are experiencing pale yellow stress.

Differentiating between these four sources of pale stress is the key to managing pale stress. Acknowledging your pale challenges and recognizing pale stressors in advance can help you pace yourself and manage pale stress. When you experience pale blue stress, use your blue with somewhat less intensity so you do not feel emotionally overwhelmed. When you anticipate or experience pale green mental fatigue, use less green and give yourself a mental break. When you have worked your fingers to the bone, are physically exhausted, run off your feet or just plain tuckered out, use less red and pace yourself for a while so your physical body has time to recharge. When you experience pale yellow organizational stress and get wound up tight like a clock, take a break so your yellow has time to unwind. When any colour becomes overwhelmed by pale stress, use it less intensely for a while so it can recuperate and be more effective later.

I have been describing pale stressors one at a time. The reality is that many situations are stressful because they challenge more than one colour at a time. For example, if you have blue and red as pale colours, you may experience a party as exceptionally challenging. You might experience the "social gathering" as a pale blue stressor because "being friendly" non-stop for hours challenges your pale blue. At the same time you might experience the "non-stop action" as a pale red stressor because "being active" challenges your pale red. If yellow and green are your pale colours then a long formal strategic planning meeting might do you in. You might experience the "intellectual discussions" as a pale green stressor because "being intellectual" challenges your pale green. At the same meeting you might experience the "formal procedures" as a pale yellow stressor because "staying on task" is challenging.

Multiple Bright and Pale Stressors

Situations may involve any combination of bright and pale stressors occurring simultaneously.

Rob's Reflection

I am reminded of an all-day workshop in which I presented the introductory workshop in the morning and when we broke for lunch I noticed that three participants went to their respective offices and closed the doors. The rest of us went out together for lunch.

When we began the afternoon session one of the participants who had gone to her office explained that she did not join the group for lunch because she had developed a headache during the latter part of the morning session. The other two participants who had also gone to their offices both chimed in, "You too?!" As it turned out, all three had developed headaches. All three had green as a brightest colour and had experienced bright green stress during the busy session because they didn't have time alone to think. Just as importantly, all three had blue as a palest colours and they explained how interacting with people all morning had been challenging — a pale blue stressor. All three needed time away from the group to regroup.

And that's the way it often is with stressful situations. We often experience bright and pale stress simultaneously.

Death, Loss and Grief

The death of a loved one is an extremely stressful event because it can cause eight kinds of stress simultaneously. In the process of death, loss and grief all four of our colours are impacted.

The death of a loved one can be

1) A bright blue stressor because the bright blue need to be loved by someone who has passed is disrupted. Emotions include feelings of despair, sadness, loneliness and depression and eventually hope for the future.

2) A bright green stressor because the bright green need to explain or make sense of death cannot be satisfied. It is profoundly confusing. This is the stage of denial. When the green brain can't make sense of what is real it experiences it as surreal. "This can't be real." "This can't be happening." "It can't be true." "How could this happen to me?" "This doesn't make sense." "It is inconceivable." "It is unthinkable."

3) A bright red stressor because the bright red need to be spontaneous, enthusiastic and resilient is disrupted. Red is our most resilient function. It bounces back quickly. The red fight response can also trigger the grieving stage of anger.

4) A bright yellow stressor because the bright yellow need for stability and control is at risk. In latter stages of death, loss and grief this becomes acceptance as life becomes increasingly more stable.

Section 3: Stress Management — Look on the Pale Side

The death of a loved one can also be

5) A pale blue stressor because it is a challenge for one's pale blue to express emotions during the grieving process.

6) A pale green stressor because it is a challenge for one's pale green to consider the diverse complex implications.

7) A pale red stressor because it is a challenge for one's pale red to respond immediately to such a sudden unexpected event. This is the stage of shock.

8) A pale yellow stressor because it is a challenge for one's pale yellow to organize a funeral or reorganize one's life.

Two Kinds of Stress: Good Stress and Bad Stress.

Some stress is good for you but too much or too little isn't.

Eustress is good stress.

Some stressors have positive effects. Stressors can motivate us to respond effectively so we can we grow, develop and mature.

Bright stressors that keep us from satisfying our needs can also be good stress because we learn self-control, self-restraint and delayed gratification rather than self-indulgence, self-centredness and immediate gratification.

Hans Selye, one of the pioneers in the field, called this stress eustress, "eu" from the Greek meaning "good."

Pale stressors that challenge our pale colours can be good stress because they stimulate and motivate us to use our pale colours more intensely. Pale stressors keep us attentive and responsive. The expectation to wake up in the morning and get to work or go to school, for instance, keeps us motivated. We rise to the challenge so we can respond effectively. Getting up in the world and getting up in the morning are closely related. Without eustress you would still be sleeping. Just as a slight push can keep you alert and keep you on your toes, eustress can keep your colours stimulated and functioning.

Dystress is bad stress.

Some stressors are overwhelming and have negative effects. Intense stressors, or an accumulation of many stressors, can overpower us to the point where our stress responses cannot cope effectively; we cannot return to a balanced state. This is not the good stress that gets us up in the morning; rather, this is the stress that keeps us awake at night and instead of getting up in the morning and getting up in the world, we phone in sick or stay in bed. Good stress keeps us on our toes. Too much stress knocks us off our feet.

Hans Selye called this dystress, "dys" from the Latin meaning "bad."

Intense bright stressors that keep us from satisfying our needs can be detrimental. When core needs are unmet for extended periods of time, we lose energy and self-esteem.

Pale stressors that overwhelm us can also be detrimental because they can overwhelm, discourage, intimidate and inhibit our personal and professional development.

Three Variables Influence Stress

Three variables determine the amount of stress that bright stressors and pale stressors will cause:

1) Frequency

   Coming face-to-face with a saber-toothed tiger once a day is more stressful than running into one once a year. The more frequently you encounter the saber-toothed tigers of your life, the more often you experience bright stressors or pale stressors, and the greater your overall stress will be.

2) Intensity

   Coming face-to-face with an adult saber-toothed tiger is more stressful than coming face-to-face with a saber-toothed kitten. The more intensely you experience bright stressors or pale stressors, the greater your stress will be.

3) Duration

   A brief encounter with a saber-toothed tiger is less stressful than being stalked for days. Long drawn-out encounters with the saber-toothed tigers in your life will cause more stress than brief encounters. The longer you experience bright stressors or pale stressors, the greater your stress will be.

Calculating Your Stress Distribution

Refer to the ColourSpectrums StressCheck on page 5.

Previously, in the left-hand column, you calculated the total number of situations that are stressful because your brightest colour needs are not being met. In the right-hand column you calculated the total number of stressful situations that are stressful because your palest colour is being challenged.

Now count the total number of stressful situations you have written in the centre column and write that total at the bottom. If you have written a complete list of 10 stressful situations the total will be 10. If you have written eight, then your total will be 8 and so on.

Section 3: Stress Management — Look on the Pale Side

Here is a completed example:

ColourSpectrums™ StressCheck

Total Personal Stressors

Brightest	10 Stressful Situations	Palest
☐	_____	☑
☑	_____	☐
☐	_____	☑
☑	_____	☑
☐	_____	☐
☑	_____	☐
☐	_____	☑
☑	_____	☐
☐	_____	☑
☑	_____	☐
5	**10**	**5**
Total Brightest Stressors	Total Personal Stressors	Total Palest Stressors

Refer to the illustration below.

Write your total brightest stressors in the top circle of the illustration.

Write your total palest stressors in the bottom circle of the illustration.

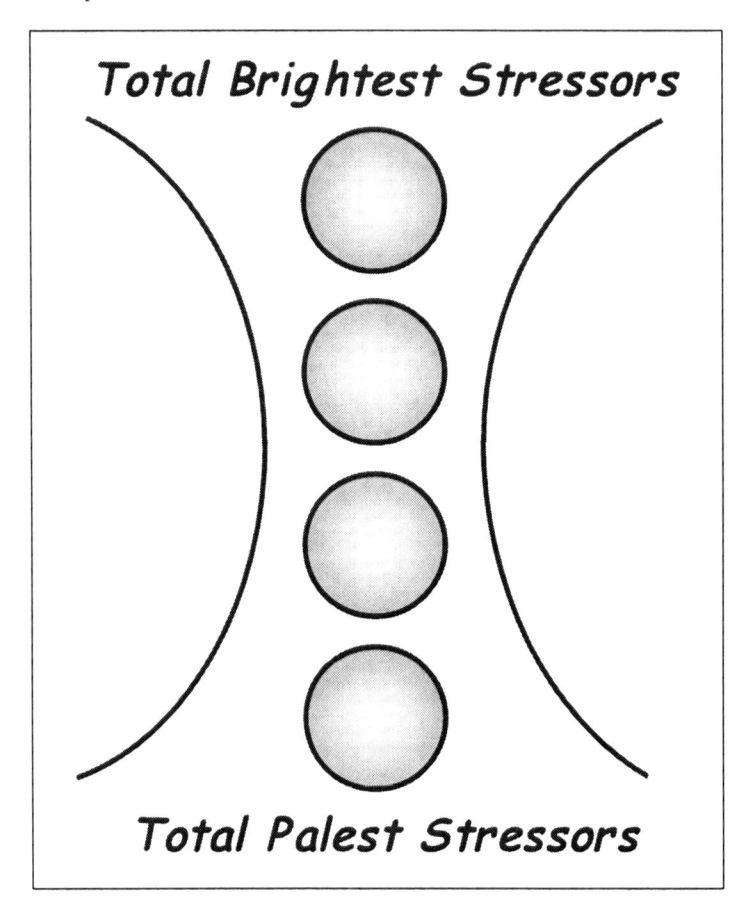

Total Brightest Stressors

Total Palest Stressors

Calculating Stress Distribution in Groups

In ColourSpectrums workshops each participant writes a list of 10 stressful situations and calculates column totals the same way you have. Facilitators then calculate a grand total — for the whole group — for each of the three columns.

Here is an example:

1) The number of participants in the group is 45.

2) The total number of stressful situations is 441.

(Most participants wrote 10 stressful situations but some wrote less)

Section 3: Stress Management — Look on the Pale Side

3) The column totals for the entire group of 45 participants is:

Total Brightest Stressors	Total Personal Stressors	Total Palest Stressors
202	441	189
(45.80%)	(100%)	(42.86%)

45.80% of the stressors are a result of brightest colour needs not being met. 42.86 % of the stressors are a result of palest colours being challenged.

These percentages are written in the corresponding circles below.

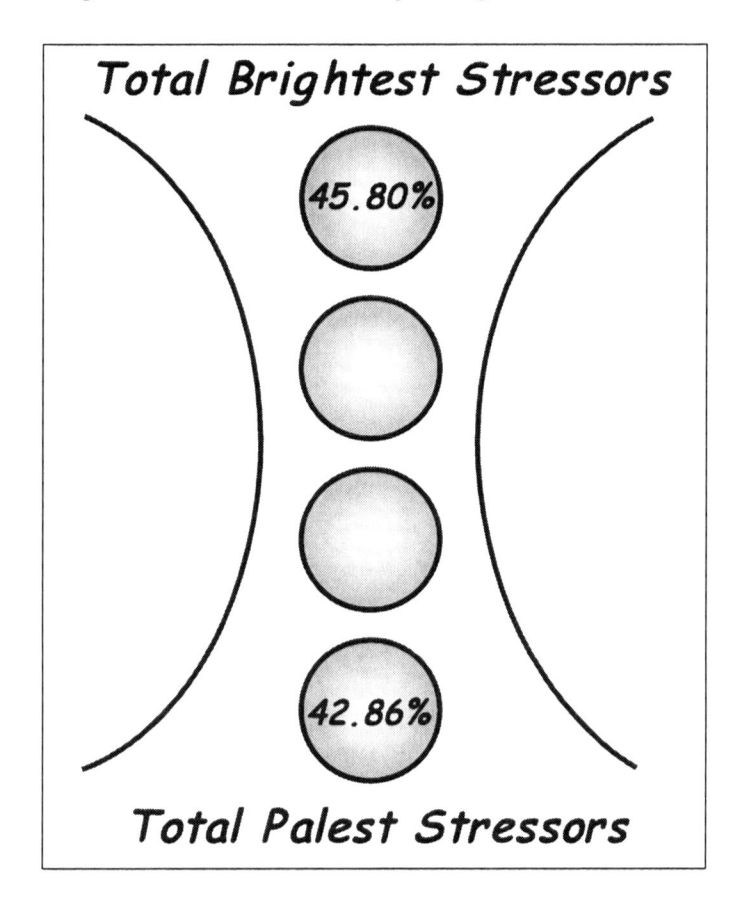

Total Brightest Stressors

45.80%

42.86%

Total Palest Stressors

This group calculation is typical of most groups. Predictably and consistently in group after group, stress is distributed in an hourglass shape with 45% of stress being bright stress — the result of brightest colour needs not being met, and 45% of stress being pale stress — the result of palest colours being challenged.

How does your stress distribution compare with the general population? Is your stress distributed in an hourglass shape as well? If you have written a total of 10 stressors then simply add a zero to each total to calculate your percentages. Five bright stressors would be 50% and four pale stressors would be 40% and so on.

So here is the big question! If almost half of your stress is the result of brightest colour needs not being met and almost half is the result of palest colours being challenged... where is your best balance? Of course! In the middle!

The Strength of Middle Colours

Generally speaking our middle colours experience less stress because they are the most functional and flexible. They have two major advantages over our brightest and palest colours. First, we have the capacity to use middle colours effectively without experiencing pale stress. Second, we have the ability to use them less intensely without experiencing bright stress. As a result we use our middle colours with more intensity when it is effective and appropriate to do so and we use them with less intensity when is it appropriate to do that. We use them more flexibly because we can. As it turns out, our middle colours are more functional and more balanced than our brightest and palest colours, which live on the edge of the light in close proximity to the bright and pale shadows, respectively. Stress is only experienced in the shadow. Our brightest colours are at risk of being too bright and being in the bright shadow while our palest colours are at risk of being too pale and being in the pale shadow. Our middle colours are at less risk of moving into the bright and pale shadows. They are more reliable and more functional because they are more in the light more of the time.

We do not usually over use our middle colours because it is relatively easy to satisfy those colours' needs by using them with medium intensities. As a result, your middle colours' fight responses are not triggered as easily and they are not inclined to move into the bright shadow in desperate attempts to satisfy deep-seated needs in the same way that your brightest colour is inclined to do.

> If half your stress is bright stress... and half your stress is pale stress... where is your best balance?

We do not usually under use our middle colours because they are readily accessible and fairly easy to use. Your middle colours' flight responses are not triggered as easily as your palest colour so they are not as inclined to move into the pale shadow in desperate attempts to avoid challenges.

Your middle colours can be your greatest resource for stress management because they are the most balanced in terms of bright and pale stress. Your middle colours can be the most functional! Your brightest and palest colours can be the most dysfunctional.

Each of our colours has a preferred intensity that seems to be the most comfortable. What is comfortable? Comfort seems to be the intensity that we use most often and is most familiar. We experience bright stress when we have to use any colour with less intensity than we are comfortable with. Our brightest colours experience this kind of stress most often. We experience pale stress when we use any colour with more intensity than we are comfortable with. Our palest colours experience this kind of stress most often.

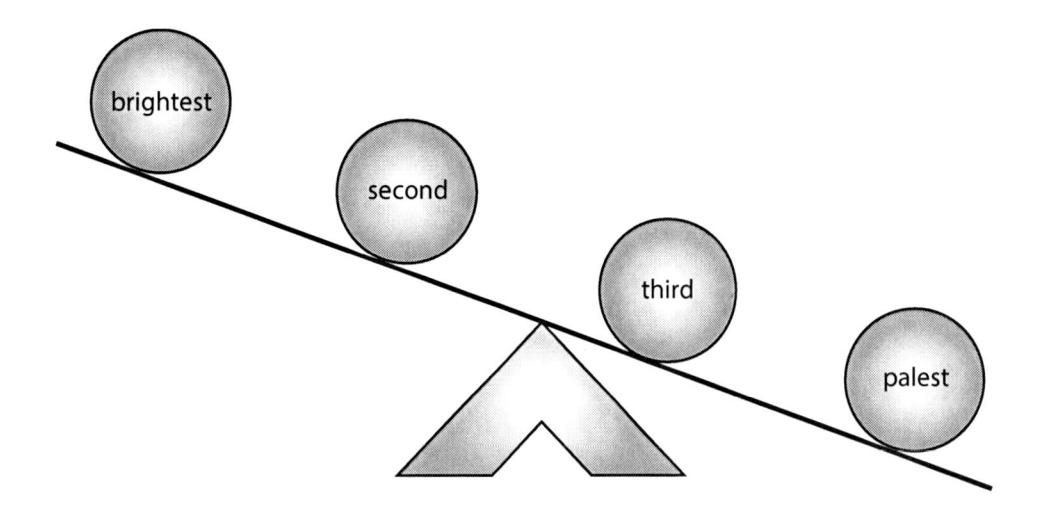

Section 3: Stress Management — Look on the Pale Side

Your middle colours are your centre. They act as a fulcrum, like the point of balance on a teeter-totter with your brightest colour up in the air at one end of your colour spectrum and your palest colour down towards the ground at the other end.

Your middle colours are less susceptible to the bright and pale stress experienced at either end of the spectrum. They are a reliable and constant source of self-esteem and empowerment. They are the unsung heroes in your life, the dependable, balanced and constantly reliable functions that you use effectively with confidence day in and day out.

Your middle colours also have a capacity that your palest colour does not have: the ability to be more intense for brief periods of time when needed. Your middle colours also have an advantage that your brightest colour does not have and that is the ability to be used with less intensity when it is effective to do so. This is particularly important in communication. You can brighten and diminish your middle colours to match other people's intensities more easily than you can brighten and diminish your brightest and palest colours to match intensities. Brightening your palest colour to match a person who has it as a brightest colour or diminishing your brightest colour to match a person who has it as a palest colour can be a real stretch.

It is important to understand the role of your brighter colours in interactions. It is just as important to understand the role of your paler colours in interactions. It is natural to perceive your brightest colours as more important to you because you identify closely with them. Your paler colours, however, are just as important because you do not identify closely with them. More accurately, you may identify closely with not using them.

When we look at a person's full ColourSpectrums personality, it is clear that all four colours have equally important and different implications whether we identify closely with bright colours because we do use them effectively or whether we identify closely with not using pale colour because we do not use them effectively.

Imagine not using, or not being able to use, one of your five senses. If you couldn't use your eyes you would be blind. If you couldn't use your ears you would be deaf. The implications would be so profound that you might even define yourself by what you cannot do. You might define yourself as a deaf person or a blind person.

It is critical to understand that all of your colours have important implications regardless of how bright or pale they are. Your brightest colours have a profound influence on how you are. Your palest colours have a profound influence on how you are not. Both influences are equally important but they are also distinctly unique and separate because each colour performs different functions that occur along distinct and separate continuums.

Consider your brightest colour for a moment. You are an expert on what it is like to have this colour as a brightest colour. Your brightest colour has a tremendous influence on the kind of person you are. It embodies your highest priorities, delights and talents.

You have a reputation for using your brightest colour.

Now consider your palest colour. You are also an expert on what it is like to have this colour as a palest colour. Your palest colour has major implications for the kind of person you are (not.) It embodies your lowest priorities, delights and talents. While you have a reputation for using your bright colours you also have another reputation — the reputation you have for not using your palest colours. To be effective in life, it is important to be aware of what you are doing. It is just as important to be aware of what you are not doing.

Four Glasses

The four glasses in the following illustration represent your four colours. The smallest glass represents your smaller capacity to use your palest colour and the largest glass represents your larger capacity to use your brightest colour. Take the time now to colour the water in the smallest glass the same colour as your palest colour. Colour the two glasses in the middle that correspond to your second and third colours. Colour the water in the largest glass the same colour as your brightest colour.

When you use a colour you experience the self-esteem associated with the colour and the glass fills with esteem. You can be full of emotions, full of ideas, full of excitement, or full of plans. The amount of self-esteem available is proportional to your capacity to use the colour effectively. When your glass is full, your esteem needs really are fulfilled.

Section 3: Stress Management — Look on the Pale Side

When you use your palest colour, your resources are rapidly exhausted and your capacity to be effective is quickly exceeded. It doesn't take long until you've had your fill. The overflow is experienced as pale stress. Your limited capacity to use this colour effectively also limits your capacity to experience this kind of self-esteem. Any of your colours can become overwhelmed and saturated but your pale colours experience this pale stress sooner, more frequently and to greater extent.

Regardless of how bright or pale your blue is, when you use your blue beyond your emotional capacity you experience emotional exhaustion and fatigue.

> *John is a counsellor for a social services agency. Blue is his brightest colour. He is passionate about his work with people. As a human services professional he uses his blue to establish therapeutic relationships, to empathize with clients and to be emotionally supportive. At the end of his work day he feels emotionally exhausted and looks forward to unwinding and having a quiet evening at home. He has had his fill and his blue is looking forward to some down time. As John walks in the door, his wife, Judy, who has been at home all day with their two preschool children, excitedly tells John how much she is looking forward to spending time with him ... and the company she invited over for the evening. John's blue is saturated while Judy's blue is thirsty for friendly adult company.*

Regardless of how bright or pale your green is, when you use green beyond your mental capacity you experience mental exhaustion and fatigue.

> *Jane has been studying for a final exam. She has been reviewing her study notes to gather her thoughts and reviewing her textbooks for three evenings in a row. She is mentally exhausted. Her best friend, Laurie, invites her over for a visit. Jane is eager to take a mental health break so she accepts the invitation. Jane arrives to discover that Laurie has recently developed a keen interest in crossword puzzles and is looking forward to working with Jane on solving one of the tougher intellectually challenging puzzles. Jane senses a headache coming on.*

Regardless of how bright or pale your red is, when you use your red beyond your physical capacity you experience physical fatigue. What starts off as physical exhilaration ends up as physical exhaustion.

> *Bill has been working in his yard all day, mowing the grass, pulling weeds, raking leaves, pruning trees, trimming the hedge and picking up bits and pieces of litter on the ground. He is physically exhausted and at the end of the day as the sun goes down he sits down on his deck to rest and catch his breath. As he begins to unwind he looks around the yard to admire his handiwork and notices that his car has a flat tire. Bill is a handy kind of guy but the challenge of changing the flat tire overwhelms him. He phones the local automobile club and has them drop by to change the flat tire as he sits relaxing on the deck.*

Regardless of how bright or pale your yellow is, when you use your yellow beyond your organizational capacity you experience the pale stress of organizational exhaustion and fatigue.

> *Theresa has spent all day at work filing papers and organizing schedules. She has a spotless reputation for being a responsible and well-organized professional. At the end of the workday her yellow is saturated. She has had enough. The last thing she wants to do is continue using her yellow when she gets home. As a result, Theresa's office is spic and span, prim and proper, neat and tidy, neat as a pin, shipshape, squeaky clean and, yes, spotless. Her house is chaos.*

When any of your colours become saturated, exhausted or fatigued, a change is as good as a rest. Using the saturated colour less intensely and using another colour more intensely can reduce stress, enhance esteem and restore balance.

The middle glasses in the previous illustration represent your middle colours. Your capacity to use these colours effectively is greater than your pale colour so these colours are not as easily overwhelmed. Your capacity to use these colours more effectively also means that you have a greater capacity to experience the kinds of esteem that these colours provide.

The largest glass represents your brightest colour. You have a great capacity to use this colour effectively. You are also highly motivated to satisfy those esteem needs. Your capacity to use this colour is not easily exceeded and these esteem needs are not often saturated. While your palest colour experiences pale stress as "too much," your brightest colour experiences bright stress as "not enough." The emptiness at the top of the large glass represents bright colour stress, your unmet brightest colour needs.

Each of your colours needs to be experienced in different proportions. You have a natural tendency to avoid situations that saturate your paler colours and you naturally seek out experiences that satisfy your brighter colours. The brighter the colour, the more unquenchable the thirst.

If blue is your brightest colour, how often is your blue ever completely satisfied? When does your blue experience enough intimacy, love and affection? Not often. If green is your brightest colour, how often is your green's thirst for knowledge actually quenched? Not often. If red is your brightest colour, how often does your red get

Section 3: Stress Management — Look on the Pale Side

enough action, adventure and variety? Not often. If yellow is your brightest colour, how often are you satisfied that you have experienced enough order, organizing, arranging and planning? Probably not often and certainly not for long.

If your palest colour is continuously overflowing perhaps your glass is too small.

If your brightest colour is continuously unfulfilled ask yourself:

1) Is your large glass half full?
2) Is your large glass half empty?
    or
3) Is your large glass too big?

In some situations our glass may be too big and our need to fill it too strong. In some situations our bright colour needs may not get met. When our esteem needs have been satisfied we can sustain ourselves for some time. In time, however, our glasses run low and we get thirsty. We return to the well again and again to fill our glasses and quench our thirst by experiencing each colour as needed.

Take another look at the couple that seems to be having a problem with their relationship. See if you can make better sense of their relationship dynamics and the stress that each is experiencing.

What kind of stress is the man on the left experiencing?

What kind of stress is the woman on the right experiencing?

> *"The problem with our relationship is...*
>
> *we spend too much time apart!"*
>
> *"The problem with our relationship is...*
>
> *we spend too much time together!"*

As it turns out, the man on the left is experiencing the bright blue stress of unmet emotional needs because the couple spends too much time apart. His bright blue glass feels empty. The woman on the right is experiencing the pale blue stress of the challenge of being too close because the couple spends too much time together. Her pale blue glass is overflowing. You may even venture a guess that his blue is brighter than her blue. In this example the roles of the man and woman could be reversed.

Rob Chubb

Eight Stressors

We often talk about "stress" and try to deal with it, but we usually don't define it very well. If we don't define it we can't manage it. ColourSpectrums delineates eight stressors that cause eight specific kinds of stress. Because there are eight different sources of stress, there are eight different solutions.

In the illustration below, the four glasses that show the capacities of each colour are superimposed on the hourglass distribution of stress in the general population.

Four Bright Stressors

Four kinds of stress occur at the top of the hourglass — the emptiness of unfulfilled needs at the top of the large glass.

1) Bright blue stressors   obstruct bright blue needs   causing bright blue stress
2) Bright green stressors   obstruct bright green needs   causing bright green stress
3) Bright red stressors   obstruct bright red needs   causing bright red stress
4) Bright yellow stressors   obstruct bright yellow needs   causing bright yellow stress

Colour the water in the top glass the same colour as your brightest colour. This represents your bright colour needs that have been satisfied. The emptiness at the top of this large glass represents your unmet bright colour needs caused by bright stressors.

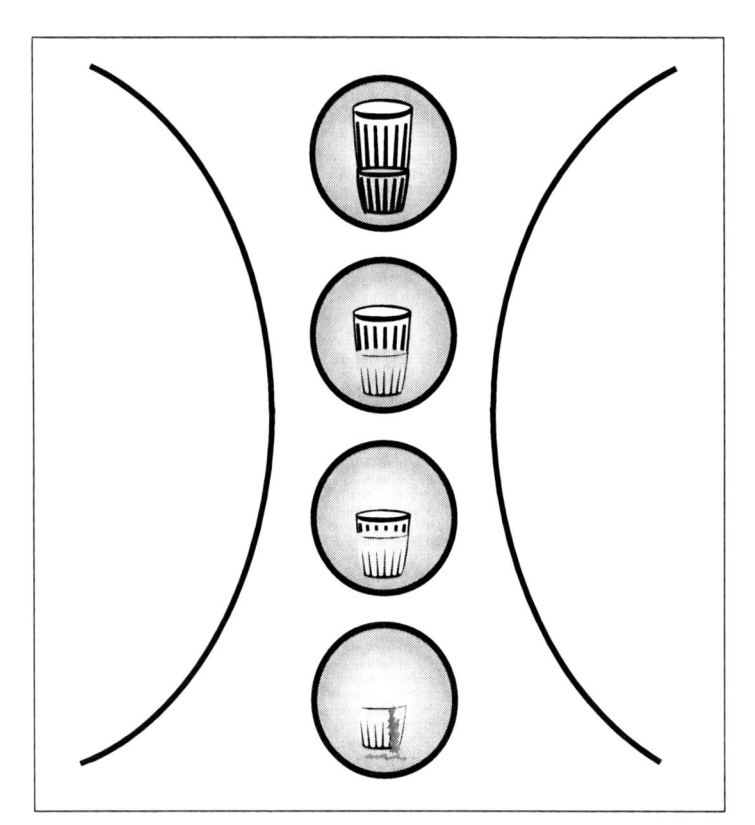

88

Section 3: Stress Management — Look on the Pale Side

Four Pale Stressors

Four kinds of stress occur at the bottom of the hourglass — the overflow of challenges that exceed the capacity of the small glass.

1) Pale blue stressors   challenge pale blue capacities   causing pale blue stress
2) Pale green stressors   challenge pale green capacities   causing pale green stress
3) Pale red stressors   challenge pale red capacities   causing pale red stress
4) Pale yellow stressors   challenge pale yellow capacities   causing pale yellow stress

Colour the water in the bottom glass the same colour as your palest colour. The water in this glass represents your capacity to cope. Colour the water that is overflowing to represent challenges caused by pale stressors that exceed your palest colour's capacity to cope.

Colour the two glasses in the middle that correspond to your second and third colours.

Simply put, stress comes in two forms: not enough and too much. Not experiencing enough blue, green, red or yellow causes four kinds of bright stress. Experiencing too much blue, green, red or yellow causes four kinds of pale stress.

When your blue is balanced and in the light, you experience emotional wellness. When your green is balanced, you experience good mental health. When your red is balanced, you are in good physical health, and when your yellow is balanced, you experience good organizational health.

Stress is an internal response to an external event. You may not be able to change external events but you can certainly change your internal response to those external events by using your colours effectively.

Interruptions

We lead busy lives. One of the hallmarks of a hectic modern lifestyle is the countless constant interruptions we experience that force us to stop one activity and start another. These interruptions are a significant sources of stress because they require us to quickly diminish a high energy activity and brighten a low energy activity, like the effort it takes to stop the momentum of a large rolling ball and the effort needed to get another ball rolling. Interruptions are especially challenging because, by definition, they are abrupt. They don't give us the time or courtesy of making a smooth transition from one activity to another.

Interruptions cause bright stress

An interruption is a bright stressor because it disrupts a high energy, esteeming experience and requires us to diminish that bright colour. Because you use your brighter colours more frequently and more intensely, your brighter colours will be interrupted more often than your pale colours.

> For example:
>
> If you are interrupted while absorbed in an engaging, personal conversation with a close friend, you will experience bright blue stress. If you are

interrupted while in deep solitary contemplative thought as you read this informative book, you will experience bright green stress, your train of thought would be interrupted. If you are interrupted in the middle of an exciting game of soccer, whether you are on the soccer field or experiencing your red vicariously while sitting on the edge of your seat while cheering for your favorite team on television, you will experience bright red stress. If you are interrupted while organizing your desk or sorting out your paperwork, you will experience bright yellow stress.

Interruptions cause pale stress

An interruption is also a pale stressor because it often challenges you to brighten a colour that is pale at the moment of the interruption.

For example:

If a distraught friend drops by unexpectedly and you have to suddenly exert greater effort to listen closely to his or her personal experiences, you will experience the challenge of being empathetic as pale blue stress. If you are giving your mind a mental break and are suddenly expected to concentrate hard because someone starts explaining a complex idea, the challenge will cause pale green stress. If you have to force yourself to get up from your seat and move a chair to make room for someone you might experience pale red stress. If you are unexpectedly told to organize a meeting, the extra effort needed to reschedule your day and prepare for the meeting can be a source of pale yellow stress.

Because you do not usually use your paler colours as frequently, as intensely or as naturally as your brighter colours, interruptions will challenge your paler colours more often than they will challenge your brighter colours.

Interruptions cause both bright and pale stress

An interruption, then, is often a combination of two simultaneous stressors: the bright stress of diminishing the colour you are using and the pale stress of brightening the pale colour you need to use. Interruptions like this are worst-case scenarios: an esteeming experience is being interrupted at the same time that a pale colour is being challenged. When you experience bright stress and pale stress simultaneously, it can be irritating. It can also be confusing because it is difficult to identify the source of the stress when we experience bright and pale stress simultaneously. The key to managing stress then is to consider each colour one at a time and identify how each colour is experiencing stress.

For example:

When you are sharing your blue emotions or a personal experience with a person who responds by suggesting a green problem-solving solution, the interruption of your blue need to express your emotions is experienced as a bright blue stressor while the challenge of brightening your green to contemplate the well-intended strategic solution is experienced as a pale green stressor.

Section 3: Stress Management — Look on the Pale Side

For example:

When you are physically exercising, a phone call that interrupts that red activity will be experienced as a bright red stressor. If it is your travel agent calling to discuss the detailed travel arrangements, flight schedules, hotel reservations and budget details for your next business trip, the challenge of brightening your yellow to attend to those detailed organizational tasks will cause pale yellow stress.

Internal Interruptions

I stated earlier that anything that interrupts the colour you are using is a bright stressor because it disrupts an esteeming experience. There is a source of interruptions that may not be readily apparent. Your own colours interrupt each other. When you are experiencing deep blue emotions, for example, your green thoughts, second thoughts and after thoughts can interrupt your blue experience. When you are deeply intrigued by an interesting idea, a sudden physical urge to get up and eat or go to the bathroom will interrupt those esteeming green thoughts. Interrupted thoughts are a bright green stressor. When you are participating in a physically stimulating red activity, your yellow judgments of right and wrong can interrupt your red experience.

> A distraction is only a distraction until you attend to it.

You can minimize the stressful effects of interruptions by giving yourself space and time to make transitions. Give yourself a few seconds or a few minutes to intentionally diminish the colour you are actively using and to intentionally brighten the colour you will be using. This strategy will reduce bright stress by giving your bright colours time to diminish. This will also reduce pale stress by giving your pale colour time to warm up.

Social Readjustment Rating Scale

The Social Readjustment Rating Scale (SRRS) is based on the premise that good and bad events in a person's life can increase stress levels and cause a person to be more susceptible to illness and mental health problems. It makes sense that "bad" events cause stress, but why would "good" events cause stress? Consider the top 10 stressors, according to the SRRS:

Life Event	Stress Value
1. Death of a spouse	100
2. Divorce	73
3. Marital separation	65
4. Jail term	63
5. Death of a close family member	63
6. Personal injury or illness	53
7. Marriage	50
8. Fired at work	47
9. Marital reconciliation	45
10. Retirement	45

What do all of these good and bad events have in common? The title, "social readjustment scale," provides a clue. Each situation involves change or readjustment. These situations can be bright stressors because they interfere with bright colour needs being met, and they can be pale stressors because they challenge pale colours. In all events the person is pushed or pulled off balance and must exert effort to respond to the stressor to regain balance and equilibrium.

An even closer look at this scale reveals that the greatest stressors are stressful in more ways than one. The life events with the greatest stress values involve multiple combinations of the eight bright and pale stressors occurring at the same time. The death of a spouse, for example, can disrupt the needs of four bright colours while simultaneously challenging four pale colours. These life events involve various combinations of the eight stressors so regardless of your ColourSpectrums personality you are vulnerable one way or the other. This is why these life events are so stressful for so many people. No one is immune.

Bright Esteem and Pale Challenges Can Occur Simultaneously

An event is not inherently esteeming or challenging in and of itself. Rather, it is the perception of an event that determines the impact. Keep in mind that your colours perceive an event simultaneously, each from different perspectives. An event that is esteeming for your blue may challenge your green; an event that is esteeming for your red may challenge your yellow. You can experience esteem and stress simultaneously.

For example, a job promotion can satisfy your yellow esteem needs for job security, increased income, career advancement up the corporate ladder of an organization to a hard-earned position of higher authority and status. At the same time your blue needs for personal relationships may be at risk because the colleagues you have been friends with become your subordinates so you may experience a loss of interpersonal relationships and those longer work hours mean less time with loved ones. Your yellow esteem is enhanced while your blue needs are placed at risk.

Tight Rope Walker

> *The little girl gazed up in amazement as the tightrope walker inched his way step by step along the high wire suspended above her head in the circus big top. "How do you keep your balance mister?" she asked curiously. The tightrope walker glanced down at her briefly and continued step by step. Then in a voice as wise as the ages he responded, "I am never in balance. I struggle to find balance and the moment I find it I lose it again."*

Life is a balancing act. Being out of balance...is how we learn to regain balance. Being in the bright or pale shadow motivates us to step back into the light once again.

Using Colours Passively

You will recall that each colour moves up and down along a continuum of varying brightness depending on how intensely the colour is being used. Colours can be used effectively with varying intensities ranging from a passive "0" to an assertive "10." When colours are perceived as being used appropriately and effectively they are considered to be within this range, "in the light."

Intensity Scale

Assertive	10	○ ↑
		○
Mid-range	5	○
		○
Passive	0	○ ↓

"In the Light"

Diminishing Colours

In many situations you naturally brighten your paler colours to respond effectively. As you experience your paler colours more intensely than you prefer, you become uncomfortable and experience the challenge as a pale stressor. You react by diminishing the colour to alleviate the pale stress. As you diminish the colour it moves back down and becomes paler.

As you diminish your blue in an effort to reduce the pale blue stress of feeling too emotional, too personal or too friendly, you become less emotional, less personal and less friendly. As you diminish your green in an effort to alleviate the pale green stress of thinking too much, reasoning too much and contemplating too much, you start to do less thinking, less reasoning and less contemplating. When you diminish your red in an effort to ease the pale red stress of being too active, too energetic and too physical, you become less active, less energetic and less physical. As you diminish your yellow in an effort to lessen the pale yellow stress of planning, preparing and organizing too much, you begin doing less planning, less preparing and less organizing.

The colour at the bottom of this spectrum has been diminished so it is now passive and in a state of low energy.

Diminishing Colours

"In the Light"
- Assertive   10   ○
- Mid-range   5   ○
-              ○
- Passive   0   ●   ↓

When you are not actively using a colour, you are using it passively. It performs basic minimal functions without your conscious attention...as if on standby. There are several reasons we use colours with less intensity:

- Diminishing a pale colour's intensity and being more passive can be an effective way to reduce the pale stress of pale challenges.

- When you use a bright colour with a great deal of intensity over a long period of time, that colour will eventually become exhausted. When a bright colour gets wound up, diminishing it helps it unwind. Diminishing a brighter colour and "letting go" or "giving it a rest" alleviates fatigue and gives the colour time to rejuvenate.

- You may want to diminish a colour in interactions. If you continue using a colour with a great deal of intensity with someone who has it as a paler colour, you may overwhelm the other person and turn them off.

- You may choose to use your colours less intensely so other people have the opportunity to use <u>their</u> colours more effectively. Creating opportunities for other people to use their colours is especially important in your role as a parent, an employer, an educator and as an effective team member.

- In some situations you can be more effective by doing less. If you constantly use bright colours with full intensities, you will be inappropriate in many situations. Not every situation needs what your bright colour has to offer. Just because you can doesn't mean you should. Just because you want to doesn't mean it's wanted. On the other hand, just because you can't use your pale colour well, doesn't mean you shouldn't.

Being able to use your colours with diverse intensities (more and less) empowers you to be more effective more often, in more situations, with more people. Using colours with diverse intensities also creates better personal balance and wellness.

Section 4: Pale Shadows — Understanding and Managing Them

The Evolution of Stress: The Flight Response

What happens when you diminish a colour in an effort to reduce a pale colour's stress and still experience too much stress? What happens when you continue to be challenged and continue to diminish a colour's intensity?

Do you remember your cave dwelling days and your fight response to the saber-toothed tiger? Imagine once again that you are a cave dweller lazily gathering cool, juicy tropical fruit in the hot and humid prehistoric jungle. As usual your mouth drools with delicious anticipation. Suddenly you find yourself face-to-face with a saber-toothed tiger...again! While you were gathering, he was hunting...again! You are having a bad week.

Just as before... Your fight/flight response immediately triggers a rapid sequence of physiological responses as described on page 26.

The physiological arousal stage of the fight/flight response is complete again. Fighting and fleeing both require this same biological readiness. Whether you fight or flee is not the point. Your supercharged body is again ready for either course of vigorous action.

The saber-toothed tiger salivates and licks his lips one last time as he prepares to lunge for lunch. Inspired by his two long protruding teeth, you spin around and run faster than you ever have in your life! In what seems like seconds, you are valleys away! Only when you are finally safe and sound back in your cave do you dare lie down...exhausted...and fall soundly asleep.

Sometimes we fight! Sometimes we flee!

The first scenario (p. 25) detailed the physiological responses to stress that trigger fight behaviour. This second scenario illustrates how these same physiological responses trigger flight behaviour. The physiological response stage is the same for both. The dramatic difference occurs at the behavioural response stage: fight behaviour or flight behaviour.

As the tension of the physiological response stage builds, a moment of truth is reached, a breaking point at which further tension cannot be tolerated. It is at this point of high tension that the behavioural response stage is suddenly triggered and tension is rapidly expended through vigorous fight or vigorous flight behaviours.

Literally, figuratively and metaphorically, in a fight response, the body turns squarely toward the threat to face it head on, and in a flight response, the body angles away from the perceived threat and takes flight.

> *Imagine walking along a railway track and precariously balancing yourself on the rail. You begin to lose your balance and fight to stay on. You regain your balance and keep walking. A few steps later you begin to lose your balance again. This time as you fight to stay on the track, you suddenly realize you are going to fall off in spite of your best efforts. At the critical point of no return your fight response to stay on the rail switches rapidly and transforms into a flight response to jump off the rail...there is no in between. At first glance fight and flight responses appear to be opposite reactions and yet they have so much in common because they are both triggered by the same physiological response stage.*

The Flight Response: For Better or Worse

When you experience a colour too intensely you may react by diminishing that colour to reduce the pale stress. The greater the challenge is perceived to be and the greater the stress, the more you will diminish the colour. Refer to the previous illustration and you will see that as a colour becomes less intense and more passive it approaches the bottom edge of the lighted area.

Using colours with less intensity can be an effective way to lower stress, but there is a high cost. The priorities, delights and talents are also diminished. What happens when we continue to diminish a colour? We already know that the fight response can bring out the worst in us and reveal our bright shadow characteristics. Well... the flight response can also bring out the worst in us and reveal... our pale shadow characteristics. If diminishing a colour and using it passively does not alleviate pale stress then a person may diminish the colour even further. When a colour continues to be diminished it moves down into the pale shadow. Welcome to the other dark side.

Pale Shadow Characteristics

Pale shadow characteristics appear when a colour is not used, or is perceived as not being used, intensely enough. The more intense the flight response is, the more diminished the colour becomes and the larger the pale shadow appears to be. Diminished blue characteristics appear as diminished emotional capacity,

Section 4: Pale Shadows — Understanding and Managing Them

diminished green presents as diminished cognitive capacity, diminished red manifests as diminished physical capacity and diminished yellow is displayed as diminished organizational capacity.

The pale blue, green, red and yellow shadows represent our challenges, shortcomings, incompetencies, weaknesses, failings, deficiencies, limitations, and inadequacies — the things we don't do well or don't do at all. These are the behaviours we procrastinate and the experiences we avoid.

Pale Shadow

- Colours move up and down and vary in brightness depending on how intensely they are being used.
- When a colour is used more intensely, it moves up and becomes brighter.
- When a colour is used less intensely, it moves down and becomes paler.
- Colours used within this range are functional and considered to be "in the light".
- Pale shadow characteristics appear when a colour is not used or is perceived as not being used intensely enough.

All of your colours are challenged from time to time; however, your paler colours are challenged more frequently and more intensely. You use your pale colours in a flight response more often because those attributes are not as important to you.

Your paler colours are also not as well developed as your brighter colours, so your odds of using them effectively to prevail in a conflict are minimal. If you use your brightest colour to respond to a conflict or a challenge, your odds of prevailing are good. If you use your second colour, your odds of prevailing are fair. If you use your third colour, your odds diminish further and if you are forced to use your palest colour, your odds of prevailing are poor which is why you rarely use your palest colour in a fight response. In flight mode you withdraw your palest colour from the conflict or challenge by "lightening" it even more.

You flight with light.

In general terms a stressor is any event that causes a stress response. To be specific in this case, a pale stressor is any event that causes a pale stress response, a flight response. Pale shadow characteristics and behaviours are best viewed as how a person reacts under pale stress.

Pale Blue Shadow Characteristics

When your pale blue is challenged by pale stressors, you may respond with fight or flight. An assessment of the challenge, your available blue resources and odds of prevailing determine your course of action.

In flight mode you attempt to alleviate your pale blue stress by diminishing your blue behaviour and using it less intensely. When you do not use, or are perceived as not using, blue intensely enough, a pale blue shadow appears and you will be perceived as having pale blue shadow characteristics. People using blue more intensely than you will perceive your pale blue shadow before you do. All it takes for a person to perceive you as not using enough blue ... is for you not to smile when you are smiled at. When you lack emotional affect, people perceive your pale blue shadow. The greater the difference in intensity is perceived to be, the larger your pale blue shadow appears to be. Not enough of a good thing ... is not a good thing. The pale blue shadow represents diminished emotional capacity, diminished emotional affect, and inadequate interpersonal responses.

The following pale blue shadow characteristics are listed on the pale side of the blue stress management card.

PALE BLUE SHADOW CHARACTERISTICS

Detached	Unemotional
Heartless	Unfeeling
Impersonal	Unfriendly
Inconsiderate	Unkind
Inhumane	Unloving
Insensitive	Unsocial
Uncaring	Unsympathetic

More Pale Blue Shadow Characteristics

Aloof	Solitary
Antisocial	Standoffish
Attachment disorder	Superficial
Callous	Thick-skinned
Cold hearted	Unaccommodating
Cruel	Unaffectionate
Dispassionate	Unappreciative of people
Distant	Unapproachable
Emotionally detached	Unattached
Lack of compassion	Uncharitable
Lack of emotional expression	Uncompromising
Lack of emotions	Uncooperative
Lack of empathy	Uncreative
Lack of self-awareness	Unforgiving
Limited self-expression	Unhelpful
Pitiless	Uninviting
Reclusive	Unromantic
Shallow	Unwelcoming

Section 4: Pale Shadows – Understanding and Managing Them

Pale Green Shadow Characteristics

When your pale green is challenged by pale stressors you may respond with fight or flight.

In flight mode you alleviate pale green stress by diminishing your green behaviour and using it less intensely. People with brighter green will perceive you as having pale green shadow characteristics. The pale green shadow represents diminished mental capacity and insufficient cognitive responses.

The following pale green shadow characteristics are listed on the pale side of the green stress management card.

PALE GREEN SHADOW CHARACTERISTICS

Bewildered	Irrational
Confused	Mystified
Ignorant	Perplexed
Illogical	Uneducated
Imprecise	Unintelligent
Inaccurate	Unprincipled
Inarticulate	Unreasonable

More Pale Green Shadow Characteristics

Baffled	Lacking insight
Bamboozled	Mixed up
Befuddled	Muddled
Clueless	Naive
Dense	Narrow-minded
Dim-witted	Not objective
Dozy	Obscure
Dull-witted	Obtuse
Dumb founded	Puzzled
Feeble-minded	Short sighted
Foolish	Simple-minded
Gullible	Stupid
In the dark	Tactless
Incoherent	Unclear
Lack of perspective	Uninformed
Lack of understanding	Unmindful
Lacking comprehension	Unrealistic
Lacking foresight	Unwise

Red Shadow Characteristics

When your pale red is challenged by pale stressors you may respond with fight or flight.

In flight mode you attempt to alleviate your pale red stress by diminishing your red behaviour and using it with less intensity. People with brighter red will perceive you as displaying pale red shadow characteristics. The pale red shadow represents diminished physical capacity and inadequate physical responses.

The following pale red shadow characteristics are listed on the pale side of the red stress management card.

PALE RED SHADOW CHARACTERISTICS

Apathetic	Lifeless
Clumsy	Listless
Idle	Repressed
Immobilized	Too slow
Inactive	Uncoordinated
Inhibited	Unmotivated
Lethargic	Unresponsive

More Pale Red Shadow Characteristics

Accident prone	Lacking initiative
All thumbs	Lackluster
Blasé	Lazy
Boring	Mundane
Cowardly	Not any fun
Dawdling	Not resilient
Deadbeat	Paralyzed
Docile	Physically awkward
Drab	Physically uncoordinated
Dullard	Plodding
Fearful	Sedentary
Frail	Shiftless
Gutless	Sluggish
Humdrum	Subdued
Humourless	Sullen
Incapacitated	Unenthusiastic
Inept	Unexciting
Klutzy	Unmoved

Section 4: Pale Shadows — Understanding and Managing Them

Pale Yellow Shadow Characteristics

When your pale yellow is challenged by pale stressors, you may respond with fight or flight.

In flight mode you attempt to alleviate your pale yellow stress by diminishing your yellow behaviour and using it with less intensity. When you do not use, or are perceived as not using yellow intensely enough, a pale yellow shadow appears. People with brighter yellow will perceive your pale yellow shadow characteristics.

People using yellow more intensely than you will perceive your pale yellow shadow before you do. The greater the difference in intensity is perceived to be, the larger your pale yellow shadow will appear to be. While a person with somewhat brighter yellow perceives you bending the rules, a person with significantly brighter yellow will perceive you as breaking the rules or breaking the law. You can be judged as establishing rules, following the rules, bending the rules, breaking the rules or being unruly depending on how bright the others person's yellow is. When your yellow is pale you may have the attitude that rules are made to be broken, that it is better to ask for forgiveness after breaking a rule than to ask permission in advance. You act first and ask forgiveness or ask questions later. While people with pale yellow look for loopholes and exceptions to the rule, people with bright yellow plug the loopholes and allow no exceptions to the rule. People with pale yellow are often not even aware of the rules until they break them, until someone with bright yellow admonishes them. People with pale yellow may overstep boundaries because they don't properly judge where to draw the line. When your yellow is pale you may be perceived as abdicating your roles and shirking responsibilities. The pale yellow shadow represents diminished organizational capacity and lack of controls.

The following pale yellow shadow characteristics are listed on the pale side of the yellow stress management card.

PALE YELLOW SHADOW CHARACTERISTICS

Disobedient	Out of line
Disorderly	Unconventional
Disorganized	Unlawful
Inattentive to details	Unprepared
Irresponsible	Unprofessional
Lacking discipline	Unreliable
Off task	Unsafe

More Pale Yellow Shadow Characteristics

Breaking rules	Not accountable
Cheating	Not being serious enough
Contravening rules	Not completing tasks
Defying authority	Not planning
Disloyal	Not prioritizing
Disobeying orders	Off schedule
Disobeying policies	Oppositional defiance
Disorderly conduct	Out of control
Disrespecting authority	Poor work ethic
Disrespecting boundaries	Squandering resources
Ignoring procedures	Tardiness
Improper	Undependable
Inconsistent	Undisciplined
Indecisive	Uneconomical
Insubordinate	Unpredictable
Lacking commitment	Unruly
Lacking self-control	Unscrupulous
Non compliant	Untidy

Reviewing Your 10 Stressors for Flight Responses

Refer to the perception check on page 5. Take a few minutes to review the stressful situations you checked off in the right-hand column of your list of 10 stressful situations. You will recall that these situations are pale stressors, stressful because your palest colour is being challenged. These situations can trigger your flight response and pale shadow characteristics. Review your palest colour's list of pale shadow characteristics above to identify the shadow characteristics you display in the situations you checked off.

Recognizing Your Pale Shadow Characteristics

It is difficult to recognize your own pale shadow because as you diminish a colour and use it less intensely, your stress is relieved so you have a sense that you are using the right intensity. For example, as you suppress your feelings because it is challenging for your pale blue to express emotions, and as you become irrational because it is challenging for your pale green to be logical, and as you slow down your activities because it is challenging for your pale red to be physically active, and as you become less organized because it is challenging for your pale yellow to maintain order...your pale stress is alleviated. Your internal frame of reference gives you the impression you are doing the right thing because it eases your stress.

While you perceive yourself being in the light, others may perceive you as being in the pale shadow. While you perceive you are being emotionally calm and cool, someone with brighter blue may perceive you as cold-hearted and callous. While you perceive yourself as mentally relaxed a person with brighter green may perceive you as mentally lax. While you while away the hours and perceive yourself as laid back, someone with brighter red may perceive you as a loafer or couch potato. While you perceive yourself as laid back your boss may perceive you as laid off. While you perceive yourself as being less controlling, someone else may perceive you as being out of control.

So, how would you know if you are using a colour with too little intensity?

Illuminating Pale Shadow Characteristics

I described earlier how illuminating bright shadow characteristics makes you consciously aware of what you are doing. Illuminating pale shadow characteristics makes you aware of what you are <u>not</u> doing. In both instances increased awareness helps us make conscious choices.

We use our colours in order of preference. We lead with our bright colours and lag with our pale colours. Our bright colours are highly tuned and quick to respond and we are energized by the opportunities to do what we do well. At the other end of the spectrum our pale colours are not highly tuned and we procrastinate what we do not do well. We can use any colour with too little intensity, but you have likely experienced the pale shadow of your palest colour more often and to a greater extent than those of your brighter colours.

Your palest colour... Use it or lose it!

One of the pitfalls of not using pale colours enough is that they become more and more diminished and more difficult to use effectively. When they are used less and less they become useless.

When you use your red, it is exercised and your physical muscles and physical coordination grow and develop. When you use your other colours, they are also exercised and grow and develop. Using blue is emotional exercise, using green is mental exercise and using yellow is organizational exercise or an exercise in self-control.

When blue is your brightest colour your initial responses are emotionally based; you wear your heart on your sleeve. When blue is your palest colour your emotional awareness is minimal and those responses occur last so you may be the last person in the room to be aware that someone is feeling emotionally distraught or elated. When green is your brightest colour, you think first; for you things (or "thinks") are easier said than done. When green is your palest colour, thinking is the last thing on your mind and you analyze situations to a far lesser extent when making decisions. When red is your brightest colour, you can go so fast that you get ahead of yourself. Things are easier done than said — acting first and feeling, thinking and judging later. When red is your palest colour, you are slow to act and may react too late because someone else has already taken the initiative to do it. When yellow is your brightest colour, the first thing you do is take charge, get organized and get control. When yellow is your palest colour, being organized is the last thing on your agenda (if you have one) and when all else fails, you desperately clean up the mess, reluctantly abide by the rules, or defiantly fall into line and follow directions.

Because your pale colours are not highly tuned functions, you do not notice the effects of not using them until the consequences become significantly loud enough to draw your pale colour's attention, as if your pale colours are hard of hearing. Only when the volume is turned up, when the negative consequences of your inactions become full blown problems, do you eventually sit up and pay attention or stand up and take action. By the time you get around to using your pale colours the damage is done.

When you have to resort to damage control mode you have to use your paler colours more intensely than you would if you had used them sooner. As a result you may associate your paler colours with desperate measures, aversive experiences, and negative consequences. You may have the impression that you use your pale colours when you are stressed. The fact is, you may experience stress because you do _not_ use your pale colours effectively enough in the first place. Although using pale colours is challenging, _not_ using pale colours effectively can create even greater challenges. The implications of not using a colour effectively can be disastrous. If you are driving down the highway and have a blow out, it is the bad tire that causes you to hit the ditch.

Because it is handy to have more than one definition of insanity, here is another one.

Another Definition of Insanity:

<u>Not</u> doing the same thing over and over again and expecting a different result.

The next time things are not going well:

1) Notice what colour you are <u>not</u> using.
2) Notice the result.
3) Use that colour.

> No problem can be solved from the same level of consciousness that created it.
>
> — Albert Einstein

Brighten-Up Phrases

When we perceive someone using a colour less intensely than we use it, rather than appreciating and valuing that intensity we often focus on the <u>difference</u> in intensity. We are inclined to perceive the difference as a negative and when we contrast and compare ourselves with others, we cast ourselves as being more in the light, and the other person as being more in the pale shadow. The more we compare and contrast, the more we cast ourselves as being in the light. When you insist on standing in the light you cast a pale shadow onto the other person.

When we perceive a person's pale shadow we often react by encouraging, persuading and pressuring the other person to use that colour more intensely. There are many common phrases that we use in everyday language to try to persuade people to use a colour more intensely. These are "brighten-up" phrases.

Section 4: Pale Shadows — Understanding and Managing Them

Your blue uses blue brighten-up phrases to persuade others to use more blue. The following blue brighten-up phrases are listed on the pale side of the blue stress management card.

BLUE BRIGHTEN-UP PHRASES
"Smile!"
"Have a heart."
"Be more caring."
"Have more faith."
"Be more sensitive."
"Trust your feelings."
"Tell me how you feel."

Your green uses green brighten-up phrases to persuade others to use more green. The following green brighten-up phrases are listed on the pale side of the green stress management card.

GREEN BRIGHTEN-UP PHRASES
"Figure it out."
"Think about it."
"Use your head."
"Be more precise."
"Put your mind to it."
"Give it more thought."
"Put on your thinking cap."

Your red uses red brighten-up phrases to persuade others to use more red. The following red brighten-up phrases are listed on the pale side of the red stress management card.

RED BRIGHTEN-UP PHRASES
"Wing it!"
"Just do it!"
"Hurry up!"
"Get going!"
"Lighten up!"
"Give it a go!"
"Take a chance!"

Your yellow uses yellow brighten-up phrases to persuade others to use more yellow. The following yellow brighten-up phrases are listed on the pale side of the yellow stress management card.

> **YELLOW BRIGHTEN-UP PHRASES**
> *"Play it safe."*
> *"Make a list."*
> *"Stay on task."*
> *"Get organized."*
> *"Stay on schedule."*
> *"Be more responsible."*
> *"Be more professional."*

Note: These brighten-up phrases are listed here as examples so you will recognize them and their variations when you say them or hear them in everyday language. They are **not** recommended things to say. In fact, as you will see, these are the phrases you ought to avoid because they can trigger a person's flight response.

We use brighten-up phrases to pressure people to use colours with more intensity so it is as intense as ours, as if pressuring people to use it more so we don't have to use it less. Brighten-Up phrases are stated with a level of urgency that is directly proportional to the perceived difference in intensity. If we perceive someone using a colour with somewhat less intensity, we use brighten-up phrases with some urgency. If we perceive someone as using a colour with a great deal less intensity, we use brighten-up phrases with a great deal more urgency.

What Brighten-up Phrases Do You Use?

What colour of brighten-up phrases do you use the most often to get people to brighten up? The brighten-up phrases that you use the most often reveal your bright colours.

What colour of brighten-up phrases do others often use to tell you to brighten up?

Those brighten-up phrases reveal your pale colours.

The intent of brighten-up phrases

On the surface it appears as if brighten-up phrases are attempts to persuade people to use colours with greater intensity, but a closer examination reveals another motivation. How often do you use a colour with more intensity just because someone tells you to? Probably not very often. And how often do people use colours with more intensity because you tell them to? Again, probably not very often.

For example, if someone seems unfriendly they don't genuinely smile just because you say "Smile!" If someone appears confused they don't use more green to think more clearly just because you try to talk some sense into them and tell them to

Section 4: Pale Shadows — Understanding and Managing Them

"brighten up," "smarten up," "wisen up" or "figure it out." If you tell an unmotivated, sedentary, lethargic person to get going and "Wing it!" the person doesn't just jump up and go for it. If you caution an entrepreneur to "play it safe" the person doesn't become more conservative as a result.

If people don't use colours with greater intensities just because they are told to, why do we continue to pressure each other in these ways? There must be something about these interactions that reinforces and maintains this common, everyday behaviour.

"Brighten-Up": A Paired Exercise

Remember the principle of physics that states, "For every action, there is an equal and opposite reaction." This principle also applies to brighten-up phrases.

In ColourSpectrums workshops, this principle of human dynamics is dramatically demonstrated in the following exercise that I encourage you to do with a partner. During this exercise you will need to refer to the brighten-up phrases that are listed on the stress management cards.

1) Stand with your partner and face each other.
2) Hold your partner's left hand with your right hand.
3) Take note of your partner's palest colour and read that colour's first brighten-up phrase aloud to your partner as if persuading him or her to use that colour more intensely. As you read the statement, pull your partner's left hand toward you as if enforcing the brighten-up phrase.
4) Read the next brighten-up phrase with increased forcefulness and pull your partner's left hand with an increased force to match.
5) Continue reading the brighten-up phrases with increasing forcefulness and pull your partner's left hand each time with increasing force.
6) Reverse roles and repeat the exercise.

Remember to apologize to each other. Say you are sorry and promise to never pressure each other again.

How did your partner respond? With each increasingly insistent brighten-up phrase and increasingly vigorous pull, your partner probably responded with an equal (in colour energy) and opposite (in direction) reaction. When you pull often enough and hard enough you will provoke this reaction. This is the <u>flight</u> response.

You will recall that a stressor is defined as any event that causes a stress response. If someone physically pulls you towards him or her and pulls you off balance, you pull back in order to maintain or regain your balance. Being pulled is a stressor because it causes a stress response — the effort exerted to pull back to regain your balance. The greater the energy you expend to regain your balance, the greater the stress you experience. A slight pull causes a little stress. An aggressive pull causes a great deal of stress.

When you have the perception a person is not using a colour intensely enough and you pressure the person to use it more intensely, you often elicit an equal and opposite reaction. The pale shadow characteristics you perceived in the person before you initiated the interaction become even more evident. Why do we pressure people to use a colour more intensely if all we get is the opposite reaction? What is our motivation?

In this exercise, you read brighten-up phrases with increasing forcefulness. Each time you increased the intensity of a brighten-up statement, you brightened and energized that colour within you. You experienced that colour with increasing intensity...and that is the payoff! As you experience greater intensity you experience greater self-satisfaction. As your partner is provoked your partner pulls back with increasing forcefulness and experiences his or her pale position with increasing satisfaction. The resistance and tension experienced by both of you is like an isometric exercise. These interactions can be blue emotional exercises of feeling emotions more or less intensely, green intellectual exercises of thinking more or thinking less, red physical exercises of being more physically active or resisting being physically active. They can be yellow exercises in exerting authority or resisting and defying authority. These interactions arouse our bright colours and suppress our pale colours, entrenching our preferred intensities.

As it turns out, brighten-up phrases and other ways you pressure people to use pale colours more intensely are not really intentions to change other people at all. They are intended to stimulate and empower your own bright colours. Brighten-up phrases are attempts to keep your bright colours from being changed by others.

Consider both of the previous push and pull exercises. When a person is pushed and pressured to use a colour less intensely, the fight response causes them to push back and use that colour even more intensely. When a person is pulled and pressured to use a colour more intensely, the flight response causes them to pull away and use that colour even less intensely. External pressures to use any colour more or less intensely is met with resistance.

Consider each of your colours one at a time and imagine being pressured to use each one less intensely. Visualize how your blue, green, red and yellow fight responses can be triggered as you resist being forced to use each one less intensely than you prefer. Visualize how your blue, green, red and yellow flight responses can be triggered as you resist being forced to use each one more intensely. Regardless of how bright or pale our colours are in our ColourSpectrums personalities, we tend to resist external forces to use them more or less intensely than we prefer.

When we are pressured to use any of our four colours more or less intensely than we prefer we tend to resist and react with equal and opposite force so we are not changed by those external forces. We resist being changed against our will.

The commonly understood technique of "reverse psychology" takes advantage of this fight or flight response. The technique, of course, is to outsmart, outwit and manipulate someone into doing or not doing something by telling them "to not do" or "to do" the opposite. Slyly delivered, the brighten-up message "to not do something" and lighten-up message "to do something" elicit the desired oppositional defiant behaviour without the manipulated person being aware of it. Interestingly enough this oppositional behaviour deceives the resisting person into experiencing a sense of autonomy and independence when in fact that person's resistant behaviour is completely dependent upon have someone to oppose and react to.

Instead of brightening and lightening our own colours to match other people's, we often pressure others to brighten and lighten their colours to match ours. It seems we want people to be more like us so we don't have to be more like them.

Dynamics of Brightest to Palest Colours

Refer to the following illustration and think of yourself as the person on the left using your brightest colour to interact with the person who has that colour as a palest colour. Think of your brightest colour's priorities, delights and talents interacting with this person who has those colour's priorities, delights and talents as a palest colour.

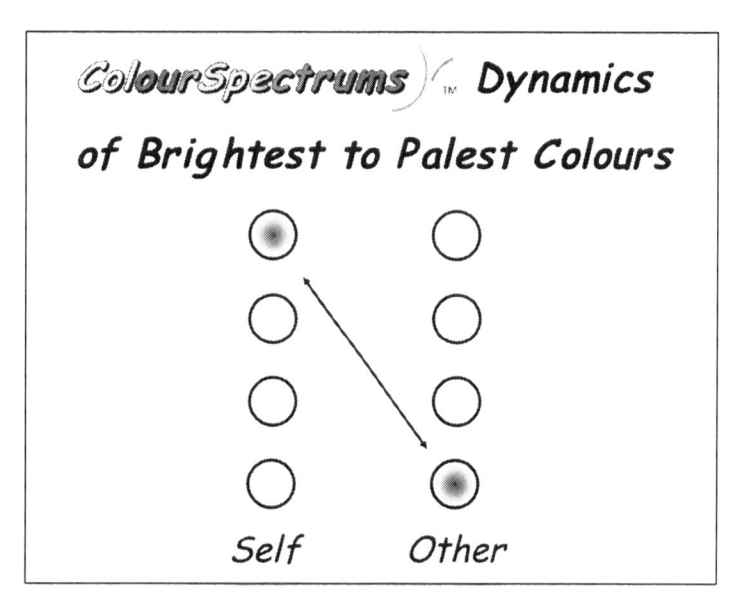

ColourSpectrums™ Dynamics of Brightest to Palest Colours

Self → Other

When you use bright blue, you may be easily disappointed by a person who uses pale blue. When you use bright green you may be easily frustrated by a person who uses pale green. When you use bright red, you can be quickly frustrated by a person who uses pale red and when you use bright yellow, you may be easily annoyed by someone who uses pale yellow.

It seems to be in our human nature to blame others for our own stresses and frustrations. If you perceive a person's pale blue, green, red or yellow as causing your bright frustration and bright stress you can be fairly certain that the other person perceives your bright blue, green, red or yellow as causing his or her frustration and pale stress.

One of the characteristics that distinguishes effective from ineffective people is how people interpret the cause of their experiences. People who are effective accept responsibility for both their positive and negative experiences. People who are not effective hold other people responsible and attribute their positive and negative experiences to external forces beyond their control, perceiving themselves as victims of negative circumstance and just bad luck or beneficiaries of positive circumstances and good luck. The person who takes responsibility is empowered and able to take charge of their own experiences, their own future. The person who abdicates responsibility is disempowered and unable to take charge of their experiences, unable to create their own path into the future. You have a choice. You can blame others for the state of your esteem and stress or you can take responsibility. To not take charge of your own esteem and stress is to let others take charge. To accept responsibility is to accept your experience and to accept your self.

Dynamics of Palest to Brightest Colours and Brightest to Palest Colours

Refer to the following illustration. Imagine yourself as the person on the left, interacting with the person on the right. Your brightest colour is the other person's palest colour and your palest is his or her brightest. Imagine the pushes and pulls and the potential fight and flight responses that can occur simultaneously.

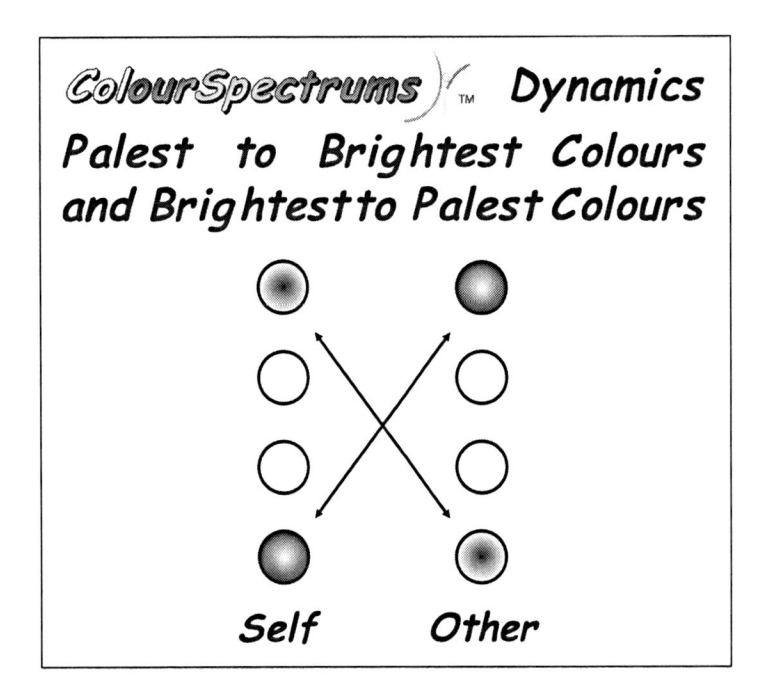

ColourSpectrums™ Dynamics
Palest to Brightest Colours and Brightest to Palest Colours

Self   Other

Your brightest colour interacts with the other person's palest colour, pulling and pushing in both directions with equal (in energy/colours) and opposite (in direction) forces in a dynamic dance of fight and flight responses.

At the same time your palest colour interacts with the other person's brightest colour, pushing and pulling in both directions with equal and opposite forces in a similar dynamic dance of flight and fight responses.

Section 4: Pale Shadows — Understanding and Managing Them

These brighten-up and lighten-up forces in equal and opposite directions occur with one person taking up a position at one end of a colour's continuum and the other person taking up a position at the other end of the same colour's continuum.

In moderation these interactions can be productive and create balance — personal balance and relationship balance. In extremes these interactions become conflicts.

There are two key principles to understanding and resolving conflict:

1) Conflicts (and collaborations) only occur between identical colours
   - blue conflicts and collaborates with blue
   - green conflicts and collaborates with green
   - red conflicts and collaborates with red
   - yellow conflicts and collaborates with yellow

2) In a conflict one person is often in fight mode and using the colour in a fight response and the other person is in a flight mode, using the same colour in a flight response.

It is common for two or three or four conflicts to occur simultaneously. This is why conflicts can be so confusing and disorienting. Remember, however, that even though multiple conflicts can occur simultaneously there are only four possible colour conflicts and that they are always distinct and separate. The key to resolving conflicts, therefore, is to deal with one colour conflict at a time.

Conflicts (arguments, debates, disagreements, dissents, disputes, quarrels, and so on) with others can perform important functions that can have positive outcomes. Because each colour performs different functions your own colours cannot interact directly with each other internally.

So how are any of your colours supposed to get any stimulation? How are your colours supposed to get experience, training, exercise or education? They can only do this by seeking out interactions with the corresponding colours in others! Just as a couple of saber-toothed kittens playfully pounce upon each other to practise their hunting and survival skills, your interactions with others provide the stimulation necessary for your colours to develop, grow, mature, and define themselves.

Your blue engages and interacts personally with others because it seeks emotional simulation. When your blue initiates emotional exchanges, your blue is aroused and you experience the intense emotional energy as emotionally validating. Bright blue emotions can be experienced as both positive and empowering as well as negative and disempowering. Empowering emotions are experienced in friendly, kind and loving interactions. In the absence of positive emotions even the arousal of intense disempowering emotions may be preferred to the apparent alternative — lack of emotional stimulation and feelings of loneliness or abandonment. Feeling full (of sadness) may feel better than feeling empty (and alone). A brief argument that temporarily stirs up disempowering emotions or an emotionally abusive relationship that stimulates intense and chronic disempowering emotions may be perceived as a better alternative than emotional numbness or an emotional void.

Your green seeks intellectual arousal and mental stimulation. Bright green thoughts can be experienced as empowering or disempowering. A bright green mind is a restless mind in perpetual thought that seeks a positive exchange of ideas, a lively debate, an intellectual discussion, an opportunity to argue a point, raise an eyebrow or open people's eyes. Opportunities to play the devil's advocate and pursue a line of questioning are perceived as welcome opportunities for mental exercise and cerebral stimulation. Entertaining thoughts is entertaining. The intellectual exercise itself is much more important than the issue or subject matter. Any subject will suffice.

> The most important thing is to not stop asking questions.
>
> — Albert Einstein

People with bright green will raise questions just for the sake of argument. In the light, people with bright green ask evocative questions that evoke positive responses and clearer thinking. In the bright green shadow, people with bright green ask provocative questions that provoke negative fight and flight reactions that inhibit clear thinking and create resistance to new ideas. When they lack mental simulation they can get bored out of their minds. A person starving for intellectual stimulation may desperately seek mental satisfaction by making a provocative statement with the intention of provoking a heated debate, starting an argument, raising a contentious or thorny issue, expressing a strong difference of opinion, locking horns, butting heads or pursuing an idea that comes to loggerheads. These desperate bright green shadow attempts to stimulate and satisfy green esteem needs are preferred to mental boredom — and who can argue with that?

Your red seeks physical arousal and visceral stimulation. Bright red physical stimulation can be experienced as empowering or disempowering. A person with bright red jumps at the chance to pull a stunt, to pull a prank, to pull a fast one or pull someone's leg or twist someone's arm. They play practical jokes (practical for them but not practical for others). This person gets excited about the unexpected and gets pumped for action. A playful nudge and a cajoling, jovial pat on the back keeps the person on their toes. Hijinx and horseplay keeps physical energy charged up. Self-esteem and elf esteem are one and the same thing. The playful competition and physical activity of rough and tumble play and games is invigorating.

Your red thrives on new and novel experiences and is interested in being there and doing that. Motto? "Been there, done that!" A person with unmet red needs may provoke a physical reaction and an altercation in an effort to experience physical arousal, to experience their red with a satisfying intensity. Even an intimidating posture, physical bullying or a physical fight invigorates and stimulates a person's red physical energy. In extremes, even physical pain or physically abusive relationships may be preferred to physical boredom.

Your yellow seeks organizational stimulation and a keen sense of order. On the positive side a person with bright yellow values traditional and formalized roles and takes pride in following through, being accountable and dependable. Duty calls them to sign on, sign up and enlist. A person with bright yellow will go above and beyond the call of duty. This loyal dedication to social order and a conventional sense of responsibility is experienced in the line of duty, in positions of authority and in positions of accountability according to rank and file. A person who asserts a position

Section 4: Pale Shadows — Understanding and Managing Them

of authority may be perceived as pulling rank. A person who needs to experience and validate their bright yellow esteem needs may exercise increasing authority that can provoke oppositional defiance in others. The person in charge may exercise controls and exert authority in order to maintain order. This bright yellow behaviour has the effect of validating, affirming and esteeming the person's bright yellow identity.

In moderation, mild conflicts and interactions provide necessary and healthy interactions that help us define ourselves and to grow and develop in social relationships with each other. In excess, however, these interactions become disempowering conflicts that interfere with healthy growth and development.

When our internal needs are satisfied we are less likely to conflict with others because our needs are not at risk. When our esteem needs have not been met we are at a higher risk of conflicting with others because we are motivated to protect our limited resources and more desperate to satisfy our unmet needs. We scramble to obtain the few small morsels of esteem that we can scrounge up. So when you are stressed and in a needy state you may blow the smallest irritations out of proportion and make a mountain out of a mole hill. When you are out of balance and desperate for esteem, the smallest bump in the road seems like the hill you are willing to die on. When you manage your stress and self-esteem, you are better able to manage conflict — internal conflict and relationship conflict.

Lighten-Up and Brighten-Up Combinations

Review the lighten-up phrases and brighten-up phrases on the stress management cards. We often use "lighten-up" and "brighten-up" phrases in combinations. We use these combinations in everyday language to discourage or pressure people from using one colour while encouraging or pressuring them to use another.

There are 12 possible combinations of lighten-up and brighten-up phrases. Here are examples of each combination.

1) "Don't take it so personally." (a blue lighten-up phrase)
   "Be more objective." (a green brighten-up phrase)
2) "Don't feel bad." (a blue lighten-up phrase)
   "Just get on with it!" (a red brighten-up phrase)
3) "Don't get your hopes up." (a blue lighten-up phrase)
   "You still have to book a reservation." (a yellow brighten-up phrase)
4) "Stop analyzing my problem." (a green lighten-up phrase)
   "I just want you to listen to how I feel." (a blue brighten-up phrase)
5) "Stop thinking about it." (a green lighten-up phrase)
   "Just do it!" (a red brighten-up phrase)
6) "That's enough debate." (a green lighten-up phrase)
   "It is time to vote." (a yellow brighten-up phrase)
7) "Don't be in such a hurry." (a red lighten-up phrase)
   "Let's make sure everyone feels okay with this." (a blue brighten-up phrase)

8) "Wait a minute!" (a red lighten-up phrase)
   "Think about the implications for the future." (a green brighten-up phrase)
9) "Don't drive so fast!" (a red lighten-up phrase)
   "Watch the speed limit." (a yellow brighten-up phrases)
10) "Bend the rules and give him a break." (a yellow lighten-up phrase)
    "John has personal problems and needs our help." (blue brighten-up phrase)
11) "Forget the formalities." (a yellow lighten-up phrase)
    "Get to the point." (a green brighten-up phrase)
12) "Don't sort them out." (a yellow lighten-up phrase)
    "Just throw them quickly into the box." (a red brighten-up phrase)

When you pressure a person to "lighten-up," the person may experience your pressure as a bright stressor. This can trigger the fight response. When you pressure a person to "brighten up" the person may experience your pressure as a pale stressor. This can trigger the flight response. When you use "lighten-up" and "brighten-up" phrases in combinations, the other person may experience both stressors at the same time, triggering the person's "fight response" and "flight response" simultaneously. At the same time you may experience your "fight response" and "flight response" simultaneously. The next exercise demonstrates what that dynamic conflict looks like.

Lighten-Up and Brighten-Up: A Paired Exercise

In the following exercise you will experience the push and pull of relationship conflicts by combining the two previous push and pull exercises. You will need to refer to the lighten-up and brighten-up phrases on the stress management cards.

Step 1: Practise exercise 1 as follows.

Exercise 1

- Stand with your partner and face each other.
- Hold the palm of your left hand up against your partner's right palm.
- Take note of your partner's brightest colour and read those lighten-up phrases aloud to your partner with increasing forcefulness and push against your partner's right palm with increasing force to match.

Step 2: Practise exercise 2 as follows.

Exercise 2

- Stand with your partner and face each other.
- Hold your partner's left hand with your right hand.
- Take note of your partner's palest colour and read those brighten-up phrases aloud to your partner with increasing forcefulness and pull your partner's left hand with increasing force to match.

Step 3: Combine exercise 1 and 2 as follows.

- Stand with your partner and face each other
- Perform exercises 1 and 2 simultaneously. You will be pushing on your partner's right hand as you read lighten-up phrases while simultaneously pulling on your partner's left hand as you read brighten-up phrases.

Reverse roles and complete the entire exercise so both of you experience both sides of the dynamic.

How did you react when your partner pushed on your right hand as if pressuring you to lighten up your brightest colour? You probably resisted by pushing back. This is your fight response.

How did you react when your partner pulled on your left hand as if pressuring you to brighten up your palest colour? You probably resisted by pulling back. This is your flight response.

Visualize your right hand as being your brightest colour pushing back with a fight response.

Visualize your left hand as being your palest colour pulling back in a flight response.

Visualize your middle colours as being halfway in between in your chest area.

As you push (and are pushed) on the one hand and pull (and are pulled) on the other hand, your body rotates around a centre of rotation in the area of your middle colours. Whether you initiate the pushes and pulls or react to the pushes and pulls, your middle colours do not experience the extreme bright and pale stresses that your brightest and palest colours do. Your middle colours are closer to your centre of balance. Your middle colours are the most centred and balanced functions as far as stress is concerned.

> Attempts to change others keep you from changing.

This simultaneous pushing and pulling is a metaphor for the pushes and pulls we experience in everyday relationships and day-to-day activities. This is how we insist and resist — our insistence that others change and our resistance to being changed by others. These are the pressures we exert on each other and the pressures life exerts on us. If you apply these pressures simultaneously to a person in real life, either intentionally or inadvertently, you run the risk of triggering the person's fight and flight responses simultaneously. Those responses can, in turn, trigger your own fight and flight responses. With this dynamic neither one of you will change. In fact both of you will become more resistant and entrenched. Brightening your green, for example, and using your bright green shadow to argue more forcefully that something is true does not make it truer. Using your green to change someone's mind keeps you from changing yours and potentially from seeing the truth.

We can lower resistance to change by minimizing these external stressors, pressures and demands. We can foster change by nurturing, encouraging, facilitating and promoting internal changes.

Rob Chubb

Your tendency to perceive others as using too much or too little of a colour blinds you to the possibility that you may be using a colour too much or too little yourself. When you pressure someone to brighten a colour you are in effect saying, "I want you to brighten up so I don't have to lighten up." When you pressure someone to lighten a colour you are in effect saying, "I want you to lighten up so I don't have to brighten up." For example, pressuring people to slow down keeps you from speeding up. This positioning polarizes your own brightest colour and palest colour at opposite ends of your colour's spectrum.

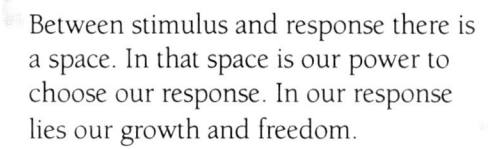

> Between stimulus and response there is a space. In that space is our power to choose our response. In our response lies our growth and freedom.
>
> — Viktor E. Frankl

It is readily apparent that we identify closely with our bright colours because those are the characteristics we associate with. What is not so apparent is that we also identify closely with <u>not</u> using our pale colours because those are the characteristics we disassociate from. When we take up a position of not using pale colours, we define ourselves by what we don't do (passive behaviours) or even worse by what we won't do (passive aggressive pale shadow behaviours and characteristics). When you resist using a colour and diminish it, you may be perceived as oppositional. If you continue to resist and become defiant you may be labeled as having an oppositional defiance disorder. Our attempts to change others demonstrate our refusal to change. When we try to change others, we cannot change. We all believe in change, as long as someone else does it.

When push comes to shove, and it sometimes does, it becomes apparent that no one wants to be forcibly changed by external forces. Once again we realize that real and lasting change must come from our free will that emanates from deep within each of us.

The next time you observe two people in conflict you will notice they take up positions at opposite ends of the same colour's spectrum and polarize their positions, with one person promoting more intensity and the other person promoting less intensity. One person will be in fight mode and the other person will be in flight mode. As the two positions become more polarized you may find yourself in the unique position of seeing both sides... seeing that one person is using too much of

> We cannot change anything unless we accept it. We cannot change ourselves as long as we are entrenched in conflict, with others, or in ourselves. Condemnation does not liberate, it oppresses.
>
> — Carl Jung

the colour and the other person is not using enough. When you have this perception it is because your colour intensity is half way between the two opposing intensities, like being a spectator standing in the middle of a tug of war with one person trying to pull the rope away from you in one direction and the other person trying to pull it away from you in the opposite direction.

Lighten-Up and Brighten-Up Phrases: A Metaphor

Personality has been defined as a person's essential being that distinguishes him or her as being unique from others, especially as a function of introspection. The push and pull of opposites has the effect of defining ourselves as being different and unique from others, delineating what we do and what we do not do, delineating who we are and who we are not.

While lighten-up phrases and brighten-up phrases are actual words that we use in everyday language, they are much more than that. They are also metaphors for all of the ways — consciously and unconsciously, behaviourally and psychologically — that we pressure each other to be different and are in turn challenged by others to be different. It is in our resisting and accommodating that we define who we are and who we are not.

We tend to think of relationship tension as being the result of <u>differences</u> between people. Similarities can be just as challenging. Imagine your employer, for example, hiring someone who has the same characteristics as you, someone who has the same priorities, enjoys the same delights, has the same talents and the same qualifications. As a matter of fact, some people at work think this person looks like you. Would you perceive this new employee as a threat to your individuality and uniqueness? Quite possibly! Conflicts can arise from similarities, as well as differences. I have seen two people with bright yellow in a power struggle over who is going to run a meeting. Conflicts often have less to do with similarities and/or differences and more to do with establishing ourselves as unique.

It is not the similarities and differences in relationships that determine their success or failure; it is your perception of those similarities and differences that makes the difference. When you have a positive attitude, when you appreciate and value similarities and differences, relationships succeed. When you have a negative attitude and depreciate or devalue similarities and differences, then the relationships are bound to fail.

Your attitude determines your altitude.

ColourSpectrums participants often ask if opposites attract, as conventional thinking often suggests. Sometimes opposites attract, sometimes opposites attack. When couples in long-lasting, positive relationships talk about the keys to their successful relationships they reveal one constant theme: that being in relationship with their partner empowers them to be their true selves. Each person in the relationship is empowered and esteemed in the presence of the other and each person experiences their colours in proportions that are naturally esteeming and validating. The experience of being together, the experience of being in the relationship esteems and empowers both people in ways that are not experienced when not in the relationship. As one workshop participant said it, "I am a better person with my partner in my life."

A Matter of Perception

Look at each object in order from left to right and mark the point on the line where you perceive the object change from a bowl to a glass.

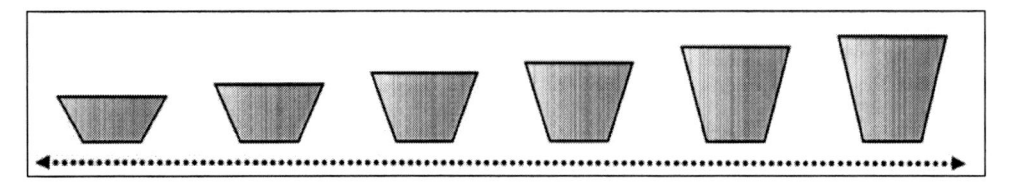

Now look at each object in order from right to left and mark the point where you perceive the object change from a glass to a bowl.

Did you find the two points you chose were different? What is happening?

You probably found that your perception changed past the mid point depending on which object you started with, the bowl or the glass. This is caused by a natural tendency to hold onto a particular perception once it has been established. In this case you tend to retain the perception of the object as being a bowl or a glass — **your first perception.**

First impressions can be lasting impressions, a fact that advertisers and marketers are well aware of. If you cut your finger, what do you put on it to make it better…a Band-Aid TM? or an adhesive bandage?

We also tend to maintain our first impressions of each other…in spite of subsequent information to the contrary. First impressions are often based on very little information and we call them first impressions as if we have second, third and fourth impressions. First impressions are often lasting impressions and as people change, our impressions may not.

Of course, you also have impressions of yourself: your self-concept. In many ways you are not the same person you were a year ago or years ago…but you may have the impression that you are. You tend to maintain perceptions of yourself that are not current and up to date.

Being Passive and Being Passive Aggressive

We use colours with varying intensities on a scale of "0" to "10." When we use a colour with a minimal intensity of "0" we use the colour passively. Passive behaviours are minimally functional but still considered to be "in the light" if they are used appropriately. When the flight response is triggered, a person who is using a colour passively begins to diminished the colour even further.

As behaviours become more and more diminished they become progressively paler and move into the pale shadow. When this occurs the person is not using the colour passively but is actively and aggressively <u>refusing</u> to use the colour. At this point, passive behaviours become passive aggressive behaviours.

Section 4: Pale Shadows — Understanding and Managing Them

```
            Passive Aggressive

Aggressive
─────────────────────────────
Assertive      10         ○
                          ○
Mid-range       5         ○
                          
Passive         0         
                          ●  ↓
Aggressive
```

It is important to make a clear distinction between being passive, which is the "absence of behaviour" and being passive aggressive, which is the active behaviour of rejecting, resisting and stubbornly refusing to use the colour. There are big differences between "do not," "can not" and "will not."

For example:

1) "Being kind" is an active bright blue behaviour.
2) Not "being kind" is the absence of that blue behaviour so it is passive, simply the absence of active kindness.
3) "Being unkind" is an active behaviour, the active pale blue shadow behaviour of being actively unkind, like the cold shoulder you might intentionally turn towards someone to display unfriendliness.

These distinctions are important to ensure accurate perceptions and guard against perceiving qualities that are not really there. Your bright blue, for instance, may mistakenly perceive a person as "being unkind" and in the pale blue shadow, when the person is just not "being kind" which is simply the absence of behaviour.

Passive behaviours are what you don't do.

Passive aggressive behaviours are what you won't do.

	Passive Behaviours	Passive Aggressive Behaviours
Blue	Lack of social behaviour	becomes unsocial or antisocial behaviour
	Lack of kindness	becomes unkindness
	Lack of cooperation	becomes uncooperative behaviour
Green	Lack of reasoning	becomes unreasonable behaviour
	Lack of logic	becomes illogical behaviour
	Lack of accuracy	becomes inaccuracy
Red	Lack of enthusiasm	becomes lethargic behaviour
	Being laid back	becomes lazy and immobilized
	Failure to act	becomes refusal to act
Yellow	Lack of order	becomes disorderly behaviour
	Lack of discipline	becomes undisciplined behaviour
	Lack of obedience	becomes disobedience

When other people think they are being passive, you may perceive them as being passive-aggressive. While you perceive yourself as using a colour passively, people using that colour with more intensity may perceive you as being passive-aggressive. These perceptions are mutual and simultaneous. As a result, our perceptions of ourselves are not the same as other people's perceptions of us.

When we are in the pale shadow we are in the dark, unaware of our behaviour and unaware of how we are perceived by others. Just because you are unaware of your pale shadow behaviour does not mean it is not having an influence on others.

Once again, we are reminded of Jung's perspective, that the acts of a person's shadow should not be taken as acts by the person, rather viewed as unintended unconscious acts.

After all, bright shadow and pale shadow behaviours are responses to stress in which we lack self-awareness. Who hasn't behaved poorly under stress or had lack of self-awareness from time to time.

Out-of-Esteem Pale Shadow Behaviour

Self-esteem is only experienced in the light. Self-esteem is not experienced in the pale shadow. Pale blue, green, red and yellow shadow behaviours are "out-of-esteem" behaviours. The greater the pale shadow becomes, the less self-esteem is experienced.

In this illustration the bottom circle represents the palest colour that is being diminished and moving down into the pale shadow. The upper half of the circle that is still in the light and represents behaviours that are diminished but still in esteem. The lower half of the circle is in the pale shadow and represents "out-of-esteem" pale shadow behaviours.

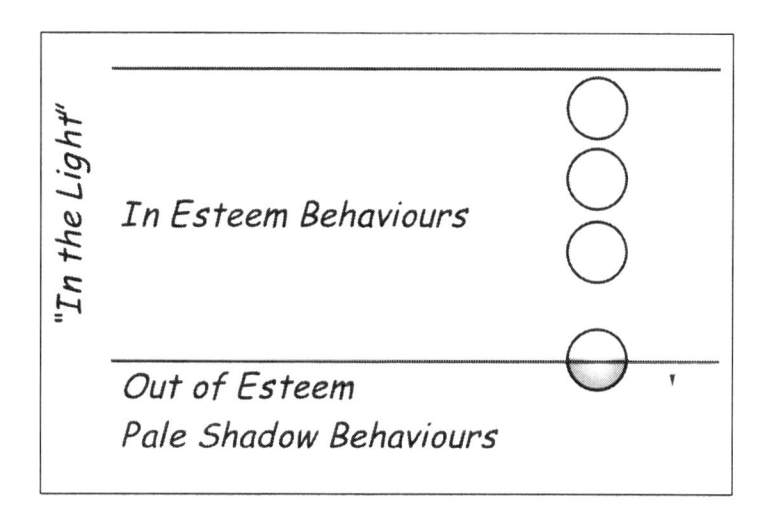

When a person withdraws and diminishes a colour there are always underlying hidden fears and apprehensions lying in the shadows. Acknowledging and validating those hidden fears and apprehensions sheds light on diminished colours and brings them back into the light, back into esteem.

Pale Shadow Sticks and Stones

The pale shadows we perceive in others are not true reflections of the person because shadow behaviours are "out-of-esteem" behaviours and are, by definition, out of alignment with the person's true self. The pale shadows we perceive in others are perceptions that are influenced by our own bright shadows, our own lack of awareness.

When we criticize a person's pale shadow behaviour we often criticize the person as well. One of the ways we degrade a person's character is by using negative labels. Pale shadow sticks and stones are negatively charged labels that we use to fault the person for not using a colour intensely enough. We are critical because their behaviours pale in comparison to our own. In short we engage in name-calling.

Reframing Pale Shadow Sticks and Stones

Pale Blue Sticks and Stones and Reframes

When your blue has the impression that someone else's blue is too pale, you will experience bright blue stress if you also perceive your blue needs are being threatened. If your blue fight response is triggered you may become more emotional, more assertive or more aggressive and perceive the person in a negative light.

Interestingly enough, there are fewer negative labels that devalue people for not using enough blue than there are for devaluing people for not using enough of the other colours. The reason is that our bright blue is naturally accommodating and accepting of differences. Our blue has the capacity to accept and value people and living things with unconditional positive regard regardless of race, gender, abilities and so on simply because our blue embraces all life unconditionally. Our true blue never seeks to dominate, overpower or devalue others.

In the left hand column is an alphabetical listing of pale blue sticks and stones — negative labels that your bright blue may use to devalue a person for not using enough blue. On the right are positive reframes.

1) For each of the blue sticks and stones on the left, write a positive reframe in the centre column before checking the suggested reframe on the right.

2) Complete each reframe one at a time and practise as you go.

Pale Blue

Sticks and Stones	Your Positive Reframe	Suggested Positive Reframe
Agnostic		Sceptical
Antisocial		Unsocial
Bully		Insecure
Callous		Insensitive
Closed-book		Introverted
Cold-blooded		Unmoved
Cold-hearted		Inattentive
Half-hearted		Detached
Hard-hearted		Firm
Heartbreaker		Dispassionate
Heartless		Unfeeling
Hermit		Independent
Loner		Shy
Mean spirited		Unemotional
Outcast		Lonely
Outsider		Private
Phony		Inexpressive
Recluse		Solitary
Thick skinned		Impersonal

This positive reframing exercise diminished your blue because you had to use your blue less intensely to perceive each negative label in a more positive light. Your blue became less intense with each reframe so reframing became easier with practice.

Section 4: Pale Shadows — Understanding and Managing Them

When you are in the bright blue shadow, diminishing your blue and being less critical diminishes your bright blue shadow and enhances your ability to perceive pale blue shadow characteristics in a more positive light.

Pale Green Sticks and Stones and Reframes

When your green evaluates someone else's green as being too pale, you will experience bright green stress if you also perceive your green needs are being threatened. If your green fight response is triggered you may become more logical, more analytical or more rational and perceive the person in a negative light.

In the left hand column is an alphabetical listing of pale green sticks and stones — negative labels that your bright green may use to devalue a person for not using enough green. On the right are positive reframes.

1) For each of the green sticks and stones on the left, write a positive reframe in the centre column before checking the suggested reframe on the right.
2) Complete each reframe one at a time and practise as you go.

Pale Green

Sticks and Stones	Your Positive Reframe	Suggested Positive Reframe
Absent-minded		Distracted
Airhead		Puzzled
Birdbrain		Free thinker
Blockhead		Uninformed
Bozo		Baffled
Dimwit		Vague
Dummy		Perplexed
Dunce		Bewildered
Fathead		Lost in thought
Halfwit		Confused
Idiot		Imprecise
Ignoramus		Uninformed
Lamebrain		Ill-informed
Moron		Innocent
Numbskull		Unclear
Scatterbrain		Unfocused
Simpleton		Down to earth
Stupid		In the dark

The positive reframing exercise above diminished your green because you had to use your green less intensely to perceive each negative label in a more positive light. Your green became less intense with each reframe so reframing became easier with practice.

When you are in the bright green shadow, diminishing your green and being less critical diminishes your bright green shadow and enhances your ability to perceive pale green shadow characteristics in a more positive light.

Pale Red Sticks and Stones and Reframes

When your red senses that someone else's red is too pale, you will experience bright red stress if you also perceive your red needs are being threatened. If your red fight response is triggered you may become more vigorous, more active or more motivated to take action and perceive the person in a negative light.

In the left hand column is an alphabetical listing of pale red sticks and stones — negative labels that your bright red may use to devalue a person for not using enough red. On the right are positive reframes.

1) For each of the red sticks and stones on the left, write a positive reframe in the centre column before checking the suggested reframe on the right.
2) Complete each reframe one at a time and practise as you go.

Pale Red

Sticks and Stones	Your Positive Reframe	Suggested Positive Reframe
Bore		Relaxed
Butterfingers		Inexperienced
Chicken		Nervous
Couch potato		Laid back
Coward		Apprehensive
Dawdler		Preoccupied
Killjoy		Conservative
Klutz		Unskilled
Lazybones		Easygoing
Party-pooper		Shy
Slacker		Unresponsive
Slowpoke		Slow and steady
Spoilsport		Unenthusiastic
Straggler		Unhurried
Wet blanket		Reserved
Wimp		Apprehensive
Wuss		Anxious
Yellow-belly		Worried

The positive reframing exercise above diminished your red because you had to use your red less intensely to perceive each negative label in a more positive light. Your red became less intense with each reframe so reframing became easier with practice.

Section 4: Pale Shadows — Understanding and Managing Them

When you are in the bright red shadow, diminishing your red and being less critical diminishes your bright red shadow and enhances your ability to perceive pale red shadow characteristics in a more positive light.

Pale Yellow Sticks and Stones and Reframes

When your yellow judges that someone else's yellow is too pale, you will experience bright yellow stress if you perceive your yellow needs are being threatened. If your yellow fight response is triggered you may become more judgmental, more critical or more authoritarian and perceive the person in a negative light. If your need to control is threatened, for example, you may become more and more controlling by laying down the law and reading the riot act. As you do so you perceive the other person as being more and more out of (your) control.

In the left hand column is an alphabetical listing of pale yellow sticks and stones — negative labels that your bright yellow may use to devalue a person for not using enough yellow. On the right are positive reframes.

1) For each of the yellow sticks and stones on the left, write a positive reframe in the centre column before checking the suggested reframe on the right.

2) Complete each reframe one at a time and practise as you go.

Pale Yellow

Sticks and Stones	Your Positive Reframe	Suggested Positive Reframe
Bad apple	_____	Wayward
Childish	_____	Childlike
Culprit	_____	Guilty party
Delinquent	_____	Youthful
Insubordinate	_____	Independent
Lawbreaker	_____	Limit tester
Maverick	_____	Spirited
Mischief maker	_____	Mischievous
Misfit	_____	Unique
Nonconformist	_____	Individualist
Offender	_____	Misguided
Outlaw	_____	Wayward
Rebel	_____	Risk taker
Renegade	_____	Adventurer
Rogue	_____	Freewheeler
Shirker	_____	Casual
Slob	_____	Carefree
Troublemaker	_____	Rascal

The positive reframing exercise above diminished your yellow because you had to use your yellow less intensely to perceive each negative label in a more positive light. Your yellow became less intense with each reframe so reframing became easier with practice. When you are in the bright yellow shadow, diminishing your yellow in this way and being less critical can diminish your bright yellow shadow and enhance your ability to perceive pale yellow shadow characteristics in a more positive light.

You may be in the bright shadow when you severely criticize others for using that colour with less intensity. The pale shadow you criticize in others is a reflection of your own bright shadow. Devaluing others for using your brighter colours less intensely than you requires you to brighten that colour even more within you even though it is already a bright colour at risk of being used too intensely and moving into the bright shadow. You are the one who can least afford to brighten it further.

> Reframing does not change the other person. It changes you.

The next time your brighter colours are intensely critical in these ways, try reframing paler colours in positive ways. As your perspective aligns more closely with a person's paler colour, your bright shadow will diminish accordingly.

When you have a different perspective than another person, you may perceive a shadow. You may perceive a person's bright shadow or a person pale shadow. The size of the shadow is directly proportional to the difference in perspective, the perceived difference in intensity. When you brighten or diminish your colours to match the other person's perception your perspective changes and the bright and pale shadows you perceived in the other are diminished.

> If you want someone to change... change.

Pale Shadow Self-Talk

Just as your subconscious recognizes your bright shadow before you are consciously aware of it, your subconscious also recognizes your pale shadow before you are consciously aware of it. By being more consciously aware of unconscious pale shadow self-talk you can heighten awareness of your pale shadow characteristics.

Self-Talk in the moment

When you listen to your internal self-talk, you will hear each colour participating in the conversation. Internal self-talk can reveal the presence of four pale shadows.

For Example:

When your blue has a feeling it is in the pale shadow, you might wonder, "Am I am being too aloof, detached or distant?"

When your green realizes it is not intense enough you might find yourself thinking, "I don't understand. This is way over my head."

If your red catches on that it is not active enough you might urge yourself to take action by saying, "Get going!" "Take a chance!" "You can do this!"

Section 4: Pale Shadows — Understanding and Managing Them

"Don't hold back," or "Just go for it!" When you are in the pale red shadow and lacking the motivation to act, your bright red self-talk is like having your own coach or motivational speaker within you urging you to take action.

When your yellow judges it is in the pale shadow you may hear yourself saying, "I should be more organized."

Self-Talk After the Fact

Have you ever failed to respond effectively, only to realize later that you should have or could have been more effective? You are left with nagging doubts and say to yourself, "that wasn't like me"? " I can't believe I how unresponsive I was!" That is your pale shadow speaking.

When your blue has the impression it has been in the pale blue shadow you may say to yourself, "I wish I had been more sensitive." When your green has sober second thoughts and becomes cognizant that it has been in the pale shadow you may find yourself thinking, "I realize I didn't give it enough thought," "How could I be so stupid?" "I didn't keep my wits about me," "I must have lost my head," or "I must have been out of my head." When it hits your red that it has been in the pale shadow it might suddenly occur to you, "I should have just done it!" When your yellow has not been intense enough, you might say to yourself, "I should have been more strict" or "I should have put my foot down."

Out-of-Esteem Bright and Pale Shadow Behaviours

Colours that are "in the light" utilize conscious awareness and effective responses. Colours that are "in the shadows" rely on unconscious awareness, distorted perceptions and ineffective responses.

Bright and pale shadows have a lot in common. When you overreact, you experience the bright shadow. Bright shadows represent all of the dysfunctional behaviours that we exhibit when we lack awareness. When you fail to respond adequately, you experience the pale shadow. The pale shadow represents all of the behaviours that we fail to use when we lack awareness and responsiveness.

```
                    Out of Esteem
                    Bright Shadow Behaviours      ○   ↑
            ───────────────────────────────────────────
    "In the Light"
                    In Esteem Behaviours          ○
                                                  ○
            ───────────────────────────────────────────
                    Out of Esteem                 ○   ↓
                    Pale Shadow Behaviours
```

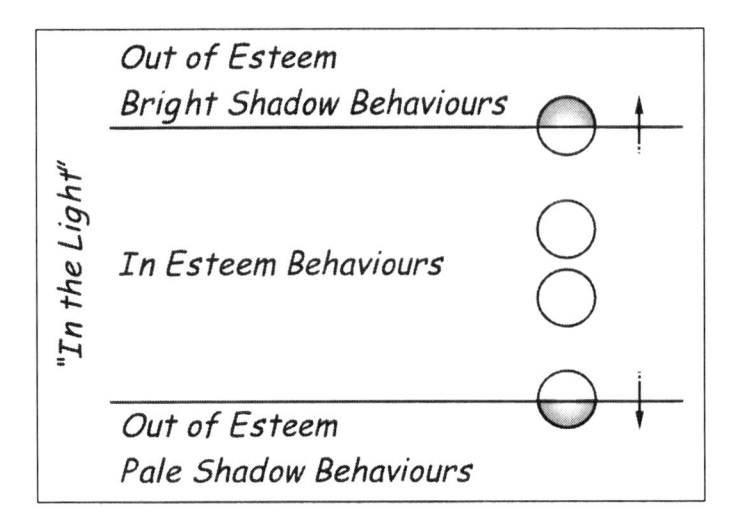

Esteem is only experienced in the light when our behaviours are congruent with our true self, in alignment with our true values and intentions. Behaviour in the shadow is "out of character" and "out of alignment" with a person's true intentions. Behaviour that does not align with the true self is out-of-esteem behaviour. The shadow has been described as the part of us that feels like it is not part of us. It feels like it can't be controlled. There is no esteem or sense of self in the shadow so when a person displays shadow behaviour there is a detachment from self. This detachment can be heard in statement such as, "I am going out of my mind," "I am beside myself," "I am not myself today," or "This is so out of character for me!"

You can visualize a person's most natural ColourSpectrums personality when you think of them being "at their best," and "in the light." The shadows explain the puzzling contradictions we experience within ourselves and the discrepancies we perceive in others. A person who acts negatively and contrary to their typical ColourSpectrums personality is likely in the bright or pale shadow.

When our behaviours are congruent with our self-concept and when we use colours in esteem we experience self-empowerment. The elusive experience of self-actualization is realized when "who we are" and "how we are" converge and align so that we experience our true selves and recognize, "I am being me!" What we can be is what we must be. This self-actualization.

Stress Management Cards: Look on the Pale Side

An Exercise in Using the Pale Sides of the Stress Management Cards

Turn the four stress management cards over so the heading: Pale Challenges is at the top of each card. Then position the four cards in their respective quadrants as indicated below.

Section 4: Pale Shadows — Understanding and Managing Them

Four Stress Management Cards — Look On the Pale Side

BLUE	**GREEN**
PALE CHALLENGES	PALE CHALLENGES
PALE STRESSORS	PALE STRESSORS
PALE SHADOW CHARACTERISTICS	PALE SHADOW CHARACTERISTICS
BRIGHTEN-UP PHRASES	BRIGHTEN-UP PHRASES
PALE CHALLENGES	PALE CHALLENGES
PALE STRESSORS	PALE STRESSORS
PALE SHADOW CHARACTERISTICS	PALE SHADOW CHARACTERISTICS
BRIGHTEN-UP PHRASES	BRIGHTEN-UP PHRASES
RED	**YELLOW**

You can use these cards to manage pale stressors in the same manner that you can use them to manage bright stressors. Simply start at any point on the pale side of these stress management cards and refer to the other related elements.

For example:

When someone appears "insensitive," locate that pale blue shadow characteristic under "Pale Shadow Characteristics" on the blue stress management card and review the related "Pale Challenges," "Pale Stressors," and "Brighten-Up phrases."

For example:

If you are intimidated by intimacy or have trouble "being intimate," locate that pale blue challenge under "Pale Challenges" on the blue stress management card and review the related "Pale Stressors," "Pale Shadow Characteristics" and "Brighten-Up Phrases."

You can use any of the other stress management cards in a similar manner.

Section 5: Using ColourSpectrums to Improve Relationships

Perceptions and Perspectives

Each of your colours is capable of distinguishing even the slightest difference in intensity, of the corresponding colour in others. When someone uses blue slightly more intensely, your blue notices. When someone uses green slightly less intensely than you, your green notices, and so on.

We do more than just notice these differences. We judge these differences. Each colour has a different motivation and we are inclined to be suspicious of people's motives when they behave differently, when they have a different colour spectrum than we do... and most people have a different colour spectrum than you do. Each of our colours has a strong tendency to perceive its current intensity as the benchmark against which it compares, contrasts and evaluates other people's intensities. People who use colours more or less intensely than we do appear to be in the bright or pale shadow; their behaviour appears shady to us, as if they are up to something, up to no good.

As you brighten and diminish your colours, your evaluations of others change accordingly.

When you perceive a person using a colour more intensely than you, you are inclined to perceive the person as using it _too_ intensely, rather than perceiving yourself as not using that colour intensely enough. When your pale colours are challenged, for example, rather than perceiving yourself as not being able to brighten the colour to match the person, you perceive the other person as using that colour too intensely and not being able to diminish it. Rather than recognizing your own pale shadow you block the light by denying it and project that shadow onto others and perceive their bright shadow, faulting the other person rather than taking ownership. The more you criticize a person's bright shadow characteristics the paler that colour becomes within you. The greater your pale shadow becomes the greater the other person's bright shadow appears to be.

When you perceive a person using a colour less intensely than you, you are likely to perceive the person as not using it intensely enough, rather than perceiving yourself as using that colour too intensely. Rather than recognizing your own bright shadow you block the light and project that shadow onto others and perceive their pale shadow, again faulting the other person rather than taking personal responsibility. The more you criticize a person's pale shadow characteristics the brighter that colour becomes in you. The greater your bright shadow becomes the greater their pale shadow appears to be.

> Everything that irritates us about others can lead us to an understanding of ourselves.
>
> — Carl Jung

Jung observed that we are much more disposed to acknowledging our positive characteristics than we are to acknowledging our negative shadow characteristics. Freud observed that we are uncomfortable with our own shadow side so we deny it in ourselves and prefer to observe it in others. He described this phenomenon as projection.

When you focus on the shadows that you project upon others, you cannot see the shadow you cast upon yourself because it is so up close and personal. Your shadow side is a mirror image of the shadow you cast upon others, a direct reflection of your own shortcomings. When you perceive someone's bright shadow ... it is a projection of your own pale shadow and when you perceive someone's pale shadow ... it is a projection of your own bright shadow. Criticizing others and perceiving shadows in others keeps <u>you</u> in the dark.

In relationships these mutual projections lead to misunderstandings, tensions and conflicts, as each person perceives the other as being in the shadow while perceiving themselves as being in the light. Each person projects and blames the other for the difference in intensity. Keep in mind that we use all four colours all the time so these projections can involve more than one colour at a time. These projections are defense mechanisms that keep both people, and the relationship, in the shadows.

> Keeping others in the dark ... keeps **you** in the dark.

We criticize and cast others in a negative light in an effort to enhance our own value. These are attempts to define ourselves by defining others. Interestingly enough, even though you use all four of your colours with different intensities, you still have the impression that you use each colour with the right intensity. Because everyone's colour spectrums are unique, the intensities you prefer will be different than the intensities that other people prefer. Just because two people are different does not mean that one of them is defective.

As long as you maintain the perception that you are the person who uses all the colours with the right intensities, as long as you perceive everyone as defective, as long as you hold other people responsible for difference in intensities, you will find it difficult to grow and develop personally and professionally. ColourSpectrums encourages everyone to use their awareness of others as opportunities to shed light on their own shadows with a view to expanding their own colour spectrums.

Section 5: Using ColourSpectrums to Improve Relationships

Consider your perceptions of other vehicles as you travel down the highway. Vehicles travelling faster than you seem to be going too fast, seem to have too much energy. Vehicles travelling slower than you seem to be going too slow, seem to have too little energy. The only vehicles that seem to be going the right speed are those travelling the same speed as you and you don't see many of them because they stay constantly ahead or behind you. (Your blue personalizes perceptions and perceives other drivers, not other vehicles.) You cannot change the speed of other vehicles or behaviours of other drivers but you can change your <u>perceptions</u> of other vehicles and drivers. If you speed up, the faster vehicles/drivers don't seem as fast. When you speed up they seem to slow down. Now there are more vehicles going too slow. If you slow down, those slower vehicles/drivers don't seem so slow. When you slow down they seem to speed up. Now there are more vehicles going too fast.

When you change your behaviour your perceptions change. It literally depends on how you look at it. When you brighten your colours, other people's bright shadows appear to diminish. When you diminish your colours, other people's pale shadows also appear to diminish. Regardless of how intense any of your colours are, there will always be people using colours more or less intensely than you. As you learn to change the intensities of <u>your</u> colours you will be able to perceive diverse perspectives that will foster your own personal growth and professional development.

> When you change,
> your perceptions change.

Stress Management Cards: Look on the Bright and Pale Sides

Have you ever wondered how people perceive you? Of course you have! We are naturally curious about how we are perceived. It is also important to know how you are perceived because it has important implications for how people respond to you in your personal and professional life.

> To know how you are perceived,
> be aware of how you perceive.

What do you see when you look in a mirror? Do you see yourself? Most of us would say, "yes." The physical reflection you see, however, is not what other people see. You literally see a mirror image and because your face and body are not symmetrical the reversed image that you see in the mirror is a different image than other's see. To understand how others really see your physical image you would have to reverse the image in the mirror.

Your perception of another person's colour spectrum is also like looking at a mirror image of your own because your colour spectrum is not symmetrical either. Your brighter colours have a different point of view than your paler colours do; your brighter colours tend to perceive a person as not using those colours intensely enough. Your paler colours tend to perceive a person as using those colours too intensely. The result is that your perception of a person's colour spectrum is a mirror image of your own. It is a mirror image of the other person's perception of your colour spectrum. People perceive a reflection of your perception.

To understand how people perceive your colours, first be aware of how you perceive theirs; reverse your perception and you've got it! When you have the perception someone is using a colour too intensely, guess what their perception of you is? Right! Their perception will be that you are not using that colour intensely enough. The other person's perception of you will be a mirror image, simply a reflection of your perception. When you have the perception that someone is not using a colour intensely enough, guess what their perception of you is? Of course! That person will perceive you as using that colour too intensity. Your perception is a reflection on you.

> You are a reflection of your perception

In a research study, subjects were shown 10 photographs of themselves and asked to choose the one they liked the best. Subjects almost always chose the one photograph that, unknown to them, was actually a reversed image.

Subsequently, friends of the subject were also shown 10 photographs of the same person and asked to choose the one they liked best. Friends almost always preferred the one photograph that, unknown to them, was actually the only true image. All the other photographs were reversed images.

Researchers suggest that we are more comfortable with familiar perceptions than we are with accurate perceptions.

An Exercise: Using Stress Management Cards to Reveal Your Bright Shadow

In this exercise you will use the ColourSpectrums stress management cards to reflect on and reveal your bright shadow characteristics.

Reflections of the Blue Shadow

When your blue perceives someone else's blue as being the same intensity, you perceive it as being in the light and it is likely the other person perceives your blue as being in the light too. However, if your blue has the perception someone is using too little blue, then you will perceive that person's pale blue shadow characteristics.

1) Locate the following pale blue shadow characteristics on the pale side of the blue stress management card.

PALE BLUE SHADOW CHARACTERISTICS

| Detached | Unemotional |
| Heartless | Unfeeling |

Section 5: Using ColourSpectrums to Improve Relationships

2) Flip the card over and read the bright blue shadow characteristics on the reverse side to see how the other person perceives your bright blue shadow characteristics.

BRIGHT BLUE SHADOW CHARACTERISTICS

| Ashamed | Moody |
| Codependent | Over accommodating |

Reflections of the green shadow

When your green perceives someone else's green as being the same intensity, you perceive it as being in the light and the other person probably perceives your green as being in the light. If your green perceives someone using too little green then you perceive that person's pale green shadow characteristics.

1) Locate the following pale green shadow characteristics on the pale side of the green stress management card.

PALE GREEN SHADOW CHARACTERISTICS

| Bewildered | Irrational |
| Confused | Mystified |

2) Flip the card over and read the bright green shadow characteristic on the reverse side to see how the other person perceives your bright green shadow characteristics.

BRIGHT GREEN SHADOW CHARACTERISTICS

| Argumentative | Opinionated |
| Arrogant | Overly analytical |

Reflections of the red shadow

When your red perceives someone else's red as being the same intensity, you perceive it as being in the light and it is likely the other person perceives your red as being in the light. If your red perceives someone using too little red then you will perceive the person's pale red shadow characteristics.

1) Locate the following pale red shadow characteristics on the pale side of the red stress management card.

PALE RED SHADOW CHARACTERISTICS
Apathetic   Lifeless
Clumsy   Listless

2) Flip the card over and read the bright red shadow characteristic on the reverse side to see how the other person perceives your bright red shadow characteristics.

BRIGHT RED SHADOW CHARACTERISTICS
Angry   Reckless
Chaotic   Restless

Reflections of the yellow shadow

When your yellow perceives someone else's yellow as being the same intensity, you perceive it as being in the light and other person probably perceives your yellow as being in the light. However, if your yellow perceives someone is using too little yellow then you will perceive the person exhibiting pale yellow shadow characteristics.

1) Locate the following pale yellow shadow characteristics on the pale side of the yellow stress management card.

PALE YELLOW SHADOW CHARACTERISTICS
Disobedient   Out of line
Disorderly   Unconventional

Section 5: Using ColourSpectrums to Improve Relationships

2) Flip the card over and read the bright yellow shadow characteristic on the reverse side to see how the other person perceives your bright yellow shadow characteristics.

BRIGHT YELLOW SHADOW CHARACTERISTICS

Authoritarian	Possessive
Bureaucratic	Punitive

The pale shadow you perceive in others is a reflection of your own bright shadow.

An Exercise: Using Stress Management Cards to Reveal Your Pale Shadows

You can use these cards in a reverse manner to reveal and reflect how others perceive your pale shadow characteristics. If you perceive someone as using too much blue, green, red or yellow, for example, then locate the <u>bright</u> blue, green, red or yellow bright shadow characteristics on the bright side of that stress management card, then turn the card over and read that colour's <u>pale</u> blue, green, red or yellow shadow characteristics on the reverse side. Those will be the pale shadow characteristics the other person likely perceives in you. The darkness you perceive in others sheds light on your own darkness.

The bright shadow you perceive in others is a reflection of your own pale shadow.

When you compare and contrast yourself with others, you cast yourself in a favourable light and cast a shadow on other people. When you insist on standing in the light you project a shadow that falls upon others but what you don't see is <u>your</u> dark side, the shadow you cast upon yourself on the half of you facing away from the light. This is the shadow you cannot see and the shadow that others see when they look back at you.

Awareness of others leads to self-awareness.

The traditional approach to improving relationship effectiveness is based on the belief that enhanced perceptions of the self enhance perceptions of others, the belief that self-awareness fosters awareness of others. I think it's true. However, it is a myth to believe that this is the only way to enhance relationship awareness; it is a myth-perception. ColourSpectrums reveals that the reverse is also true: that being aware of how we perceive others enhances self-awareness.

Finding a State of Balance

Each colour seeks balance along its own continuum. This state of balance is homeostasis — a state of equilibrium or stability. When a colour's needs are satisfied, that colour experiences a state of balance in the light — a state of high esteem and low stress. Both shadows are states of low self-esteem and high stress. When a colour's needs are not met it experiences a state of imbalance in the bright shadow — a state of low self-esteem and bright stress. When a colour is being challenged it experiences a state of imbalance in the pale shadow — a state of low self-esteem and pale stress. High stress and high self-esteem do not coexist at the same point along a colour's continuum. One is experienced at the expense of the other.

In the illustration that follows you will see that the bright shadows at the top of each spectrum are at the opposite ends of the pale shadows at the bottom of each spectrum. The yang and yang of opposites along each continuum creates balance.

Some of your colours may be in balance while some of your other colours are out of balance.

For example, your bright red need to be physically active, "on the go," or "going out" may be satisfied while your bright green need to contemplate, cogitate, ruminate, postulate, analyze and simply mull things over are not being met. Your pale yellow may be challenged to get organized while your pale red is not being challenged to get going. All combinations are possible.

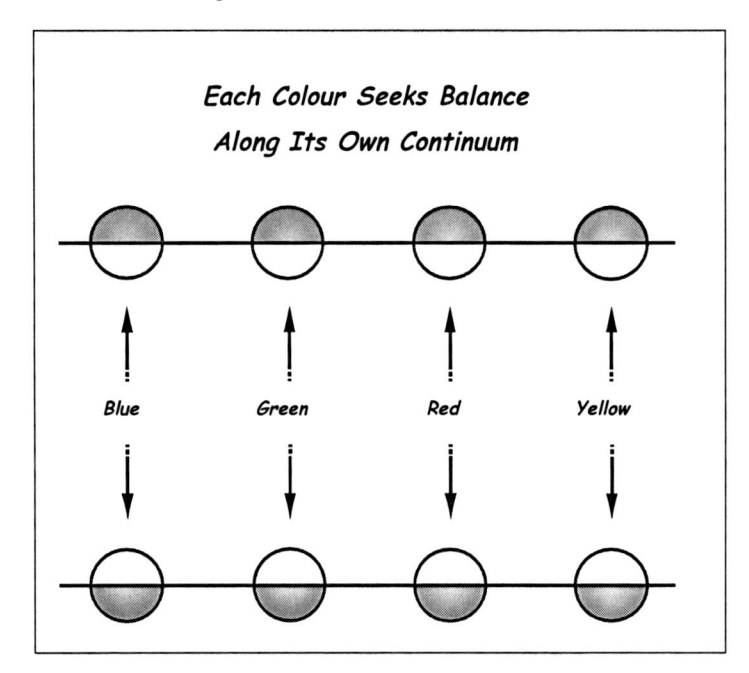

Each Colour Seeks Balance Along Its Own Continuum

Blue   Green   Red   Yellow

Section 5: Using ColourSpectrums to Improve Relationships

The Fight/Flight Shadow Connection

Refer to the illustration below. Imagine that the bright shadows at the top of this illustration extend away from you over a curved horizon and continue down the far side and reappear as pale shadows at the bottom of each spectrum, the way the far dark side of the moon extends from horizon to horizon.

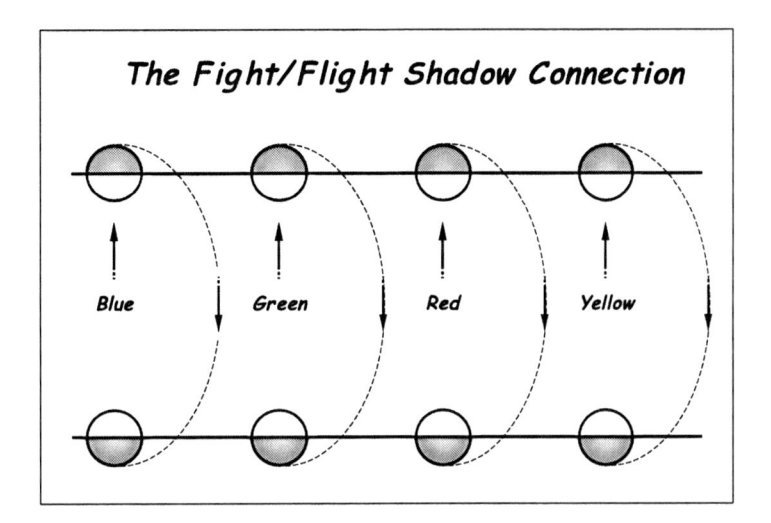

The Fight/Flight Shadow Connection

Blue   Green   Red   Yellow

Now imagine a person brightening his or her blue because they want to deepen a personal relationship with a friend. The other person remains unresponsive, so the person seeking a deeper relationship continues to brighten his or her blue, first by being assertive and then by being aggressive. In desperation he or she displays bright blue emotional shadow behaviours such as pleading for affection as the fight response kicks in. Suddenly out of frustration and out of the blue, he or she emphatically declares how much they hate the person and want nothing do with them. What happened?

When bright blue fight behaviours become too intense, pale blue flight behaviours kick in as a counter measure. This dynamic is known in psychology as a reaction formation, behaving in a way that is exactly the opposite of one's true feelings or intentions. In Aesop's fables this is sour grapes. Notice that all of the behaviours in this example occur along the blue continuum — that one's blue can be in the bright shadow one moment and in the pale shadow the next. It is as if the blue spectrum is struggling desperately to find its own balance.

The green, red and yellow spectrums must also find their own balance. These colours all vary in intensity with energy moving up into the bright shadow and down along the continuum into the pale shadow. Someone brightening his or her green in attempts to explain a complex idea may abruptly take flight and say, "Never mind!" Someone brightening his or her red in an effort to rally the troops and motivate others to action may abruptly throw in the towel and say, "Just drop it!" Someone brightening his or her yellow in a serious effort to complete tasks may suddenly quit with a sigh of resignation or a signed resignation.

The Flight/Fight Shadow Connection

Imagine that the pale shadows at the bottom of this illustration extend away from you under a curved horizon and continue up the far side and reappear as bright shadows at the top of each spectrum; in the same way the far dark side of the moon extends from horizon to horizon.

The Flight/Fight Shadow Connection

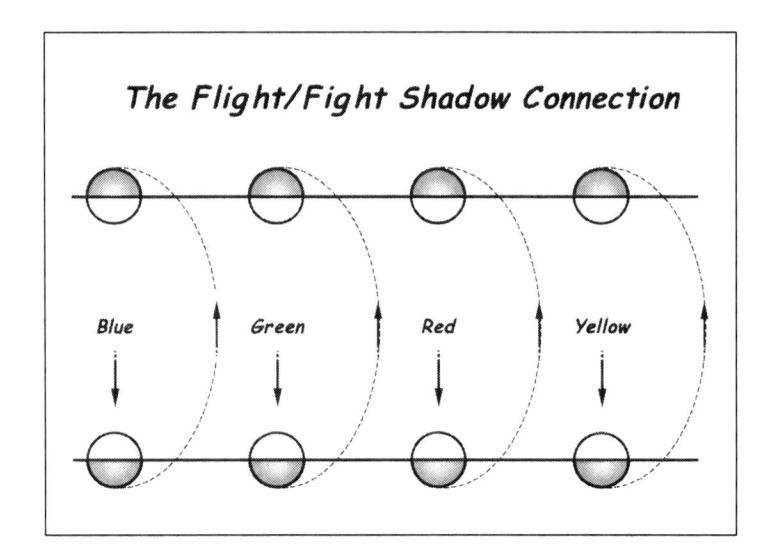

Blue   Green   Red   Yellow

Imagine someone diminishing his or her blue in an attempt to break off a personal relationship. The person diminishes his or her blue and the passive pale blue shadow becomes more obvious as the person's flight response becomes passive aggressive. He or she becomes progressively less friendly and more emotionally detached and aloof. The pale shadow expands and suddenly appears as a bright shadow at the top of the continuum...the fight response kicks in and triggers bright blue shadow behaviour as the person apologizes profusely for being distant and aloof, for hurting the person's feelings and declares his or her overwhelming love and affection.

Similarly, a person displaying pale green shadow characteristics in an attempt to avoid a research paper may suddenly display bright green shadow characteristics by announcing he or she is off to the library to pull an all-nighter researching and studying.

A person diminishing his or her red in an effort to avoid standing up in front of a group may suddenly give in, stand up and make a public speech.

Someone diminishing his or her yellow <u>and</u> red may actively avoid cleaning up their house...and then in a burst of bright yellow and red shadow energy, spend the whole day frenetically cleaning, organizing and arranging the entire contents of the house, running a tight ship so everything is ship shape.

Illuminating Bright and Pale Shadows

The bright and pale shadows are powerful influences because they are hidden from conscious awareness and often remain hidden because they are difficult to accept. Jung believed that acknowledging shadow behaviours sheds light on them and empowers people to make informed choices. Shedding light on pale shadows does not eliminate them but it does illuminate them and that is the first step to enlightenment. Revealing the shadow reveals untapped resources, gifts and talents that are lying dormant in the dark awaiting discovery. Everything you are exists whether you are aware of it or not. Without our attention this wealth of human potential never sees the light of day. Let your light shine!

> Everything you are ... exists.
> — Carl Jung

Acknowledging your bright and pale shadows minimizes their negative influences and maximizes your potential. Revealing your hidden self to your conscious self creates a strong congruent and integrated identity. Carl Jung stated, "Individuation is the process of integrating our unconscious shadows, accepting both the positive and negative aspects of our natures, of becoming whole human beings."

Chart of ColourSpectrums Continuums

Each colour is a spectrum of exclusive characteristics and behaviours that occur along a continuum. The following chart locates all the characteristics and behaviours found along each colour continuum. Each spectrum extends from the bright esteem needs at the top down through the characteristics that are "in the light" and further down to the pale shadow characteristics at the bottom.

This chart summarizes all categories found on the 12 ColourSpectrums cards:

- The four attribute cards included in *ColourSpectrums Book 1: The Introduction*.
- The four stress management cards included in this *ColourSpectrums Book 2: Stress Management and Conflict Resolution*.
- The four brightening cards included in *ColourSpectrums Book 3: Brightening Pale Colours*.

Rob Chubb

ColourSpectrums Continuums

Blue Spectrum	Green Spectrum	Red Spectrum	Yellow Spectrum
Bright Blue Shadow Characteristics	Bright Green Shadow Characteristics	Bright Red Shadow Characteristics	Bright Yellow Shadow Characteristics
Blue Lighten-Up Phrases	Green Lighten-Up Phrases	Red Lighten-Up Phrases	Yellow Lighten-Up Phrases
Bright Blue Esteem Needs	Bright Green Esteem Needs	Bright Red Esteem Needs	Bright Yellow Esteem Needs
Bright Blue Stressors	Bright Green Stressors	Bright Red Stressors	Bright Yellow Stressors
Blue Card Illustrations	Green Card Illustrations	Red Card Illustrations	Yellow Card Illustrations
Blue Card Descriptions	Green Card Descriptions	Red Card Descriptions	Yellow Card Descriptions
Blue Common Phrases	Green Common Phrases	Red Common Phrases	Yellow Common Phrases
Blue Voice Tone & Pace	Green Voice Tone & Pace	Red Voice Tone & Pace	Yellow Voice Tone & Pace
Blue Body Language	Green Body Language	Red Body Language	Yellow Body Language
Blue Facial Expressions	Green Facial Expressions	Red Facial Expressions	Yellow Facial Expressions
Blue Physical Appearance	Green Physical Appearance	Red Physical Appearance	Yellow Physical Appearance
Blue Interaction Style	Green Interaction Style	Red Interaction Style	Yellow Interaction Style
Pale Blue Challenges	Pale Green Challenges	Pale Red Challenges	Pale Yellow Challenges
Pale Blue Stressors	Pale Green Stressors	Pale Red Stressors	Pale Yellow Stressors
Blue Brighten-Up Phrases	Green Brighten-Up Phrases	Red Brighten-Up Phrases	Yellow Brighten-Up Phrases
Pale Blue Shadow Characteristics	Pale Green Shadow Characteristics	Pale Red Shadow Characteristics	Pale Yellow Shadow Characteristics

Four Distinct and Separate Continuums

Acknowledging the obvious can provide insight for understanding the more subtle but essential distinctions between each colour's spectrum. Consider the obvious: emotions are not logical, logic is not emotional, spontaneity is not planned, and plans are not spontaneous. A closer examination of these obvious distinctions reveals the underlying fact that holds true for all functions across the four continuums: that a function performed by one colour is not performed by another. This means that each colour performs exclusive functions along its own continuum. The characteristics and behaviours found in one colour's spectrum are not replicated in another colour's spectrum. There is no duplication of services.

> Your four colours function simultaneously with no duplication of services.

The Blue Spectrum of Functions

Refer to the Chart of ColourSpectrums Continuums. The blue spectrum encompasses the range of functions listed under the heading "Blue Spectrum" — from the bright blue shadow characteristics at the top — ashamed, codependent, defensive,

Section 5: Using ColourSpectrums to Improve Relationships

depressed, emotionally conflicted and so on — down through the characteristics that are "in the light" — kind, affectionate, empathic, intimate and spiritual — to the pale blue shadow characteristics at the bottom — detached, heartless, impersonal, inconsiderate, inhumane and so on.

You have probably noticed that your emotions are not logical. This is because the function of emotions only occurs along the blue continuum and the function of logic only occurs along the green continuum. Although emotions are not logical it is just as important to realize that emotions are not illogical either. Saying that emotions are illogical is like saying your eyes are deaf. The functions of logic occur along the green continuum: "being logical" is a bright green function that occurs at the top end of the green continuum, and "being illogical" is a pale green shadow characteristic that occurs at the bottom end of the green continuum. This principle holds true for all functions. A colour's functions only occur along the continuum of that colour's spectrum.

Blue functions only occur along the continuum of the blue spectrum and not along the green, red and yellow spectrums.

For example, the blue qualities of compassion, heart-felt emotions, love, affection and spirituality

> are not reasonable or unreasonable
> are not rational or irrational
> are not logical or logical
> (because the functions of reason, rationale and logic are in the
> green spectrum).

> are not physically active or lethargic
> are not physically coordinated or uncoordinated
> are not physically skilled or unskilled
> (because the functions of physical activity, physical coordination and physical skills are in the red spectrum)

> are not responsible or irresponsible
> are not organized or disorganized
> are not right or wrong
> (because the functions of responsibility, organization and judgment of right and wrong are in the yellow spectrum).

Review the blue card illustrations and descriptions (included in Book 1) and you will see that all of those attributes are unique to the blue spectrum. They are exclusive blue functions that are not duplicated on the other cards.

I AM PERSONAL: I FACILITATE HARMONIOUS RELATIONSHIPS.
I am friendly and enjoy warm-hearted interactions.
I relate genuinely and attach emotionally.

Rob Chubb

The Green Spectrum of Functions

Refer to the Chart of ColourSpectrums Continuums on page 142. The green spectrum encompasses the range of functions listed under the heading "Green Spectrum." From the bright green shadow characteristics at the top — argumentative, arrogant, condescending, controversial, cynical and so on — down through the characteristics that are "in the light" — curious, analytical, logical, pensive and reasonable — to the pale green shadow characteristics at the bottom — bewildered, confused, ignorant, illogical, imprecise and so on.

Just as your emotions are not logical, your logic is not emotional. This is because the functions of logic occur exclusively along the green continuum and the functions of emotions occur exclusively along the blue continuum. Your green can explain and rationalize emotions, but that does not make emotions logical or make your logic emotional.

Green functions only occur along the continuum of the green spectrum and not along the blue, red and yellow spectrums.

For example the green qualities of logic, intelligence, strategy, curiosity and knowledge

>are not kind or unkind
>are not friendly or unfriendly
>are not humane or inhumane
>(because the functions of kindness, friendliness and humanness are in the blue spectrum)

>are not physically active or lethargic
>are not physically coordinated or uncoordinated
>are not physically skilled or unskilled
>(because the functions of physical activity, physical coordination and physical skills are in the red spectrum)

>are not responsible or irresponsible
>are not organized or disorganized
>are not right or wrong
>(because the functions of responsibility, organization and judgment are in the yellow spectrum).

Look at the green card illustrations and descriptions and you will see that those attributes are unique to the green spectrum. They are exclusive green functions that are not duplicated on the other cards.

> **I AM ANALYTICAL: I CONCEPTUALIZE NEW IDEAS.**
> I have a curious mind and want to know more.
> I am theoretical, intrigued by mysteries and possibilities.

Section 5: Using ColourSpectrums to Improve Relationships

The Red Spectrum of Functions

Refer to the Chart of ColourSpectrums Continuums on page 142. The red spectrum encompasses the range of functions listed under the heading "Red Spectrum." From the bright red shadow characteristics at the top — angry, chaotic, disruptive, distracted, erratic and so on — down through the characteristics that are "in the light" — physically active, hands-on, physically skilled, on the go and full of life — to the pale red shadow characteristics at the bottom — apathetic, clumsy, idle, immobilized, inactive and so on.

Red functions only occur along the continuum of the red spectrum and not along the blue, green, and yellow spectrums.

For example the red behaviours of being physically active, being immediate, living in the moment, being enthusiastic and being competitive

> are not kind or unkind
> are not friendly or unfriendly
> are not humane or inhumane
> (because the functions of kindness, friendliness and humanness are in the blue spectrum)

> are not reasonable or unreasonable
> are not rational or irrational
> are not logical or illogical
> (because the functions of reason, rationale and logic are in the green spectrum)

> are not responsible or irresponsible
> are not organized or disorganized
> are not right or wrong
> (because the functions of responsibility, organization and judgment are in the yellow spectrum).

Look at the red card illustrations and descriptions and you will see that those attributes are unique to the red spectrum. They are exclusive red functions that are not duplicated on the other cards.

I AM PHYSICAL: I TAKE IMMEDIATE ACTION.
I am physically active, living moment to moment.
I act immediately on impulse to maximize opportunities.

The Yellow Spectrum of Functions

Refer to the Chart of ColourSpectrums Continuums on page 142. The yellow continuum encompasses the range of functions listed under the heading "Yellow Spectrum." From the bright yellow shadow characteristics at the top — authoritarian, bureaucratic, controlling, judgmental, materialistic and so on — down through the characteristics that are "in the light" — organized, traditional, responsible, disciplined and steadfast — to the pale yellow shadow characteristics at the bottom — disobedient, disorderly, disorganized, inattentive to details, irresponsible and so on.

Yellow functions only occur along the continuum of the yellow spectrum and not along the blue, green and red spectrums.

For example the yellow behaviours of budgeting, setting limits, staying on task, making commitments and establishing boundaries:

> are not kind or unkind
> are not friendly or unfriendly
> are not humane or inhumane
> (because the functions of kindness, friendliness and humanness are in the blue spectrum)

> are not reasonable or unreasonable
> are not rational or irrational
> are not logical or illogical
> (because the functions of reason, rationale and logic are in the green spectrum)

> are not physically active or lethargic
> are not physically coordinated or uncoordinated
> are not physically skilled or unskilled
> (because the functions of physical activity, physical coordination and physical skills are in the red spectrum).

Look at the yellow card illustrations and descriptions and you will see that those attributes are unique to the yellow spectrum. Those characteristics and functions are not duplicated on the other cards.

> **I AM ORGANIZED: I ESTABLISH AND MAINTAIN ORDER.**
> I am dedicated, reliable and prepared to serve.
> I am trustworthy and diligent in my duties.

Continuums affect each other

While it is true that each spectrum functions along distinct and separate continuums, it is also apparent that the functioning of one colour can have an impact upon the functioning of another. Consider again how your five senses function. A loud noise heard by your ears can make you blink and interfere with your eyesight. The earsplitting shout of a martial arts fighter can momentarily overwhelm and immobilize an opponent's physical responses (that's a good reason to shout!).

Similarly your green thinking can affect your blue emotions. For example, when you have empowering thoughts such as thinking that someone likes you, your blue is likely to experience pleasant empowering emotions. If you have disempowering thoughts such as thinking that someone does not like you, your blue will probably experience unpleasant disempowering blue emotions. Conversely, if your blue feels proud, self-assured and emotionally empowered, empowering thoughts will follow. and you will tend to interpret a person's behaviour as an indication the person likes you. If your blue feels disempowered, lacks confidence and feels insecure, you will have disempowering thoughts and interpret the person's same behaviour as an indication the person does not like you.

Your colours affect each other but they do not perform each other's functions. Disempowering experiences in one spectrum are likely to cause disempowering experiences in another spectrum. On the other hand, empowering experiences in a spectrum promote empowering experiences in the other spectrums.

> You have emotions attached to your thoughts.
> You have emotions attached to your actions.
> You have emotions attached to your responsibilities.
>
> You have thoughts about your emotions.
> You have thoughts about your actions.
> You have thoughts about your responsibilities.
>
> You act on your emotions.
> You act on your thoughts.
> You act on your responsibilities.
>
> You judge and control your emotions.
> You judge and control your thoughts.
> You judge and control your actions.

Does Pavlov's dog ring a bell? The repeated pairing of a ringing bell with the delivery of dog food caused Pavlov's dog to salivate at the sound of the bell in the absence of dog food. Even though the dog's tastebuds could not hear the bell, and even though the dog's ears could not taste dog food, the repeated pairing of both sensory experiences caused one sense to trigger the other. This is operant conditioning.

Similarly, the repeated pairing of our colours causes linkages over time. These linkages can be temporary or long term. Each of our colours has memories that can be triggered in various combinations. We have blue emotional memories, green cognitive memories, red physical body memories and yellow organizational memories (about how we are supposed to behave). Particular emotions can trigger specific thoughts.

Certain organizational experiences can trigger familiar physical reactions and emotional associations. You may experience this as déjà vu when a situation triggers a compelling sense of familiarity accompanied by a sense of "eeriness," "strangeness," or "weirdness" as you experience unconsciously familiar associations between your colours.

The vagus nerve transmits messages between the brain, heart, lungs and digestive tract. We feel full of blue emotions in the centre of our chest and around the heart. When we eat, we also feel full of food in our stomach, a red physical sensation. Because we experience the emotional sensation and the physical sensation in the same area of the body... we can confuse the different messages relayed by the vagus nerve and end up eating to feel emotionally good. Of course, you can eat all the comfort foods you want — and feel physically full — but that will not fulfill your blue emotional needs. Which is why emotional eating can leave you feeling full (a red physical sensation) and feeling empty (a blue emotion) at the same time — feeling physically full and satisfied while feeling emotionally guilty, ashamed, sick to your stomach and emotionally dissatisfied.

Similarly, a hoarder attaches emotionally to belongings (the only difference between a hoarder and a collector is how organized the belongings are).

Some conditioned pairings are empowering and productive and some are not. Some pairings are temporary and some are long term. Consider how your colours interact and how they might interact in increasingly empowering ways. What you have learned, you can relearn. You have been conditioned so you can be... reconditioned.

Section 6: Using ColourSpectrums to Improve Communication

Great Communicators Match Colours

Because each colour functions along distinct and separate continuums, your colours cannot communicate directly with each other. Just as your eyes cannot describe the beautiful, vibrant colours of a rainbow to your ears, and just as your tongue cannot convey the scrumptious mouthwatering fruity taste of a delicious apple to your eyes, your colours cannot perceive each other's experiences either. Your blue cannot express deep-seated emotions in a way that your green logic, red physical body or organizational yellow can understand. Your green logic cannot explain a scientific hypothesis in a way that can be understood by your blue, red or yellow. Your red cannot act in a way that conveys physical exhilaration to your blue, green or yellow. Your yellow cannot outline the serious need for order and organization in a way that your blue, green and red can appreciate.

As human beings we have a need to communicate, and each of our colours needs to express itself and be validated. So how do each of your colours express themselves in a way that they can be perceived? The answer is that your colours express themselves to, and are perceived by, and interact with the corresponding colour in other people.

Your blue seeks emotional interactions and personal validation so it expresses emotions and communicates personally with the blue in other people. Your blue performs spiritual functions. Your blue can pray and experience a personal and spiritual relationship with God, can be with God in spirit. When your blue personal experiences are valued and appreciated by someone else's blue, you experience empathy. Your blue also seeks opportunities to empathize with the blue in others. Your green seeks mental interactions and validation so it articulates and explains ideas to the green in other people and your green listens for other people's ideas. When another person's green comprehends, you experience a stimulating debate or a meeting of the minds. Your red seeks physical experiences and validation so your red responds enthusiastically to other people's red energy and seeks opportunities to be physically active with others who are also being physically active. Your red also interacts physically with the physical world. Your yellow seeks organizational experiences. Your yellow is validated by opportunities to impart stability and structure so it seeks orderly, role-oriented, formal transactions with the yellow in other people.

Communication only occurs colour to colour

The fact that each of your colours has unique functions that are not duplicated by other colours has profound implications for communication; you must use all four colours effectively to effectively communicate with the four colours that all people have. This means that you must be able to perceive, receive and process messages using all four colours. It also means that you must be able to process and send messages using all four colours.

> You must use all four colours effectively to effectively communicate with all four colours that everyone has.

Refer to the following illustration and you will see how our colours communicate.

Your blue only perceives, responds and communicates with another person's blue. This is interpersonal communication.

Your green only perceives, responds and communicates with another person's green. This is cognitive/intellectual communication.

Your red only perceives, responds and communicates with another person's red. This is physical communication.

Your yellow only perceives, responds and communicates with another person's yellow. This is organizational communication.

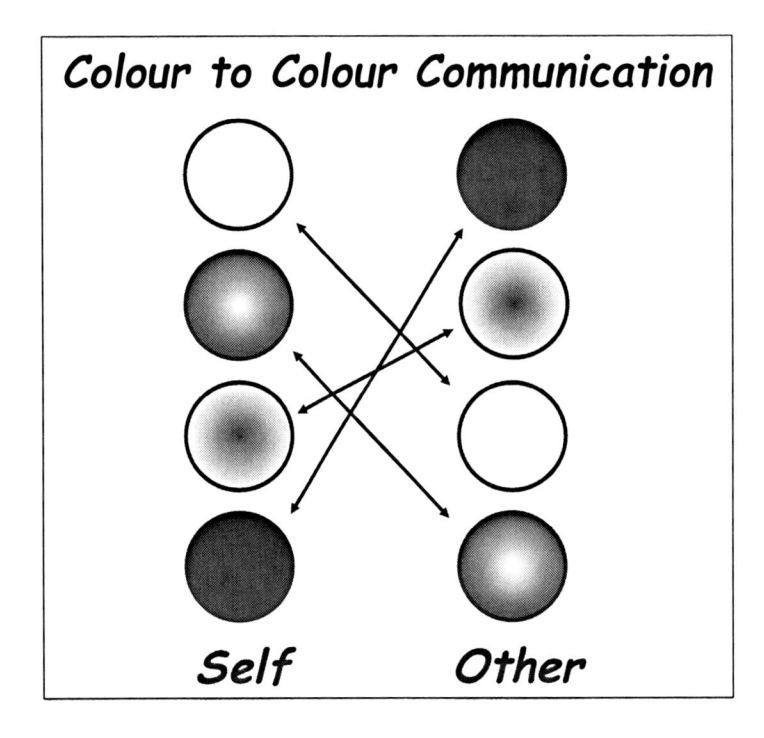

Colour to Colour Communication

Self — Other

Section 6: Using ColourSpectrums to Improve Communication

The extent to which you develop and use your colours to communicate is the extent to which you can communicate effectively with those colours in other people. If you only use one or two colours effectively, you can only communicate with half of the person.

Miscommunication is often missed communication. Communication is a two-way interaction so you must be able to speak and listen effectively using all four colours.

One way or the other we are all in the business of communicating.

Only that which is in me can perceive that which is in you. When I perceive that which is in you it becomes part of me.

As a parent, it is only the blue part of you that communicates with the blue part of your child, your green only communicates with the green part of your child, your red communicates with your child's red and your yellow communicates with the yellow part of your child. Your blue, for example, cannot communicate with the green, red or yellow part of your child and so on. If you are only effectively using your two brightest colours to communicate, you are only communicating with half of your child or half of your children.

The same communication principle is true regardless of your roles in life. As an educator, if you are only effectively using your two brightest colours to educate, you are only educating half of the student or half of the student population. As a leader, manager or supervisor you must use all your colours to communicate with all of the employee and all of your employees. As an employee, if you are only using your two brightest colours to communicate you are only communicating with half of your fellow employee, half of your fellow employees or half of your employer.

Listen with the colour of the speaker. Speak with the colour of the listener.

If you only use one or two colours effectively, you will have the impression that you are communicating effectively with a person who has the same colour spectrum as you and even then, your paler colours will not be communicating as effectively as your brighter colours. It is only when you use all four colours effectively that you will be a highly effective communicator in all areas of your life, as a friend, partner, parent, caregiver, educator, leader, manager, supervisor, employee, and so on.

How audience members' brightest colours influence perceptions of brightest colour presentations

When ColourSpectrums workshop participants work in brightest colour groups to make presentations on the priorities, delights and talents of using their brightest colour, they use their brightest colours and diminish their paler colours as much as possible.

Let's join a ColourSpectrums workshop in progress to see what this communication looks and sounds like in action. Following each of the brightest colour presentations, the audience is invited to ask questions of the presenters to better understand the priorities, delights and talents of the presenting group's brightest colour. At this point in the ColourSpectrums workshop, audience members are seated in brightest colour groups so when they ask questions it is easy to see what their brightest colour is and how it influences their perceptions of the presenting group.

Audience members with blue as a brightest colour ask green, red and yellow presentation groups, "Aren't you worried about hurting people's feelings?" or "Don't you care if people like you or not?" Because green, red and yellow presentations do not include blue priorities, delights and talents, audience members with blue as a brightest colour, who naturally listen for blue compassion, are troubled when they don't hear it. These audience members are actually trying to use their blue to perceive, process and communicate with presenters who are not using blue. It's like using a radio to tune into a television station and complaining about a poor signal. These audience members perceive pale blue shadow characteristics. The only way for these audience members to perceive a presenting group's green, red or yellow priorities, delights and talents is to diminish their bright blue and brighten the colour that corresponds to the presenting group's brightest colour.

Audience members with green as a brightest colour ask blue, red and yellow presentation groups, "When do you get time to think things through?" or "Why don't you think more?" Because blue, red and yellow presentations do not include green priorities, delights and talents, audience members who have green as a brightest colour, who naturally listen for green information, are puzzled when they don't hear it. These audience members are actually trying to use their green to perceive, process and communicate with presenters who are not using green. These audience members perceive pale green shadow characteristics. The only way for these audience members to perceive a presenting group's blue, red or yellow priorities, delights and talents is to diminish their bright green and brighten the colour that corresponds to the presenting group's brightest colour.

Audience members with red as a brightest colour are quick to ask blue, green and yellow presentation groups, "When do you have any fun?" or "How do you handle surprises?" Because blue, green and yellow presentations do not include red priorities, delights and talents, audience members who have red as a brightest colour, who naturally listen for red information, are surprised when they don't hear it. These audience members are trying to use their red to perceive, process and communicate with presenters who are not using red. These audience members perceive pale red shadow characteristics. The only way these audience members can perceive a presenting group's blue, green or yellow priorities, delights and talents is to diminish their bright red and brighten the colour that corresponds to the presenting group's brightest colour.

And lastly, audience members with yellow as a brightest colour ask blue, green and red presentation groups, "When do you get your work completed?" or "How can you work without getting organized first?" Because blue, green and red presentations do not include yellow priorities, delights and talents, audience members who have yellow as a brightest colour, who naturally listen for organized yellow information, get concerned when they don't hear it. These audience members are trying to use their yellow to perceive, process and communicate with presenters who are not using yellow. These audience members must diminish their bright yellow and brighten the colour that corresponds to the presenting group to perceive their blue, green or red priorities.

The questions that audience members ask reveal how their brightest colours expect other people to use it to communicate. Our brightest colours have high expectations. Being highly tuned into our brightest colours can interfere with other colour communication. If the reception and volume of your brightest colour is turned up too high, you may not be able to hear and respond to the other colour messages that people are sending.

How audience members' middle colours influence perceptions of brightest colour presentations

The question period that follows each brightest colour presentation also reveals the influence of middle colours on perceptions of brightest colour presentations. Audience members who have middle colours that are the same as the presenting group's brightest colour can identify with the presenting group's priorities, delights and talents because those qualities are just under the surface for them. These audience members experience the brightest colour presentations as somewhat more intense than they are comfortable with, however, they usually rise to the occasion and are able to identify with many of those priorities, delights and talents.

How audience members' palest colours influence perceptions of brightest colour presentations

The question period that follows each brightest colour presentation reveals the influence of palest colours on perceptions. Our inability to experience our pale colours as highly esteeming can make it difficult for us to identify closely with people who do experience it as highly esteeming. We are particularly perplexed by people's motivations.

Audience members who have blue as a palest colour frequently ask the presenters who have blue as a brightest colour, "What is it like to be so sensitive?" or "Don't you get tired of being so friendly and accommodating?" Because blue is challenging for them they find it difficult to empathize, and may be suspicious of the motives of presenters who experience blue as highly esteeming.

Audience members who have green as a palest colour frequently ask the presenters who have green as a brightest colour, "Why do you have to think so much?" or "Why do you need to know why?" Because green is their greatest challenge they are naturally puzzled by and suspicious of people who have green as a brightest colour.

Audience members who have red as a palest colour frequently ask the presenters who have red as a brightest colour, "How do you keep your energy up?" or "Why do you do everything so fast?" These audience members can be overwhelmed and even shocked by this group's high energy, zeal and enthusiasm for using a colour that is their greatest challenge. These audience members wonder what they are up to and what they will do next.

Audience members who have yellow as a palest colour frequently ask the presenters who have yellow as a brightest colour, "How do you stay so organized?" or "How come you are so serious?" Because yellow is their palest colour, these audience members perceive the bright yellow presentation as too formal. They listen and watch with utter disbelief as the presenters describe their greatest delights as organizing and completing detailed tasks on time.

Audience members' questions and brightest colour groups' responses reveal a natural inclination for us, as human beings, to be suspicious of people who behave and communicate differently than us. We are especially suspicious of people who have different motivations than we do, and each of our colours really does have different motivations.

Your ability to experience your bright colours as highly esteeming can make it difficult for you to appreciate that other people experience that same colour as challenging and stressful. It can appear to you as if they just don't get it. Brightest colour groups are sometimes taken aback when audience members don't readily understand or appreciate the intensity of their presentation. Because your brighter colours are so naturally esteeming and easy to use you may unconsciously and mistakenly assume that other people have the same capacity. You may be intuitively suspicious and unconsciously wary of people who use those colours less intensely.

No matter how bright your brightest colour is, there are still many people who use it more intensely than you. To appreciate how people experience your brightest colour when it is their palest colour, find someone who uses your brightest colour even more intensely than you do. Hang out with them for a while and notice how overwhelming it can be.

To get a sense of how people experience your palest colour when it is their brightest, find someone who uses your palest colour even less intensely than you do, spend some time together and notice how your palest colour reacts.

Brightest Colour Groups Communicate Colour to Colour

The presenting groups use their brightest colours to communicate. The only way that audience members can appreciate the priorities, delights and talents of a presenting group's brightest colour is to use that same colour to perceive the presentation.

The presenters with blue as a brightest colour use their blue to communicate with the blue in the audience members and audience members must use their blue to perceive those blue messages. The same is true of the other presenters. The presenters with green, red and yellow use their brightest colours to communicate with that corresponding colour in the audience members and the audience members must use matching colours to perceive the intended brightest colour messages.

You can improve your communication skills by visualizing this principle of perception in your interactions. Feel your blue empathizing, listening, observing and communicating with the other person's blue. Think of your green visualizing, listening, observing and communicating with the other person's green and make a point of using your green to understand and comprehend the other person's green. Picture yourself using your red to react and interact with the other person's red and using your yellow to give your undivided attention to listen to, observe and communicate with the other person's yellow. Visualize yourself communicating colour to colour. It will keep your communication clear and focused in person, on the phone, by letter, by email and so on.

There are a number of common phrases that emphasize the importance of matching colours to communicate effectively:

"Having a tête-à-tête"
"I know where you are coming from."
"Let's have a head to head debate"
"Let's have a heart to heart talk."
"Let's meet face to face."
"Let's put our heads together."
"Two hearts beating as one."
"We are in step."
"We are like minded."
"We are on the same wave length."
"We are soul mates."
"We have a meeting of minds."
"We see eye to eye."

Humour: a matter of perception

Great communication occurs when the message sent equals the message received. Take humour for example. Imagine watching a couple of clowns walk past and one suddenly sticks her foot out and trips the other who falls flat on his face. This pratfall is red physical comedy. It is intended to be funny and entertaining to your red. Consider how something as simple as a pratfall might be perceived by your four colours. Keep in mind that all four colours perceive the event simultaneously with various intensities.

To your blue, the pratfall is a mean and nasty trick played at someone's expense. Your blue would enjoy shared humour in which everyone is laughing together in harmony but certainly not at the expense of someone's hurt feelings. Blue humour is laughing with, not laughing at someone. Blue humour is relationship humour that is shared in a spirit of friendship, companionship, kinship and relationship. Blue laughter creates a sense of group cohesion and unity and is used in conflict to heal strained relationships. For your blue, laughter is the shortest distance between two people. When there is conflict humour alleviates emotional and relationship tension. Blue humour is gentle and uplifting humour that acknowledges, embraces and celebrates the joys and softens the impact of the relationship blunders that come with being fully human.

Your green values cognitive intelligence. If your green thinks about the pratfall, it is stupid. If your green really thinks about it, it is really stupid. Your green makes sense of things and can't make sense of this nonsense. What is the meaning of this? Your green perceives the clowns as foolish, and there is no sense in fooling around. Your green prefers to muse and this is not amusing. Green humour is intellectual humour. Your green enjoys intellectual wit, puns, satire, parody, double entendres and double meanings. Our green has a way with words so likes to play with words and play on words "jest" for fun but it does not appreciate "prac-tickle" jokes. Green likes to play with meanings so playing with words and wordplay are one and the same thing and "fun-da-mental" to green humour. This musing is amusing. But a pratfall?! We are not amused. Entertaining these thoughts is entertaining. An oxymoron, for example, delights the mind as a figure of speech or expressed idea in which apparently contradictory terms appear in conjunction. Our green delights in mental exercises of riddles and quizzes that keeps one mentally sharp as a tack and on the ball. For your green, laughter and learning go hand in hand. Green humour includes the mental gymnastics of paradoxes, irony, intellectual banter, razor-sharp clever wit and wise cracks. Green humour is often used to make a point and so it can be blunt and to the point. This intellectual dry, wry wit can be deadpan and droll, without external expression. As it moves into the bright green shadow it becomes increasingly satirical, tongue in cheek, facetious, snide, sarcastic and caustic.

Rob's Reflection

When I had finished photographing Rodin's sculpture "The Thinker" for use on the green ColourSpectrums card, I realized I was the proud owner of the impressive 2-foot high replica. I subsequently gave the sculpture to my oldest daughter Brittany, who has green as her brightest colour, reasoning that she would be interested in it. About two weeks later I walked into our bathroom at home and there was Rodin's sculpture of the thinker sitting on the toilet tank. Later that day as my family sat around the supper table, I commented, "I see that 'The Thinker' is sitting on the toilet tank" and as I looked over at Brittany she returned my glance with a slight smile and suppressed chuckle of amusement. Talk about an inside joke. With green humour you have to figure it out for yourself. You either get it or you don't. Our green delights in learning so when we have a sudden insight we experience the internal joy of ah-ha learning on the inside and the subtle sound of ha-ha laughter on the outside.

To your red, the clown's pratfall is funny physical comedy. Your red enjoys funny-bone funny slapstick antics, stand up comedy, practical jokes, jesting, clowning around, playing around, and tomfoolery just for a lark, just for fun, just for laughs, just for a hoot and a holler. People with bright red are full of surprises and full of mischief. They get a real charge out of it. For people with bright red, physical comedy is funny till someone gets hurt...then it's hilarious. Red humour delights in the element of fun and element of surprise. It can be surprisingly shocking, outrageous and risqué. Red levity defies the gravity of a situation and red cajoling helps us laugh it up and laugh it off. Humour makes light of serious situations. Red humour is comic relief that keeps things light, upbeat and entertaining. Red humour is the side-splitting, knee-slapping, back-slapping physical gotcha humour of the stunt, the hoax, the prank, the trick and pie in your face gag delivered by the practical joker, jester, comic or chuckles the clown.

Yellow is about control. Humour is about letting go of control and taking things lightly. Your yellow is serious and does not take anything lightly. Your yellow does not have a sense of humour. To your yellow the clowns are childish, immature, unsafe and irresponsible. This is no laughing matter. Stop being silly, get serious... and get back to work. No clowning around on my watch. They have crossed the line. Just to be on the safe side, there should be a law that safeguards against this sort of behaviour... or a local bylaw or safety code. That clown must be held responsible for her actions or held irresponsible for her undisciplined behaviour. This clowning around is out of line and out of control and must be stopped. Arrest that clown! Read her rights. Take her to the clown prosecutor.

Just as great communication occurs when the message sent equals message received, a great comical moment occurs when the intended humour is perceived as it is intended. As it turns out, your red is the only colour that can laugh at a pratfall. How much you end up laughing depends on two things: how bright your red is when that pratfall occurs and how bright it is in comparison with your other colours. The brighter your red is the greater your capacity for a great big hilarious belly laugh. Because you experience all four colours simultaneously, the brighter your other colours are the more they will modify your overall humour experience. The paler they are the less they will modify your overall experience. To perceive the humour that the clowns intended, to experience the opportunity for uproarious laughter that the pratfall offers, you have to let go of your other colours and just go for the comical relief and hilarious, side-splitting entertainment of the moment.

300 Social Workers Can't Be Wrong

Our ColourSpectrums influence our perceptions of people

> *The ColourSpectrums workshop was coming to an end and the 300 social workers who had been participating sat at tables in brightest colour groups of 10 people throughout the auditorium. Each table had either blue, green, red or yellow balloons to identify each group's brightest colour. The director of child welfare came up to the front of the room to formally thank me for presenting the workshop. In closing, he turned to the audience and challenged the participants to guess my brightest colour. "Raise your hand if you think Rob's brightest colour is blue." Most of the participants who raised their hands were in the bright blue groups. "Raise your hand if you think his brightest colour is green" and most of the participants who raised their hands were sitting at the green tables. "How about red?" and most of the participants who had red as a brightest colour stood up and cheered enthusiastically. "And how many of you think Rob's brightest colour is yellow?" at which point almost all the participants with yellow as a brightest colour raised their hands with arms straight up.*

What happened? How could so many people perceive me in so many different ways? Upon reflection, it became clear to me that perception is everything. During the workshop I had intentionally used all four colours with equal intensity. I used my blue to ensure the participants focused on positive self-esteem and interpersonal communication. I used my green to be cognizant and concise regarding the underlying philosophical concepts. I had used my red to have fun and keep the workshop upbeat, funny, fast-paced and physically active. I used my yellow to give step-by-step instructions and to stay on task and on time. I had been sending out the same messages to everyone simultaneously; they all heard me say the same things and they all saw me do the same things... or had they?

Our brightest colours are more perceptive than our paler colours. As a result our brightest colours are more highly tuned and more receptive to those colour messages. Our brightest colours simply perceive and process more information than our other colours.

Conversely our paler colours are less perceptive than our brighter colours. As a result our palest colours are not as highly tuned and are less receptive to those colour messages. The result is that we do not perceive or process as much paler colour information. These missed perceptions lead to misperceptions.

When you perceive someone's blue, green, red or yellow, it is because you are using that colour with enough intensity to perceive it in that person. When you do not notice someone using blue, green, red or yellow it is because you are not using that colour intensely enough to perceive it.

Ultimately, the participants' perceptions of my spectrum was a reflection of their own ColourSpectrums; each person perceived more of their brighter colours in me because they could, and did not perceive as much of their own paler colours in me because they couldn't. Diminished colours have diminished perceptions.

What do you suppose would have happened if those same social workers had been sitting in palest colour groups and been asked to identify my palest colour? I am convinced that participants with blue as a palest colour would have perceived blue as my palest colour, that participants with green as a palest colour would have perceived green as my palest colour and so on. In other words, your failure to use your palest colour effectively, diminishes your ability to perceive that colour in others. Your pale colours are hard of hearing. They are hard of hearing blue emotions, green thoughts, red actions and yellow organizational messages. Those messages can fall on deaf ears. Your palest colour can be tone deaf, unable to hear the subtle voice tones and nuances that differentiate each colour. Your pale colours can make you colourblind. Your pale colours are your blind spots and you do not easily see these visual messages.

> We don't see people as they are. We see them as we are.

Each of your colours perceives different information with each of your colours only perceiving the corresponding colour in another person. You must use all of your colours to accurately perceive a person's full colour spectrum. You must use your full spectrum to perceive the whole person.

Our ColourSpectrums influence our perceptions of experiences

Taken to the next logical step, it is apparent that we perceive life experiences according to our capacity to perceive. Our brighter colours have a great capacity to perceive and process information that corresponds to that colour. Our paler colours have a diminished capacity to perceive and process that colour's information.

> " Tell me to what you pay attention and I will tell you who you are. "
>
> — José Ortega y Gasset

ColourSpectrums is presented to groups by certified facilitators who are specially trained to use all four colours effectively in the workshops. The workshop format is also specifically designed so participants experience all four colours in the process.

At the end of ColourSpectrums sessions participants complete a written feedback form. On the form participants have the option of indicating their brightest and palest colours. The range of feedback from participants attending the same workshop reveals how people experience the same event in diverse ways. Participants' brightest and palest colours are reflected in their written feedback.

Here are examples of actual comments by ColourSpectrums workshop participants.

Participants with blue as a brightest colour:

> "I really got to know myself and other people better."
> "I liked the facilitator. He was personable and approachable."
> "I loved the interaction."
> "I believe this will help us get along better."

Participants with blue as a palest colour:

> "The facilitator was encouraging but not too intrusive, thanks."
> "I would have preferred a little less group work."
> "This takes the confusion out of personal interactions."
> "I usually don't like group work but this was pretty good."

Participants with green as a brightest colour:

> "Very interesting."
> "Intriguing concepts. Made a lot of sense."
> "The facilitator knew what he was talking about."
> "Really gives one something to think about."

Participants with green as a palest colour:

> "Now I understand why I don't understand things."
> "Thanks for making it understandable."
> "Easy to understand."
> "Even I understood the ideas!"

Participants with red as a brightest colour:

> "Fun!"
> "Great time!"
> "The presentations were fun to do."
> "Great! I can't wait to start using this."

Participants with red as a palest colour:
> "A bit too noisy at times."
> "I didn't know what to do with the props."
> "I felt a bit rushed at the end."
> "Presenting was sort of fun, once I got warmed up."

Participants with yellow as a brightest colour:
> "The facilitator was well prepared."
> "Well organized. Started and stopped on time."
> "Very professional. Clear step by step instructions."
> "I appreciated the certificate of completion but mine wasn't signed."

Participants with yellow as a palest colour:
> "Thanks for helping me with the scoring procedure."
> "I liked the informal atmosphere."
> "Easy to follow directions."
> "I liked the flexible format."

When ColourSpectrums facilitators receive balanced feedback across all four colours it indicates they have used their four colours effectively. It also indicates that participants' four brightest colours have been positively validated at the bright end of the four colour continuums and that their four palest colours have been appropriately challenged at the pale end of the four continuums. When facilitators use all four colours to present a workshop the feedback reflects this balance. ColourSpectrums has something for everyone.

If you are in the business of creating growth experiences for others, it is worth paying attention to how people perceive your efforts, as a parent, an educator, a leader, a manager, a supervisor, an employer, an employee and so on. The implication is that when you use all four colours effectively you are better able to meet the needs of all of your children, all of your students, all of your employees, all of your colleagues, all of your customers and those who follow your leadership.

A matter of Perception

> *A friend and colleague of mine — I'll call him Chris, because that is his name — had been interested in attending a ColourSpectrums workshop for some time. I was setting up a classroom for a ColourSpectrums workshop at the college where he was an instructor. About half an hour before the workshop, he chanced to walk past and decided to attend on a moment's notice. You would be correct if you guessed red was his brightest colour and yellow was his palest colour. During the introductions, Chris mentioned that he just happened to be walking by and decided to attend on the spur-of-the-moment. One of the other participants with bright blue offered her perspective by commenting, "It was meant to be." Chris was quick to respond with his bright red perspective, "I'm just lucky!"*

Great Communicators Match Colours and Intensities

The first step in being a great communicator is to use the same colour or colours that the other person is using. Of course the reality is that everyone is using all colours with varying intensities. So the second step to being a great communicator is to use your colours with the same <u>intensities</u> as other people. In the same way that you use your ears to tune in and listen closely to what someone says and use your eyes to focus and see what someone is showing you, you must use each colour in a focused way to perceive the corresponding colours and messages people use to communicate.

> You are a great communicator when you match colours and intensities. It is that simple. It is that challenging.

Each of your colours has a natural ability to tune into the corresponding colour of the other person and sense the relative difference in intensity. Consciously attending to these sensitivities will enhance your communication skills.

For example:

Your blue can sense whether someone is being more or less friendly than you are.

Your green detects whether someone is thinking more or less clearly than you are.

Your red is quick to notice whether someone is more or less active than you are.

Your yellow takes note of whether someone is more or less organized than you are.

When you use a colour more intensely than another person, that person may perceive that colour as being too bright and perceive that colour's bright shadow in you. When you use a colour with less intensity than another person, that person may experience that colour as too pale and perceive that colour's pale shadow in you.

A person experiencing intense blue affection may give a well-intended warm embrace. If the person being embraced is experiencing the same blue intensity then the affection is well received. However, you can imagine a person's response to a hug if their blue is not as intense. The hug would be experienced as a pale blue stressor, too blue! If the other person is looking forward to a warm embrace and does not get one, then that person will perceive the pale blue lack of affection as not being friendly enough, a bright blue stressor.

These illustrations show how you must sometimes brighten a colour to match another person's intensity and how you must sometimes diminish a colour to match a person's intensity.

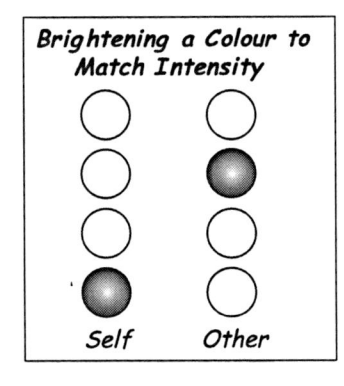

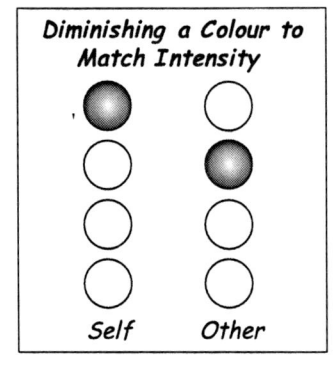

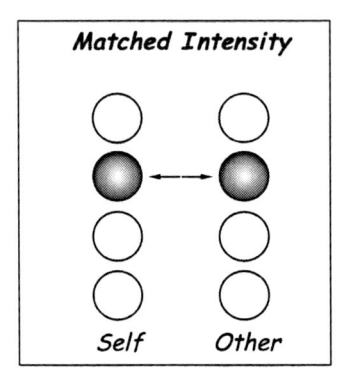

| Brightening a Colour to Match Intensity | Diminishing a Colour to Match Intensity | Matched Intensity |

When you use different colours with different intensities than another person, you are reacting. When you brighten or diminish colours to match the other person, you are responding. When you match colours and intensities, you both experience rapport.

An Exercise in Matching People's Intensities

Some of your colours may be a natural match with the other person, and some of your colours may not. The following exercise will heighten your awareness of differences in intensities.

> I have learned silence from the talkative, toleration from the intolerant, and kindness from the unkind; yet, strange, I am ungrateful to those teachers.
>
> — Kahlil Gibran

Matching Blue

Imagine a friend greeting you with the blue statements below.

Place a check mark beside the statement that best matches your blue's natural intensity.

Blue   **Intensity**

_____ "Hi! I missed you soooo much!"   10 Bright blue
             (accompanied by a warm embrace)

_____ "Hi! It's good to see you."   5   Mid-range blue

_____ "Hi."   0   Pale blue

You would have to brighten or diminish your blue to match the two intensities you did not check off.

Section 6: Using ColourSpectrums to Improve Communication

Matching Green

Imagine someone saying these green statements to you.

Place a check mark beside the statement that best matches your green's natural intensity.

Green   **Intensity**

_____ "Review this demographic analysis and write a 10-page assessment of your findings."   10   Bright green

_____ "Read this report and write your comments on it."   5   Mid-range green

_____ "So, what do you think?"   0   Pale green

You would have to brighten or diminish your green to match the two intensities you did not check off.

Matching Red

Imagine someone saying these red statements to you.

Place a check mark beside the statement that best matches your red's natural intensity.

Red   **Intensity**

_____ "Hey! Let's go for it big time!"   10   Bright red

_____ "Let's do it now."   5   Mid-range red

_____ "Let's do it later."   0   Pale red

You would have to brighten or diminish your red to match the two intensities you did not check off.

Matching Yellow

Imagine someone saying these yellow statements to you.

Place a check mark beside the statement that best matches your yellow's natural intensity.

Yellow   **Intensity**

_____ "Our responsibility is to coordinate the team so let's prepare a detailed agenda and schedule a meeting in room 305 at 3:00 pm sharp — on the dot."   10   Bright yellow

_____ "Let's get organized at 3:00."   5   Mid-range yellow

_____ "Maybe we should organize something around 3-ish."   0   Pale yellow

You would have to brighten or diminish your yellow to match the two intensities you did not check off.

Our colours are constantly changing in intensity, sometimes slowly and sometimes quickly. It is important then to exercise caution when you know what someone's ColourSpectrums personality is because you must pay attention to the colours and intensities the person is using in the moment. When you use a different colour or intensity than another person, your communication is not a match. Recall an interaction you have had in which you experienced great communication. The chances are you and the other person were using all four colours with matched intensities; your colour spectrums communication matched during the interaction. When you interact with a person and match all four colours and intensities simultaneously you resonate with each other and experience great communication and exceptional rapport. If you only use your natural colour spectrum to communicate, you can only communicate effectively with people who have the same colour spectrum as you. Remember how many ColourSpectrums there are? When you brighten and diminish your colours to match others you can create a ColourSpectrums communication match with almost anyone.

Good communication gives good results. Great communication gives great results. When you match colours and intensities, you are a great communicator, as a partner, as a parent, as a spouse, as a family member, as an educator, as a leader, as a manager, as a supervisor, as an employer and as an employee.

Effective People Match Intensities

An Exercise in Matching Situational Intensities

Brightening and diminishing your colours will help you communicate effectively with diverse people. Brightening and diminishing your colours will also help you respond effectively to diverse situations. You can be effective in some situations by using colours passively and you can be effective in other situations by using colours assertively. If you use colours with unmatched intensities you can be highly ineffective. On the positive side, when you use colours with matched intensities, you can be highly effective.

Matching Blue

Imagine using your blue to respond effectively to the following situations.

Place a check mark beside the behaviour that best matches your blue's natural intensity.

Blue		**Intensity**
_____	Write a heart-felt letter of deep sympathy and genuine compassion.	10 Bright blue
_____	Write a thank you card.	5 Mid-range blue
_____	Say thanks.	0 Pale blue

You would have to brighten or diminish your blue to be effective in the two situations you did not check off.

Section 6: Using ColourSpectrums to Improve Communication

Matching Green

Imagine using your green to respond effectively to the following situations.

Place a check mark beside the behaviour that best matches your green's natural intensity.

Green   **Intensity**

_____ Explain how to write a research   10 Bright green
proposal for a corporation.

_____ Explain how to play chess.   5 Mid-range green

_____ Explain how to play checkers.   0 Pale green

You would have to brighten or diminish your green to be effective in the two situations you did not check off.

Matching Red

Imagine using your red to respond effectively to the following situations.

Place a check mark beside the behaviour that best matches your red's natural intensity.

Red   **Intensity**

_____ Play football.   10 Bright red

_____ Play Frisbee.   5 Mid-range red

_____ Play tiddleywinks.   0 Pale red

You would have to brighten or diminish your red to be effective in the two situations you did not check off.

Matching Yellow

Imagine using your yellow to respond effectively to the following situations.

Place a check mark beside the behaviour that best matches your yellow's natural intensity.

Yellow   **Intensity**

_____ Organize a wedding banquet.   10 Bright yellow

_____ Organize supper.   5 Mid-range yellow

_____ Organize a snack.   0 Pale yellow

You would have to brighten or diminish your yellow to be effective in the two situations you did not check off.

Shifting to Match Intensity

Be understanding then be understood.

We all have a deep basic human craving to be understood. Being understood is naturally validating and reassuring. Listen to anyone and just beneath the surface of the content is the rarely stated, but implicit message, "Please understand me!" Please listen to my blue, green, red and yellow experiences.

Unfortunately our enthusiasm to be heard exceeds our enthusiasm to listen. We would rather bend an ear than lend an ear. We know great listeners are hard to come by so we may offer the rare gift of listening: "Call me if you need someone to talk to."

We know great talkers are easy to come by so no one says, "Call me if you need someone to listen to."

Given our need to be understood, who will understand?

The key to great communication and effective conflict resolution is to momentarily suspend your need to be understood so you can understand. You can initiate great communication by first matching the other person's colours and intensities. When you demonstrate your willingness and ability to understand, you set the stage for being understood. Temporarily suspending your need to be understood is a small price to pay for mutual understanding, a small investment in time with huge dividends in relationship.

> " Every man supposes himself not to be fully understood or appreciated. "
>
> — Ralph Waldo Emerson

The phenomenon of motherese

Our inclination to match colours and intensities occurs naturally and unconsciously in some situations. The term "motherese," for example, is used to describe the high-pitched voice tone and pace used by parents to talk to their babies and young children. The adult may hold the baby's face inches from their own, they may soften their voice, use simple words or none at all. The adult may coo, hum, sing a song or use a sing-songy voice. If the child is a few years old, the adult may kneel down so the two are face-to-face at equal eye level and use age-appropriate words and short simple sentences to facilitate mutual understanding. The adult begins to look and sound like the child. This "baby talk" is rapport at its finest. This is empathy at its best. Interestingly enough, research indicates that this method of communicating with a child actually helps them learn words faster and communicate more effectively than if normal adult voice tone and words are used.

We continuously change our behaviours intuitively to match others all the time. We change our words, voice tone and pace, body language and topics of conversation to match people we are interacting with.

As two people brighten their blue to match each other they sound more and more alike. As they establish blue empathy and rapport they share each other's emotional voice tones and may even adapt each other's accents. Two people being intimate with each other, two people having a personal conversation or two people having a friendly chat match behaviours and look alike.

As two people brighten their green intellect to match each other they look and sound increasingly similar. Two people involved in an intellectual conversation, two people having a debate, two people studying together or two people playing chess have many similar behaviours.

As people brighten their red to match each other their physical behaviours become increasingly similar. Two people walking together, two people golfing together or two people setting up tables and chairs for a meeting, act similar.

As people brighten their yellow to match each other they behave in increasingly similar ways. Two colleagues sitting at a staff meeting display similar organizational behaviour. Two students organizing their desks and two soldiers in uniform marching in lockstep have the same organizational behavior.

The next time someone at home answers the telephone, try to guess who the person is talking to simply by listening to the person's telephone voice, how the person changes voice tone and pace to match the person they are talking to.

What does all this mean? Research and life experiences demonstrate that these adaptations dramatically improve communication. If using these adaptations unconsciously and intuitively improves communication, imagine how using them consciously, deliberately and skillfully can improve your communication.

The question of manipulation

You might be reluctant to intentionally adapt your communication to match someone else's because the idea of adapting doesn't seem real or genuine. The truth is that just because your natural communication is familiar and comfortable, doesn't mean it is the most effective way to communicate. It depends on your priorities. Sometimes it is more important to be ourselves. At other times it is more important to adapt to be an effective communicator. You may also be reluctant to intentionally use the same colour and intensity as someone else because it seems manipulative.

Consider, however, that it is not the matching of colours and intensities that is manipulative, rather it is the intention that makes the difference. If your intention is to improve communication and mutual understanding, then matching is a good thing. As it is now, you unconsciously match your communication to some extent but are usually unaware of it. If you are concerned about manipulating others, it will help you to know that the more conscious you are of your communication, the less likely you are to unconsciously manipulate others.

If you were travelling to a country where people spoke a different language, you would probably spend some time learning the language that is foreign to you so you could communicate ... not manipulate. When in Rome, it helps to speak Italian. It would be unreasonable to travel the world and expect everyone to speak your language. It is just as unreasonable to expect everyone in your family, workplace or community to use your colour language. You are fluent in the language of your brighter colours. To communicate effectively with everyone you need to communicate using all four colours effectively. You could think of your paler colours as your second, third or even fourth languages — perhaps less natural, but certainly well worth learning to speak and understand fluently.

Matching Colours

To listen effectively you must shift from your colours' natural intensities and brighten or diminish them to match the other person. You will have to brighten and diminish your blue emotions, green thoughts, red physical activity and yellow organizational skills. As you learn to brighten and diminish your colours you will become a great communicator, understanding and being understood in all four colours. With practice you will be equally fluent in all four languages.

> In order to lead you must first be willing to be led.

For example:

Practise your red matching skills the next time you are walking with someone. Begin by walking beside the person. If you have to speed up to keep pace, you must brighten your red to match. If you have to slow down, you must diminish your red to match. Hone your skills by walking side-by-side, shoulder-to-shoulder and step-by-step. Match the person's physical body movements — the swing of the arms, the gait of each step, the cadence, rhythm and tempo of each body movement.

Matching colours and intensities in this manner establishes rapport and effective communication because you are using the same body language. There are many roles and relationships in which establishing rapport is not enough. It is often important and appropriate to help the other person shift; as parents, as leaders, as managers, as supervisors, as educators and so on we take the role of facilitating change in others. The first step, however is to match colour and intensity. Once you have established rapport you can facilitate change in others.

For example:

First match the other person's walking style and pace as just described. Once you have established a match, begin walking slightly faster and guess what happens. Yes! The person will follow your lead and speed up to keep pace with you. Begin walking slower and guess what. Yes! The person will follow your lead and slow down to match your slower pace. The same principle applies to all of the colours: establish a match, shift, and the other person will follow your lead, follow your leadership.

> " Be the change you wish to see in the world.
>
> — Mohandas Gandhi

You can assist others in brightening and diminishing their colours so they are more effective in their lives. The key is to establish the match first. The key is to change so others can change.

Paraphrasing and Active Listening

Paraphrasing

An effective way to match colours and intensities is to use paraphrasing and active listening. A paraphrase is a brief statement by the listener that restates the original core message back to the speaker. A paraphrase is a shorter, concise summary of the original message and does not add to it. An accurate paraphrase confirms to the listener and the speaker that original the message has been understood, that the message sent equals the message received. If the paraphrase is not accurate, the speaker will naturally correct the listener. A paraphrase does not imply agreement or disagreement. It simply demonstrates understanding.

> One of the most sincere forms of respect is actually listening to what another has to say.
> — Bryant H. McGill

For example:

"I hear you saying... you feel disappointed because you didn't get invited."
"I hear you saying... you think we need to find a better solution."
"I hear you saying... you are going to take action right away."
"I hear you saying... you want me to organize it by the end of the week."

Paraphrasing and active listening have four powerful effects:

1) Paraphrasing and active listening require the listener to focus intently on understanding the incoming messages from the speaker. This also has the powerful effect of silencing the listener's distracting internal self-talk.

2) Paraphrasing and active listening suspend the listener's critical judgment and reduce the tendency of the listener to react to the speaker. As a result the listener is not preoccupied with rehearsing their reaction; rather, the listener is focused on listening attentively and responding accurately. The listener moves from reacting to responding.

3) Paraphrasing and active listening interrupt the push and pull dynamics of conflict. When you paraphrase and actively listen the adversarial positions and oppositional dynamics of power struggles are suspended and understanding emerges.

4) Paraphrasing and active listening change you. When you paraphrase and actively listen, your colours match the person you are listening to. When you experience what the other person is experiencing you maximize your capacity to understand the other person. It is this matching that empowers you to be a great communicator.

Use paraphrasing and active listening to listen to a child, to listen effectively to your partner, to hear where your boss is coming from and to listen to your clients. Give people the gift of listening. You will be amazed what you will learn about others and you will learn how to be a highly effective listener and communicator. Open listeners open doors.

Endings and Beginnings

In the first book of this trilogy, *ColourSpectrums Personality Styles Book One: The Introduction*, you learned the fundamental principles of ColourSpectrums. In this second book, *ColourSpectrums Personality Styles Book Two: Stress Management and Conflict Resolution*, you have learned about ColourSpectrums human dynamics and how to enhance interaction. I am confident these principles and strategies will contribute significantly to your personal growth and professional development. In the next book, *ColourSpectrums Personality Styles Book Three: Brightening Pale Colours*, you will further your communication skills and learn how to empower all of your colours in a highly effective balanced manner.

ColourSpectrums Applications

The journey and discoveries continue. ColourSpectrums continues to develop with a view to advancing human understanding and personal and professional effectiveness. I encourage you to visit our website www.colourspectrums.com for current developments, new applications and learning opportunities.

ColourSpectrums workshops have been presented to diverse groups around the world.

Diverse Applications Include:

Anti Bullying	Life Skills
Business Management	Marketing
Career Counseling	Marriage Preparation
Career Development	Parenting Styles
Child Care	Personal Counseling
Child Development	Rehabilitation Services
Communication Skills	Self-Esteem
Community Relations	Solution Focus
Conflict Resolution	Stress Management
Correctional Services	Supervision
Couples Communication	Teaching Styles
Customer Service	Team Building
Family Communication	Team Diversity
Family Dynamics	Team Esteem
Family Violence Prevention	Youth Development
Foster Parenting	Youth at Risk
Learning Styles	Values Clarification

About the Author

Rob Chubb was born in Grande Prairie, Alberta, in 1951. Rob is the middle child of five children. His father was a United Church minister and his mother, a former nurse, dedicated herself to raising the family of four boys and one girl. Rob lived in Alberta and British Columbia until the age of 15 when he moved with his family to California. He graduated from North Hollywood High School in 1969. When he returned to Canada he worked extensively with children and youth at risk throughout western Canada. In 1976 he graduated from Grant MacEwan College in Edmonton with a diploma in Child and Youth Care. He was a faculty member at MacEwan for the next 20 years. He also graduated with his girlfriend Laurie. They married in 1978 and live in Sherwood Park, Alberta. They have five adult children. In 1997 Rob graduated from the University of Victoria, B.C., with a Bachelor's Degree (with distinction) in Child and Youth Care. Rob and Laurie have been foster parents to over 20 children during the last 25 years. They have managed group homes for at-risk pregnant teens, managed a group home in Cambridge Bay in the Arctic and dedicated their lives to improving the lives of children and families. Rob has worked extensively as a foster parent trainer for the Government of Alberta and in Australia.

Rob is the author and director of ColourSpectrums promoting human development and self-empowerment through education, interaction and fun. Rob presents regularly at local, provincial, national and international venues. He has presented ColourSpectrums to over 20,000 participants over the past 15 years. Clients include Government, Educational, Business, non-profit and private agencies. Rob has trained over 1,000 facilitators throughout Canada, the United States and Australia.

Call for Facilitators

We are actively seeking people who would like to be trained and certified to present ColourSpectrums. ColourSpectrums is presented to groups only by certified facilitators. If you would like to be trained to present ColourSpectrums to groups or would like to participate in an depth session please contact Rob at www.colourspectrums.com

Rob welcomes your enquiries and comments. You can contact him through www.colourspectrums.com.

ColourSpectrums Personality Styles Book 1: The Introduction

Sort the cards to reveal your personality as a unique spectrum of:

Blue   Emotional intelligence
Green   Intellectual intelligence
Red   Physical intelligence
Yellow   Organizational intelligence

You are more intelligent than you "think"!

You will:
- Use four intelligences to make more intelligent choices
- Identify your bright colour strengths
- Acknowledge your pale colour challenges
- Easily identify anyone's ColourSpectrums personality
- Communicate more effectively and enhance relationships

Includes:
- Four Introductory Cards and scoring system
- Written exercises with individual and paired activities

Benefits:
- Personal, professional and team development for:
  Leaders, managers, students, coaches, educators and families
  Thousands have benefitted. You can too!

This ground-breaking work synthesizes personality styles into one seamless developmental model.

"So brilliantly simple, it's simply brilliant!"
"Profoundly insightful aha! learning."
"Entertaining ha-ha! learning."
"Hands-on practical and user friendly."

In the series:

ColourSpectrums Personality Styles Book 1: The Introduction
ColourSpectrums Personality Styles Book 2: Stress Management and Conflict Resolution
ColourSpectrums Personality Styles Book 3: Brightening Pale Colours

Author

Rob Chubb is the founding director and author of ColourSpectrums. Rob has trained over 1,000 ColourSpectrums facilitators worldwide. He draws from a wealth of practical experience and dynamic presentations to diverse audiences of children, youth and adults including local agencies, national organizations and multinational corporations. Rob is the father of five children and lives with his wife, Laurie, in Sherwood Park, Alberta.

www.colourspectrums.com

ColourSpectrums Personality Styles Book 3: Brightening Pale Colours

Use Brightening Cards and In-ChargeCards to brighten pale colours:

Blue   Emotional skills
Green Cognitive skills
Red   Physical skills
Yellow Organizational skills

TM

*Who you are is constant.
How you are is
constantly changing.*

You will:
- Learn the common phrases, voice tone and pace of each colour
- Recognize each colour's body language
- Brighten your palest colour
- Use four colours to communicate effectively
- Use four colour to balance your life

Includes:
- Four Brightening Cards with goal setting In-ChargeCards
- Written exercises with individual and paired activities

Benefits:
- Personal, professional and team development for:
  Leaders, managers, students, coaches, educators and families
  Thousands have benefitted. You can too!

This ground-breaking work synthesizes personality styles into one seamless developmental model.

"**So brilliantly simple, it's simply brilliant!**"
"**Profoundly insightful aha! learning.**"
"**Entertaining ha-ha! learning.**"
"**Hands-on practical and user friendly.**"

In the series:

ColourSpectrums Personality Styles Book 1: The Introduction
ColourSpectrums Personality Styles Book 2: Stress Management and Conflict Resolution
ColourSpectrums Personality Styles Book 3: Brightening Pale Colours

Author

Rob Chubb is the founding director and author of ColourSpectrums. Rob has trained over 1,000 ColourSpectrums facilitators worldwide. He draws from a wealth of practical experience and dynamic presentations to diverse audiences of children, youth and adults including local agencies, national organizations and multinational corporations. Rob is the father of five children and lives with his wife, Laurie, in Sherwood Park, Alberta.

www.colourspectrums.com

Enjoy all three books in this series:

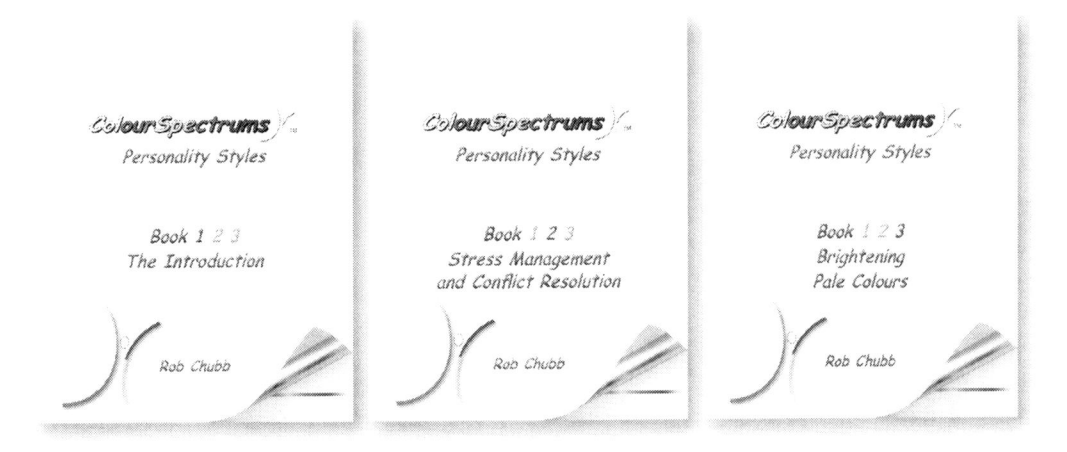

ColourSpectrums Personality Styles
Book 1 2 3
The Introduction
Rob Chubb

ColourSpectrums Personality Styles
Book 1 2 3
Stress Management and Conflict Resolution
Rob Chubb

ColourSpectrums Personality Styles
Book 1 2 3
Brightening Pale Colours
Rob Chubb

1) Order by phone 780-922-6877
2) Order on line at www.colourspectrums.com
3) Fax (780-922-6877) or Mail this form to: ColourSpectrums
   #13, 53046 Range Road 222
   Ardrossan, Alberta   T8E 2E8
   Canada

Your name _____

Address _____

_____

City _____

Province/State _____   Postal Code _____

Quantity	Stock #	Product Description	Unit Price	Total
	CS 022	ColourSpectrums Personality Styles Book 1 The Introduction	$30.00 (includes $5.00 S&H)	
	CS 023	ColourSpectrums Personality Styles Book 2 Stress Management and Conflict Resolution	$30.00 (includes $5.00 S&H)	
	CS 024	ColourSpectrums Personality Styles Book 3 Brightening Pale Colours	$30.00 (includes $5.00 S&H)	
		Our GST #: 104085691	Subtotal	
			Add 5% GST	
			Total Payable	

Method of Payment: ☐ Visa   ☐ Mastercard

Card Number _____   Expiry Date _____

Card Holder's Name _____

Signature _____

Rob Chubb

Blue

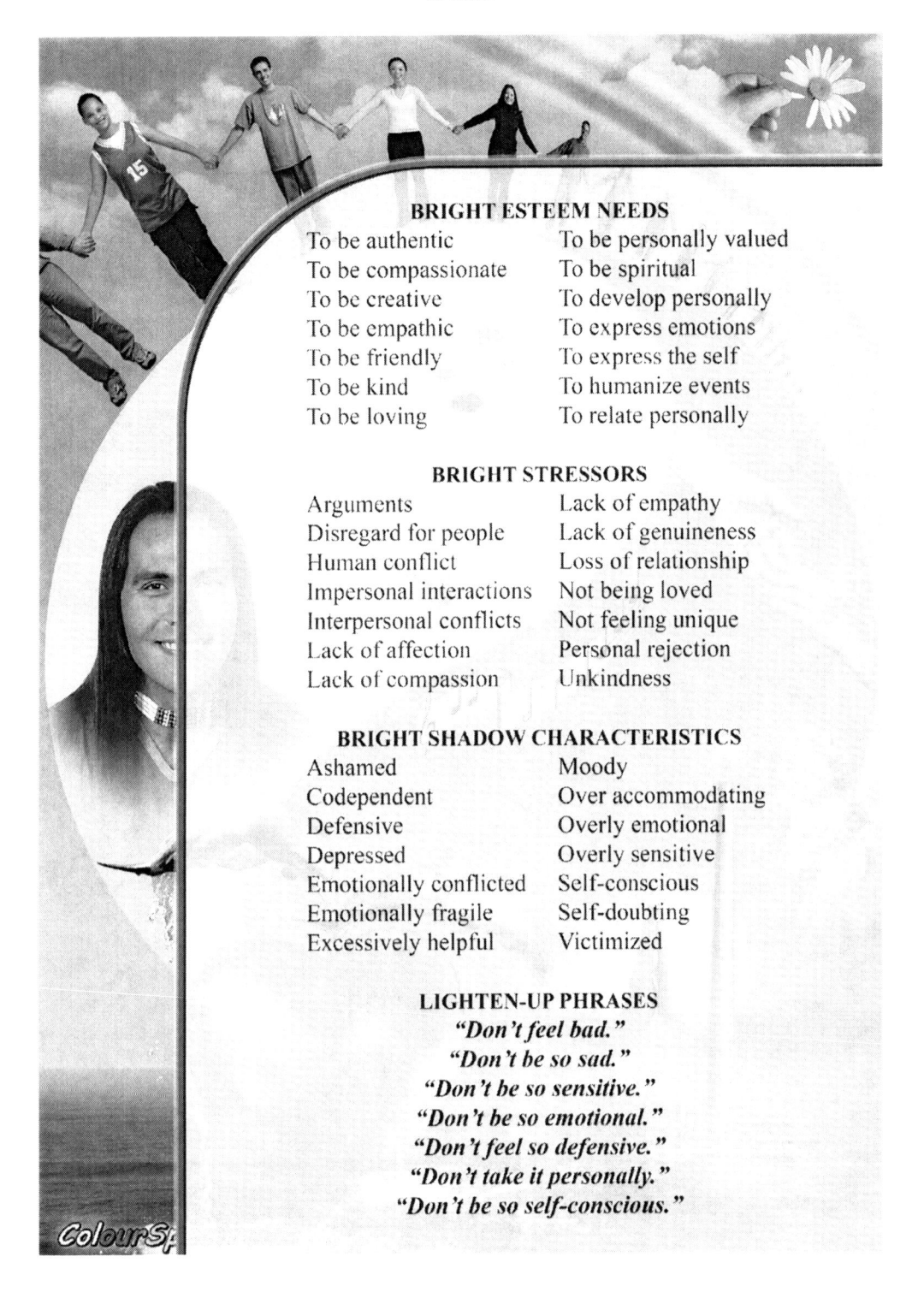

BRIGHT ESTEEM NEEDS

To be authentic
To be compassionate
To be creative
To be empathic
To be friendly
To be kind
To be loving
To be personally valued
To be spiritual
To develop personally
To express emotions
To express the self
To humanize events
To relate personally

BRIGHT STRESSORS

Arguments
Disregard for people
Human conflict
Impersonal interactions
Interpersonal conflicts
Lack of affection
Lack of compassion
Lack of empathy
Lack of genuineness
Loss of relationship
Not being loved
Not feeling unique
Personal rejection
Unkindness

BRIGHT SHADOW CHARACTERISTICS

Ashamed
Codependent
Defensive
Depressed
Emotionally conflicted
Emotionally fragile
Excessively helpful
Moody
Over accommodating
Overly emotional
Overly sensitive
Self-conscious
Self-doubting
Victimized

LIGHTEN-UP PHRASES

"Don't feel bad."
"Don't be so sad."
"Don't be so sensitive."
"Don't be so emotional."
"Don't feel so defensive."
"Don't take it personally."
"Don't be so self-conscious."

Blue

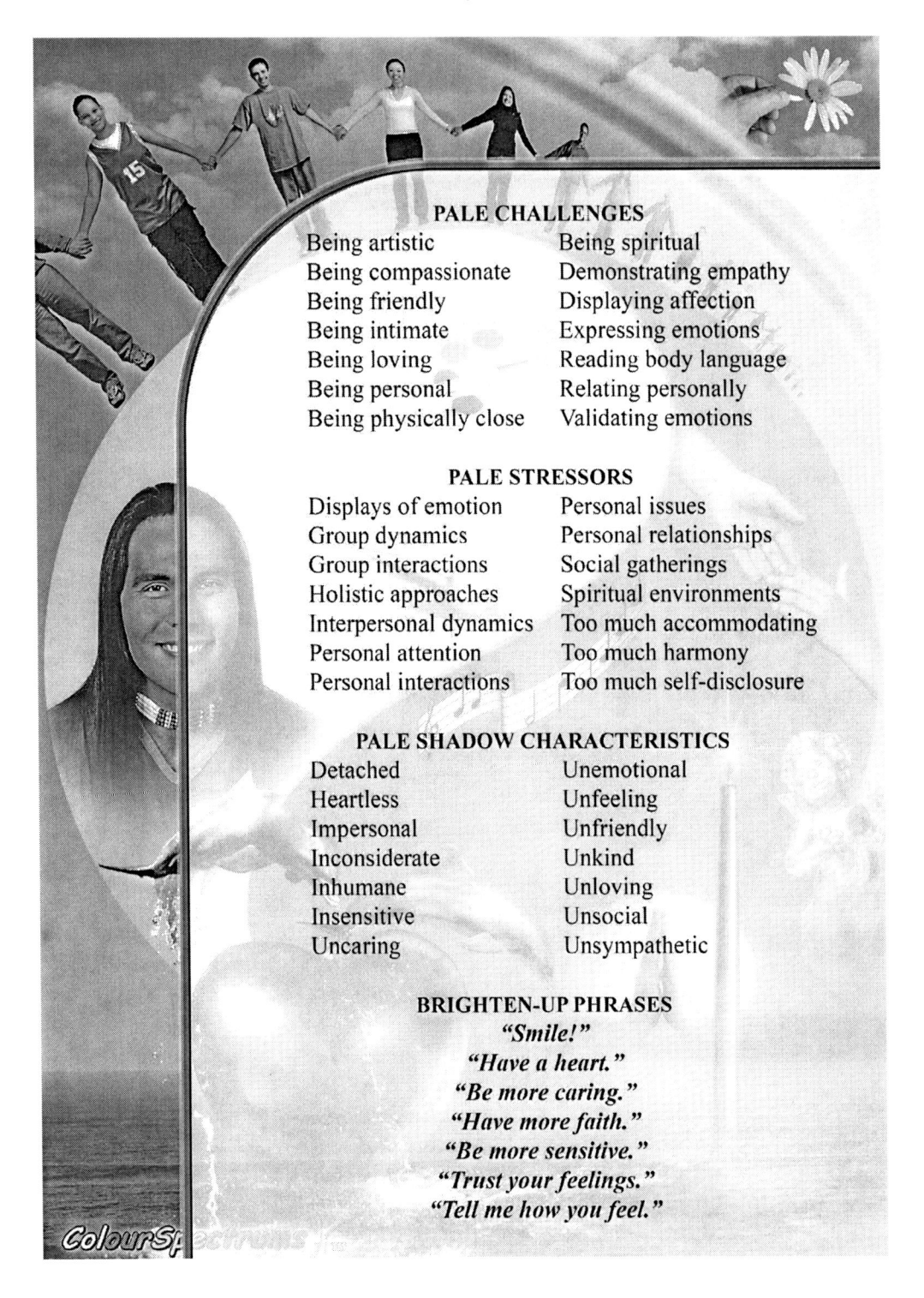

PALE CHALLENGES

Being artistic
Being compassionate
Being friendly
Being intimate
Being loving
Being personal
Being physically close
Being spiritual
Demonstrating empathy
Displaying affection
Expressing emotions
Reading body language
Relating personally
Validating emotions

PALE STRESSORS

Displays of emotion
Group dynamics
Group interactions
Holistic approaches
Interpersonal dynamics
Personal attention
Personal interactions
Personal issues
Personal relationships
Social gatherings
Spiritual environments
Too much accommodating
Too much harmony
Too much self-disclosure

PALE SHADOW CHARACTERISTICS

Detached
Heartless
Impersonal
Inconsiderate
Inhumane
Insensitive
Uncaring
Unemotional
Unfeeling
Unfriendly
Unkind
Unloving
Unsocial
Unsympathetic

BRIGHTEN-UP PHRASES

"Smile!"
"Have a heart."
"Be more caring."
"Have more faith."
"Be more sensitive."
"Trust your feelings."
"Tell me how you feel."

Stress Management Card Set

Green

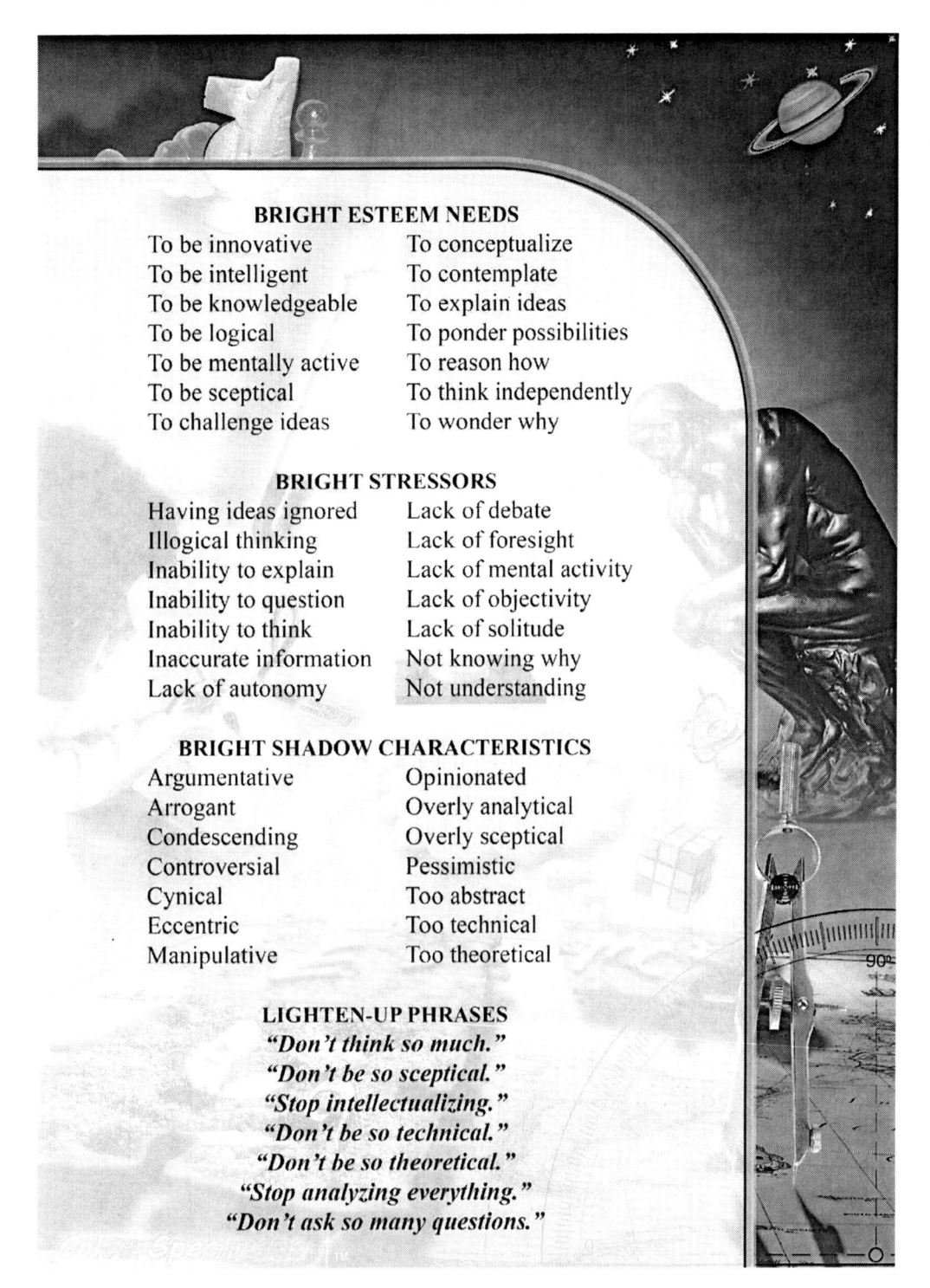

BRIGHT ESTEEM NEEDS

To be innovative
To be intelligent
To be knowledgeable
To be logical
To be mentally active
To be sceptical
To challenge ideas
To conceptualize
To contemplate
To explain ideas
To ponder possibilities
To reason how
To think independently
To wonder why

BRIGHT STRESSORS

Having ideas ignored
Illogical thinking
Inability to explain
Inability to question
Inability to think
Inaccurate information
Lack of autonomy
Lack of debate
Lack of foresight
Lack of mental activity
Lack of objectivity
Lack of solitude
Not knowing why
Not understanding

BRIGHT SHADOW CHARACTERISTICS

Argumentative
Arrogant
Condescending
Controversial
Cynical
Eccentric
Manipulative
Opinionated
Overly analytical
Overly sceptical
Pessimistic
Too abstract
Too technical
Too theoretical

LIGHTEN-UP PHRASES

"Don't think so much."
"Don't be so sceptical."
"Stop intellectualizing."
"Don't be so technical."
"Don't be so theoretical."
"Stop analyzing everything."
"Don't ask so many questions."

Rob Chubb

Green

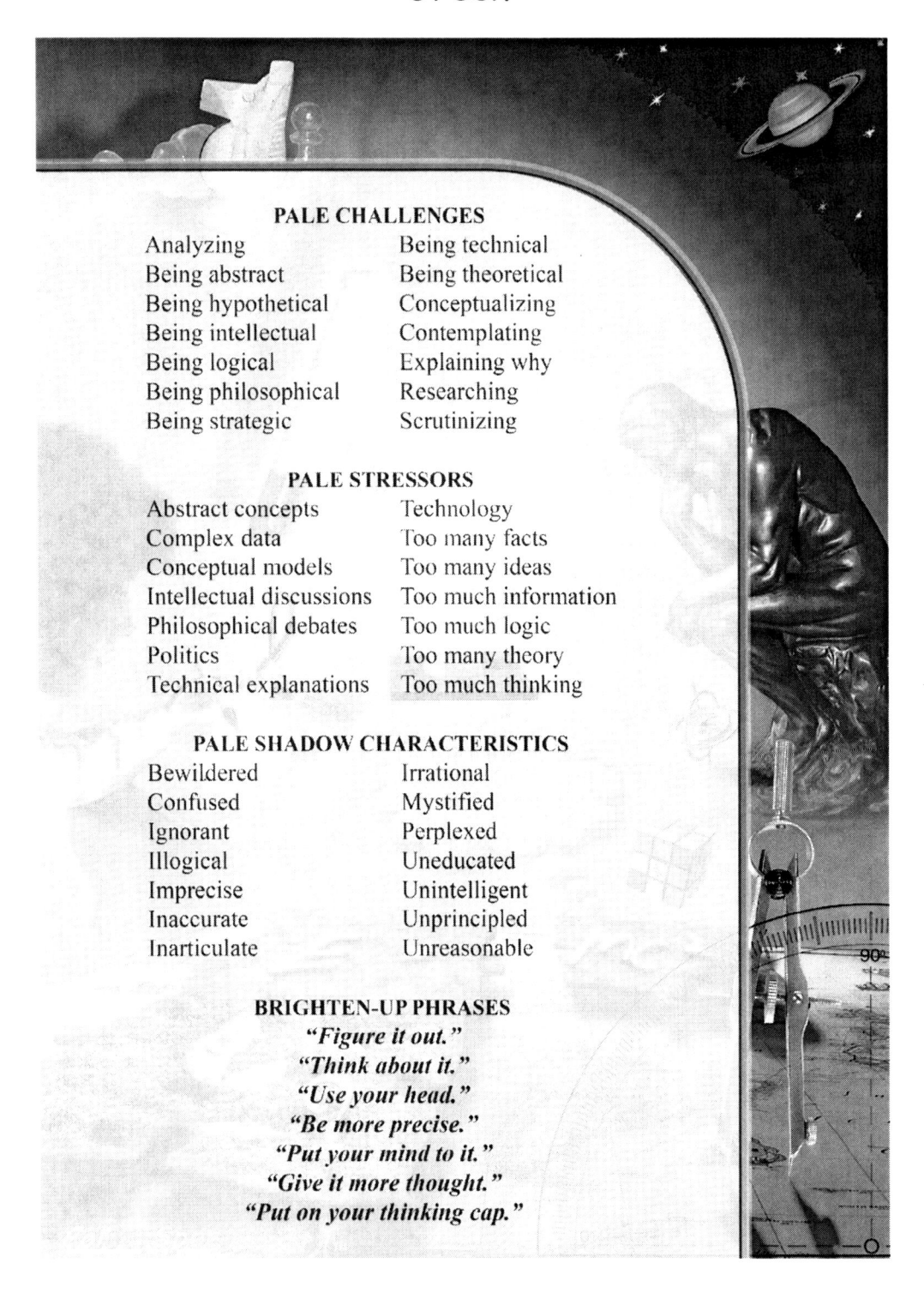

PALE CHALLENGES

Analyzing
Being abstract
Being hypothetical
Being intellectual
Being logical
Being philosophical
Being strategic
Being technical
Being theoretical
Conceptualizing
Contemplating
Explaining why
Researching
Scrutinizing

PALE STRESSORS

Abstract concepts
Complex data
Conceptual models
Intellectual discussions
Philosophical debates
Politics
Technical explanations
Technology
Too many facts
Too many ideas
Too much information
Too much logic
Too many theory
Too much thinking

PALE SHADOW CHARACTERISTICS

Bewildered
Confused
Ignorant
Illogical
Imprecise
Inaccurate
Inarticulate
Irrational
Mystified
Perplexed
Uneducated
Unintelligent
Unprincipled
Unreasonable

BRIGHTEN-UP PHRASES

"Figure it out."
"Think about it."
"Use your head."
"Be more precise."
"Put your mind to it."
"Give it more thought."
"Put on your thinking cap."

Stress Management Card Set

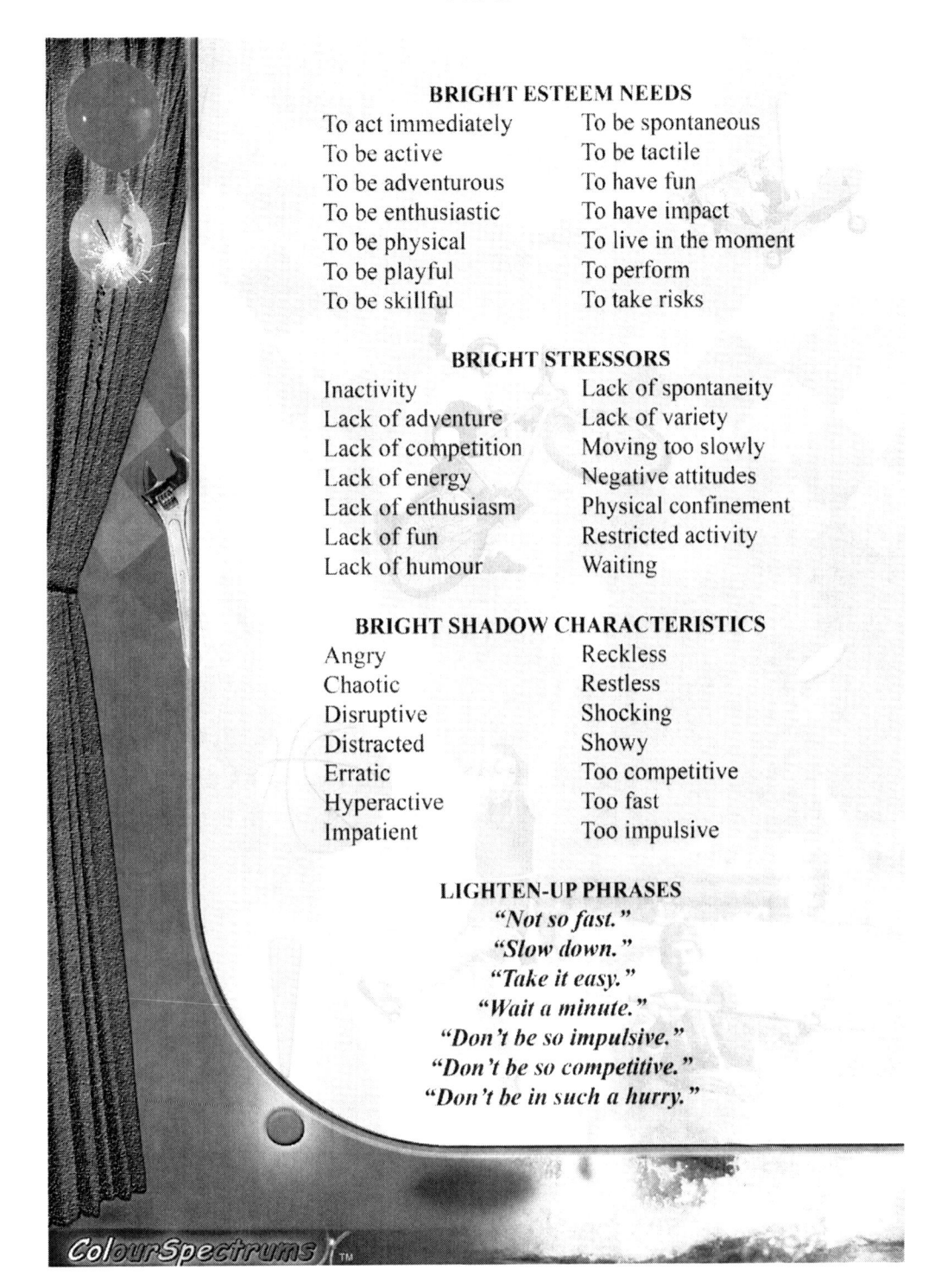

Red

BRIGHT ESTEEM NEEDS

To act immediately · To be spontaneous
To be active · To be tactile
To be adventurous · To have fun
To be enthusiastic · To have impact
To be physical · To live in the moment
To be playful · To perform
To be skillful · To take risks

BRIGHT STRESSORS

Inactivity · Lack of spontaneity
Lack of adventure · Lack of variety
Lack of competition · Moving too slowly
Lack of energy · Negative attitudes
Lack of enthusiasm · Physical confinement
Lack of fun · Restricted activity
Lack of humour · Waiting

BRIGHT SHADOW CHARACTERISTICS

Angry · Reckless
Chaotic · Restless
Disruptive · Shocking
Distracted · Showy
Erratic · Too competitive
Hyperactive · Too fast
Impatient · Too impulsive

LIGHTEN-UP PHRASES

"Not so fast."
"Slow down."
"Take it easy."
"Wait a minute."
"Don't be so impulsive."
"Don't be so competitive."
"Don't be in such a hurry."

ColourSpectrums™

Red

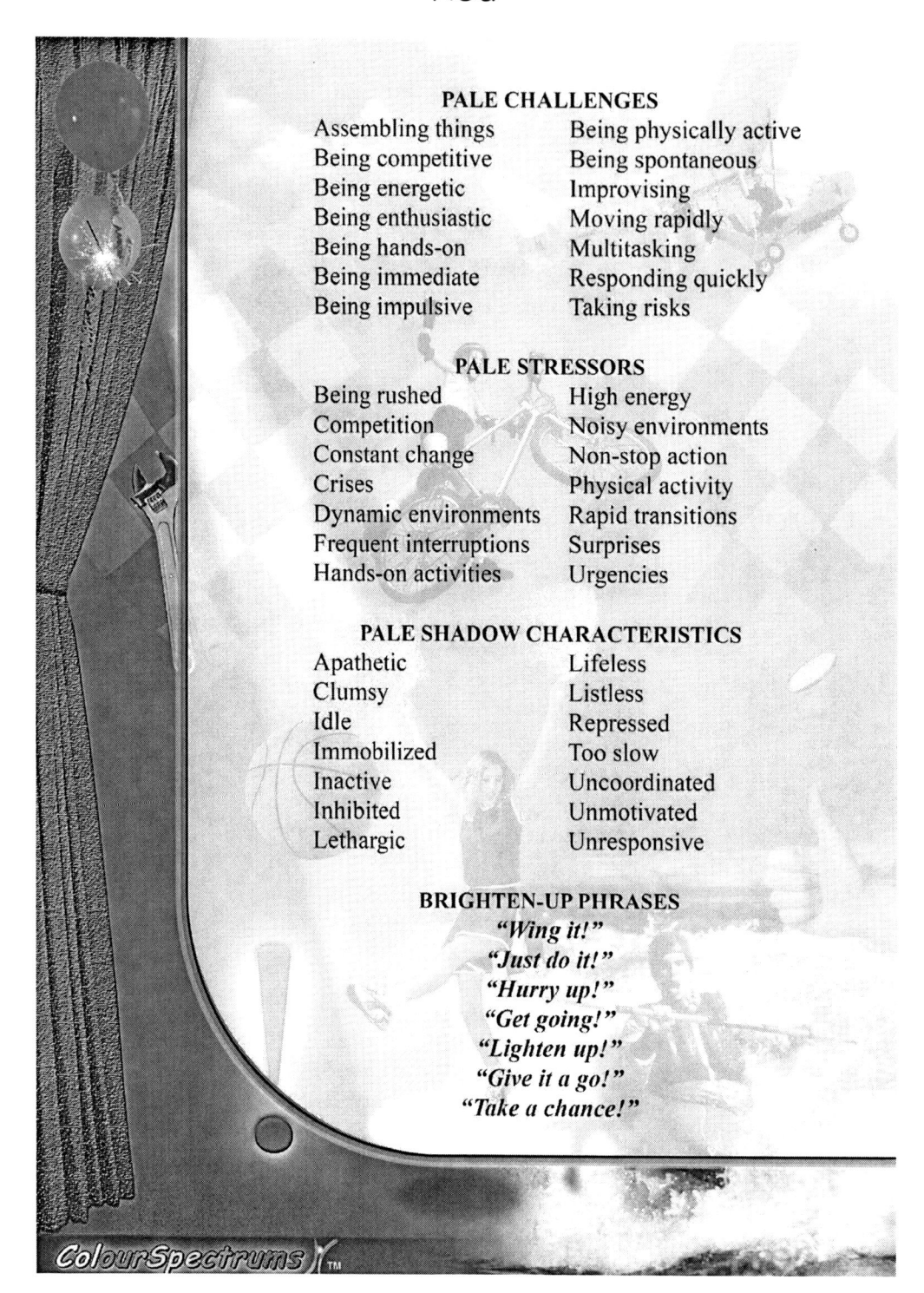

PALE CHALLENGES

Assembling things
Being competitive
Being energetic
Being enthusiastic
Being hands-on
Being immediate
Being impulsive
Being physically active
Being spontaneous
Improvising
Moving rapidly
Multitasking
Responding quickly
Taking risks

PALE STRESSORS

Being rushed
Competition
Constant change
Crises
Dynamic environments
Frequent interruptions
Hands-on activities
High energy
Noisy environments
Non-stop action
Physical activity
Rapid transitions
Surprises
Urgencies

PALE SHADOW CHARACTERISTICS

Apathetic
Clumsy
Idle
Immobilized
Inactive
Inhibited
Lethargic
Lifeless
Listless
Repressed
Too slow
Uncoordinated
Unmotivated
Unresponsive

BRIGHTEN-UP PHRASES

"Wing it!"
"Just do it!"
"Hurry up!"
"Get going!"
"Lighten up!"
"Give it a go!"
"Take a chance!"

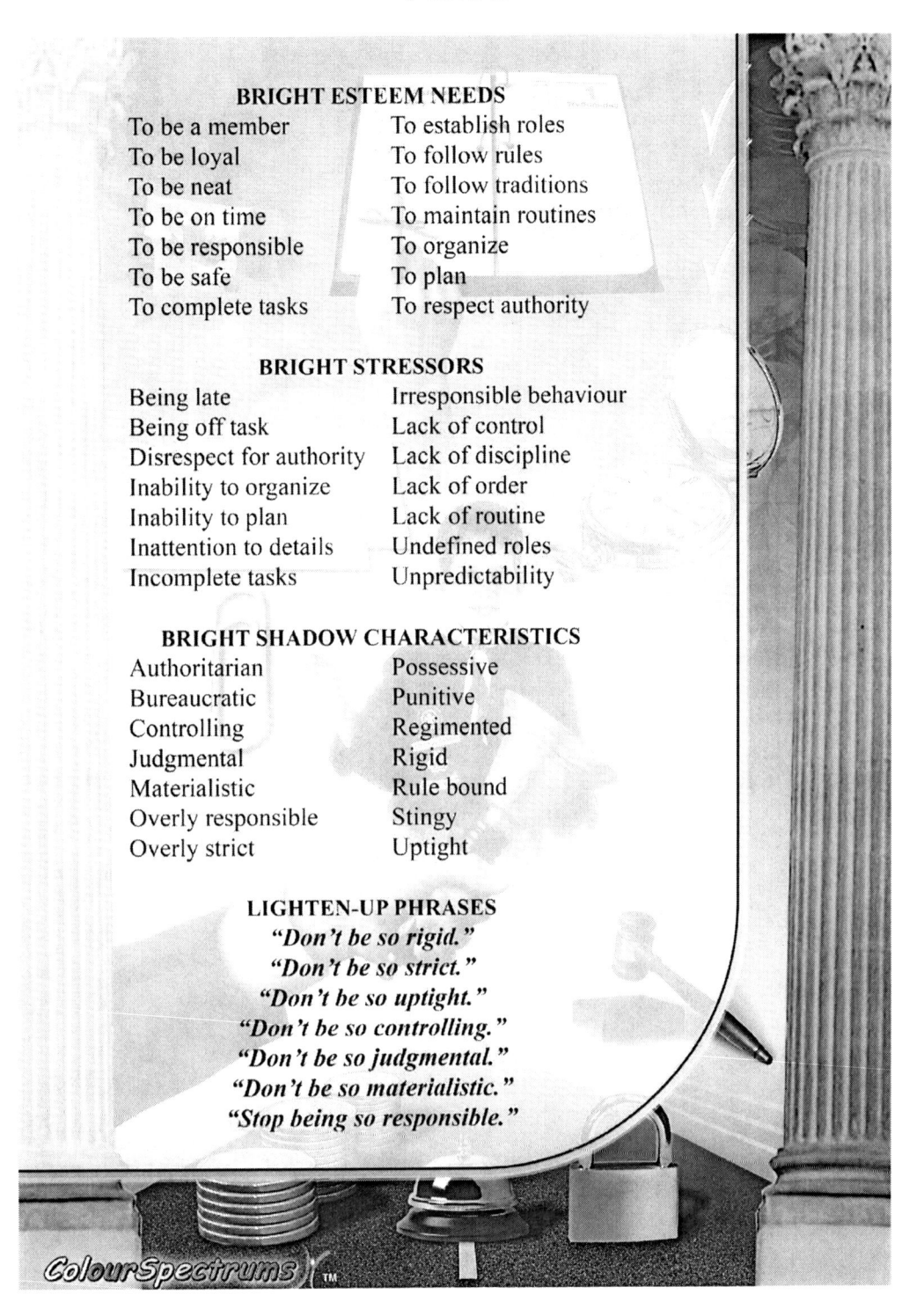

Yellow

BRIGHT ESTEEM NEEDS

To be a member
To be loyal
To be neat
To be on time
To be responsible
To be safe
To complete tasks
To establish roles
To follow rules
To follow traditions
To maintain routines
To organize
To plan
To respect authority

BRIGHT STRESSORS

Being late
Being off task
Disrespect for authority
Inability to organize
Inability to plan
Inattention to details
Incomplete tasks
Irresponsible behaviour
Lack of control
Lack of discipline
Lack of order
Lack of routine
Undefined roles
Unpredictability

BRIGHT SHADOW CHARACTERISTICS

Authoritarian
Bureaucratic
Controlling
Judgmental
Materialistic
Overly responsible
Overly strict
Possessive
Punitive
Regimented
Rigid
Rule bound
Stingy
Uptight

LIGHTEN-UP PHRASES

"Don't be so rigid."
"Don't be so strict."
"Don't be so uptight."
"Don't be so controlling."
"Don't be so judgmental."
"Don't be so materialistic."
"Stop being so responsible."

Yellow

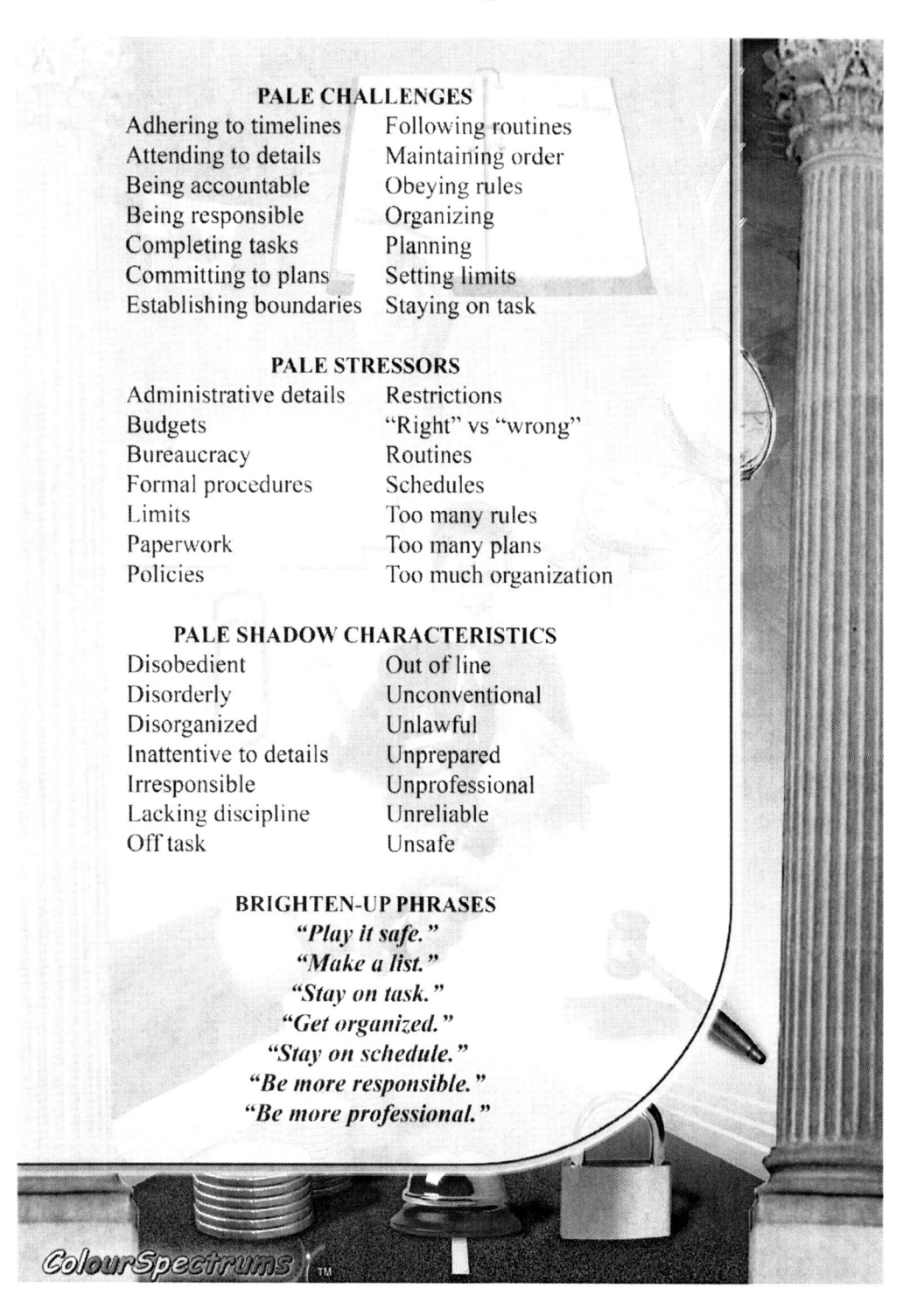

PALE CHALLENGES
Adhering to timelines   Following routines
Attending to details   Maintaining order
Being accountable   Obeying rules
Being responsible   Organizing
Completing tasks   Planning
Committing to plans   Setting limits
Establishing boundaries Staying on task

PALE STRESSORS
Administrative details Restrictions
Budgets   "Right" vs "wrong"
Bureaucracy   Routines
Formal procedures   Schedules
Limits   Too many rules
Paperwork   Too many plans
Policies   Too much organization

PALE SHADOW CHARACTERISTICS
Disobedient   Out of line
Disorderly   Unconventional
Disorganized   Unlawful
Inattentive to details Unprepared
Irresponsible   Unprofessional
Lacking discipline   Unreliable
Off task   Unsafe

BRIGHTEN-UP PHRASES
"Play it safe."
"Make a list."
"Stay on task."
"Get organized."
"Stay on schedule."
"Be more responsible."
"Be more professional."